GRAHAM GREENE

Yours etc.

LETTERS TO THE PRESS

Selected and Introduced by
Christopher Hawtree

REINHARDT BOOKS
IN ASSOCIATION WITH
VIKING

REINHARDT BOOKS
in association with Viking

Distributed by the Penguin Group
27 Wrights Lane, London w8 5 tz, England
Viking Penguin Inc., 40 West 23rd Street, New York, New York 10010, USA
Penguin Books Australia Ltd, Ringwood, Victoria, Australia
Penguin Books Canada Ltd, 2801 John Street, Markham, Ontario, Canada l3r 1b4
Penguin Books (NZ) Ltd, 182–190 Wairau Road, Auckland 10, New Zealand

Penguin Books Ltd, Registered Offices: Harmondsworth, Middlesex, England

First published 1989

Typeset in 10½/13 pt Linotype Janson by
Rowland Phototypesetting Ltd, Bury St Edmunds, Suffolk
Printed in Great Britain by
Butler and Tanner Ltd, Frome and London

A CIP catalogue record for this book is available from the British Library

ISBN 1-871061-22-9

Library of Congress Catalog Number 89–62859

CONTENTS

Introduction / ix

Editor's Note and Acknowledgements / xix

Prologue / xxiii

YOURS ETC. / 3

Epilogue / 254

Index / 255

'It is a rule that letters to the newspapers may not be written on the club writing paper.'

(Evelyn Waugh to Graham Greene,
after successfully proposing him for White's)

INTRODUCTION

'I've always liked reading newspapers. My enemies might say I get my ideas from theological works and newspapers.'

Graham Greene, interview with V. S. Naipaul
(*Daily Telegraph Magazine*, 8 March 1968)

The product of innumerable decisions, judicious or otherwise, the course of each life could have been – can yet be – far different. Sixty years ago, the world almost lost a prolific novelist. The author of *The Man Within* was about to resign from *The Times* after four years' sub-editing; this was despite having been told that, if only he were patient, he might well become correspondence editor.

As Graham Greene recalls in *A Sort of Life*: 'Already, when the correspondence editor was on holiday, I tasted the glory of deputizing for him and this brought me into direct contact with the editor, Geoffrey Dawson himself. Closeted with the editor every afternoon at four o'clock I argued the merits of the letters and we decided which was to lead the page. I was exalted by the contact, especially when, as sometimes happened, I won the argument and even perhaps secured the promotion of one of Walter Sickert's frequent letters which offended Dawson's tidy mind by being almost illegibly written over large sheets of lined paper in thick black ink, apparently with a matchstick and usually with an impenetrable smudge over an operative word, a calligraphy which suited his savage *non sequiturs* on subjects far removed from painting.'

He added, in a letter to *Books and Bookmen* (June 1976), that, had he succumbed, 'my whole life would have been changed disastrously for the better'.

Rarely has life – especially a writer's – taken as many turns.

Greene has frequently given a few months – or less – to experience which others spin out for a decade or more. These letters to the press, combining reminiscence and contemporary comment, form another sort of life, which could hardly have been printed had he remained in Printing House Square.

Exactly why he should have chosen to produce what amounts to a couple of volumes' worth of free copy is part of an ambiguous attitude to the press which perhaps goes as far back as the *School House Gazette*, a periodical edited by his eldest brother, in whose pages he tried to publish 'a coloured drawing of a bit of shit' under guise of a cigar. This was spiked by the sharp-eyed sibling sub, but a sense of glory was restored, enterprisingly, by adolescent publication in the *Star* and his diverse Oxford journalism.

That this should have led to a stint on the *Nottingham Journal* was less than cheering, the high point of the evening's work a sweepstake on the football results, chips for all to be bought by the winner. 'I was unreasonably lucky, so that around eight, more often than not, I would get a breath of fresh air while I fetched the chips from a fish-stall. They were wrapped up in an old copy of the *Journal*, but never in the *Nottingham Guardian*: the *Guardian* was the respectable paper.' Even now, when the hygiene laws have been tightened up, the image of one's work going out in the world to wrap fish can only make a journalist shudder (and a haddock never looks best pleased at being squashed against a mugshot of Paul Johnson).

Despite this experience, Greene 'can think of no better career for a young novelist than to be for some years a sub-editor on a rather conservative newspaper: a writer with a sprawling style is unlikely to emerge from such an apprenticeship.' This was in fact a hard-won lesson. His second and third novels display all the faults for which he would later berate the novelist and *Times* drama critic, Charles Morgan ('The Seed Cake and the Love Lady', *Life and Letters*, August 1934). As has often been remarked, Greene's fiction became very much a part of the contemporary world, sometimes presciently so, and this can first be seen in the inexplicably little-known *It's a Battlefield*, published a few months before the attack on Morgan.

Among the characters in this is Conder, a journalist beset by a fantasy-life, and one can almost say of Greene's fiction that the figure in the carpet is the foot in the door: from the fittingly-named Chase of *Rumour at Nightfall* to Jim in *The Captain and the Enemy*, the novels contain an array of journalists for whom glory of a sort is the motive but scarcely describes their methods.

Throughout the thirties, Greene was himself ever on the lookout for ways of earning money by those products of the pen that come more readily than a novel. There is much that has not reached the stout volumes of *The Pleasure-Dome* and *Collected Essays*, and it is by no means inferior to them. Such were these nerve-end labours of the freelance that it was with some relief that he accepted the co-editorship of the 1937 weekly *Night and Day* and, even after the success of *Brighton Rock*, the less congenial post of literary editor on the *Spectator* under the dour Wilson Harris, who is now only remembered for keeping pornographic photographs between the pages of his Bible.

These office-bound periods were haunted by those trips abroad, far from the piles of galley-proofs and endless, pointless 'meetings'. His surname has become an adjective, the *OED* quoting the essay later collected in *Ways of Escape*: far from perversely favouring the down-at-heel, 'I have sometimes wondered whether they [critics] go round the world blinkered. "This is Indo-China," I want to exclaim, "this is Mexico, this is Sierra Leone carefully and accurately described. I have been a newspaper correspondent as well as a novelist. I assure you that the dead child lay in the ditch in just that attitude. In the canal of Phat Diem the bodies stuck out of the water . . ." But I know that argument is useless. They won't believe the world they haven't noticed is like that.'

In a conversation with Marie-Françoise Allain in 1980, he pointed out that 'the amateur journalist is closer to the writer than is the professional journalist, because he's entirely free in his movements and opinions'. The strength of the fiction – the art of the matter – is in its allying observation and imagination, a continual awareness of technique, one part of which is transcription: although it uses much the same words, how different in effect is 'A Memory of Indo-China' (*Listener*, 15 September 1955) from the vertical raid which forms a part of the complex time-scheme and narrative method of *The Quiet American*.

A novelist's approach would be a night-editor's despair; equally, admirable columns of sharp newsprint, reset and bound, can often appear lumpen. These letters to the press, however, are not diminished by time. Only some of their contents shall be revealed here, for one wishes to preserve the surprise which must have been given to those readers who were around at the time and able to keep up with all these newspapers and magazines.

At Oxford there had been a *Cherwell* dispute about Greene's verses in *Babbling April*, of whose merits Harold Acton was doubtful, even wishing to throw down the book in disgust and to cry aloud, 'For God's sake, be a man!' 'An attack by Mr Acton is a recommendation to most readers,' retorted the author, adding the subtle thrust that readers would surely be surprised to find 'Mr Acton as a professor of Manliness'. During the thirties the letters were generally confined to Restoration literature, although there was an exchange with Francis Iles in the *Daily Telegraph* after he had reviewed *The Old School* (1934) with less than pleasure. After the war, letters to the press became another of those forms – along with children's stories, film-scripts and plays – at which he was now far more successful than before.

In these letters one can sense the manic-depressive nature to which Greene first confessed when psychoanalysed at sixteen. One way or another, there is a continual wish to stir things up, and perhaps to annoy editors around the world who would pay large sums for material instead sent free to journals of more modest circulation.

Time and again, one can see a shot fired off, the author then standing back to watch a rush of other combatants enter the field. Journalists such as Nicholas Wapshott ('Badshott') are a butt for outraged humour as they coin fanciful anecdotes and perpetuate error derived from that inverted, crumbling pyramid of doubtful assertions, the cuttings-file. A number of these brief corrections have been excluded: those that remain often show the difficulty of ensuring that the truth registers in such minds.

Not that this forms a solemn chronicle. Outwardly formal announcements saw the birth of two bizarre organizations, one devoted to Anglo-Texan relations and the other to the nefarious activities of *Express* columnist John Gordon. One can detect a pecking-order in the outlets for those letters which are not a specific rejoinder. The *Telegraph* appeared more suitable than *The Times* for comments on the merits of the Great Train Robbers and on 'Rab' Butler's removal of prostitutes from the London streets.

Dr Bellows, in *The Confidential Agent*, brushes aside the evening paper with the words, 'I never read the daily press, I find that in a good weekly paper fact has been sifted from rumour. All the *important* news is there.' One contributor to the *Spectator* under the elegantly raffish Alexander Chancellor's editorship, Peter Ackroyd, has likened its sphere of operations to St Trinian's (*Sunday Times Magazine*, 9 April 1989), but from Antibes came a letter of support written to Chancellor himself in 1978: 'I can't resist quoting to you a sentence from the letters of William James which I have just been reading. He wrote in 1900 but his words seem equally true today. "The *Spectator* appears to be the only paper of the nervous system in England."' Not that Greene was partisan: consultation with a motor-car expert enabled him to suggest that, surely, the magazine was offering a dud Daimler as star-prize in a competition by which it was hoped to increase sales. Perhaps the most simply subversive of his schemes was the one to bring down the Post Office (if, however, one now wishes to support it, there is no easier way than by sending back empty all the reply-paid envelopes one receives: the funds thus accrued could pay for the restoration of a Sunday delivery). His exophthalmic eyes spot *The Times*'s wildly inaccurate weather reports, and they light on much else with amused displeasure.

Some editors might now think, 'Ah-ha, "Disgusted, Antibes" will make a good headline'; it has been pre-empted. Certainly there is a strong anti-American tone in the letters, one clear since the thirties and perhaps strengthened by SIS work and the evidence of American business dealings with Nazi Germany after Pearl Harbor and throughout the war. 'They strike me rather as the English abroad strike me,' he told Martin Amis (*Observer*, 23 September 1984). 'Noisy, and incredibly ignorant of the world. I had a woman who came to see me from Houston the other day, and she was the most incredibly stupid woman I've ever known. And she was a graduate. We talked about the Central American situation. She'd never heard about it. She'd never heard of any troubles down there.'

Enlightenment is available here. The Vatican and the Pope do not emerge unsullied. One sometimes has the impression that Greene has established his own Intelligence network. Those whom it has exposed are sometimes to be found – literally – on his doorstep: the letters to *The Times* about the dark side of Nice became *J'Accuse* but the casinos have been granted fresh licences, the shootings have resumed and – despite a court case – the story is not over. One might even supply another letter (not intended for immediate publication) of 21 December 1970 which suggested that the *Sunday Times* investigate a seaside mystery also of particular interest to him: forty years before, the hotel had welcomed Mr Colleoni as a guest, where his 'small shrewd eyes shone blankly under the concealed pervasive electric glow', and where an emphatic clerk later barred Pinkie and Rose.

'I feel strongly that the fire which destroyed the old Bedford Hotel in Brighton – in April 1964 – is well worth an investigation.

'As you will know, the old Bedford Hotel was an old Georgian building and it was burnt down with the loss of two lives on the night that a protection order had been granted which would have prevented the seventeen-storey building that has risen on the site. A curious feature of the fire was, I am told by Dr Clifford Musgrave, the late director of the Royal Pavilion, that only one small fire engine came to the scene of the fire and was quite inadequate. I believe that another hotel connected with the Bedford was also burnt down though not at the same date. It would be interesting to know what happened to the porter who gave evidence at the inquiry. Is he living in luxury in the West Indies?! I have a strong feeling that you would find a great deal to unearth in this affair. Brighton was really living up to its reputation.'

'Got him on the raw!' exclaims the atrocious Granger at the press-conference in *The Quiet American*; the phrase is echoed, with rather more justice, in *Ways of Escape* about Papa Doc's outraged reaction to *The Comedians*.

Greene has continually spoken of failure, and was once described by the *Daily Express* (17 April 1954) as wearing success like a hair-shirt; it is perhaps a spur to unceasing work and a defence against those who prey on his time.

Among those to do so was Philip Toynbee, a journalist forever on the trail of the 'significant', finding it in such trumpery as *The Outsider*. In an *Observer* interview (15 September 1957), part of a series 'on the relationship between a writer and the social problems of his times', Toynbee repeatedly urged the claims of the 'engaged'. This brought the reaction, 'I don't see how the novelist can write about anything of which he hasn't had direct personal experience.' 'So you really feel that any deliberate decision by a writer to engage himself is rather nonsensical?' 'It is to me personally.' Toynbee wondered whether a young man in the fifties could write like Firbank. 'I should be very glad if it happened,' replied Greene. The interviewer was horrified: 'You say that you wouldn't feel any offence if a writer of today wrote a good book in that sort of manner?' 'No: I'd be delighted. I hate the idea that any sort of duty is imposed on the writer from outside ... A modern

Firbank would certainly be a rather different Firbank. There would inevitably be a difference of tone in his books.' 'Perhaps a note of defiance,' asked the ever-hopeful Toynbee, only to receive the classic comment, typical of Greene, 'Or of despair. Or even of optimism.'

In a shaft calculated to annoy *Observer* readers, he added, 'There are times when one would welcome a bit of destruction. Especially in a Welfare State.' A writer's task is more complicated than the journalist's; it is to engage sympathy for characters outside the usual range, such as the traitor. 'To do this sets one a slightly more difficult task. It also makes people see something which they have failed to see. That the apparent villain is in fact human, and deserves more compassion than the apparent hero.'

After mentioning his account of the Mau Mau rebellion, where his sympathies are clearly engaged by the Africans and not the White Settlers, Greene went on to say, perhaps in the hope of further goading Toynbee: 'I should like very much to go to South Africa as a reporter. [One can perhaps see the beginning of *The Human Factor* here.] But the hero and villain of such non-fictional writing might well turn out to have their rôles reversed in a novel . . . it's in this way that one's function as a novelist seems to differ so much from one's function as a reporter of events.'

To the *Express* journalist who spoke of a hair-shirt, Greene remarked, 'Success is the point of self-deception. Failure is the point of self-knowledge.' Never less than a novel entertainment, these letters are not only a way of escape, but a product of success brought to bear upon, and deflate, those who by their vainglory ignore all that lies in wait.

In the case of politicians, this is the explanatory footnote which they never dreamed would be necessary. Such will perhaps be required one day for the overweight, chain-smoking Minister of Health, who was more correct than he realized when remarking that 'people who write letters to the press are not typical of the general public' (*Newsnight*, 22 February 1989).

Whatever has been the error of journalists' ways, one cannot help but regret the current reliance upon agency reports and the curtailment of such news reporting as Greene supplied to the *Sunday Times* in the fifties: *pace* the Health Minister, the correspondence columns could well become the press core.

EDITOR'S NOTE
AND ACKNOWLEDGEMENTS

As many letters as possible were collected and, after some debate, a fair number were eliminated: in a few instances, such as the 1987 publishing row, because the repercussions continue; in others because too much exegesis would have been necessary to explain the circumstances which prompted a sentence or two – these ranged from President Kennedy's assassination, Tito's visit to England and General Gordon in Africa, to the Theatre Workshop's finances, the Edwardian periodical *Chums*, Paul Theroux's memory and John Wells's dodgy grammar. Also dropped have been a few pseudonymous ones, under the names of M. E. Wimbush and Hilary Trench.

1945 has been taken as the starting-date, which marks the end of war-work and – in due course – the achievement of popular success with *The Heart of the Matter*. Letters are arranged chronologically so that themes become apparent of themselves (although an index is also supplied). This is a system from which there has been some deviation, and earlier letters have been fitted into the notes.

Where a carbon copy exists, it has been collated with the printed version; the original paragraphing, titles and occasional cuts have been restored but left unburdened by a textual apparatus, except for brackets around the date of those letters that went unpublished.

The letters have been gathered from a number of sources, and it is puzzling that editors of weekly magazines should not always deem letter-writers worthy of a place in their indexes: the *New Statesman*'s columns feature the first appearances in print of, among others, John Fowles and Jim Crace, not that the authors might care to admit it – Dan Kavanagh cheerfully confessed to his, while Clive James might prefer to forget a 2,000-word effort from the early weeks of 1968.

I am very grateful to Mr Graham Greene and his sister, Mrs Elisabeth Dennys, for allowing me to look through boxes of cuttings and carbons (it is curious what havoc a bundle of paper can cause when scattered across the floor); and to Mr Nicholas Shakespeare and Mr John Coldstream of the *Daily Telegraph*, and Mr Graham Lord and Mr Keith Beard of the *Express*, for access to their cuttings; and to Lady Elizabeth Bowes Lyon, Mr Max Reinhardt, Mr John Ryder and Miss Judy Taylor for bringing into shape the resultant unwieldy, ever-growing bundle of typescript and sellotape.

The staff of the British Museum Reading Room and the London Library were as helpful as ever, as were those at the Catholic Reference Library (Francis Street, SW1), 'Colindale', the Press Association, and Hove Reference Library, who cheerfully underwent what proved to be a weight-training course.

I am also grateful to Dr Fareed Ali, Lady Clare Asquith, Mr Julian Barnes, Dr Robert Baxter, Mrs Judith Bennett (*Tablet*), Mr Alexander Chancellor, Mr Michael Davie, Mr Nick Dennys, Miss Helen Ellis, Mr Keith Hawtree, Mr Ian Hislop, Mr John Hughes, Mr Bryan Marlow, Dr Seyed Moosavi (University of Texas), Miss Pepper, Ms Marion Powers (*Time*), Mr David Pryce-Jones, Mrs Isabel Quigly, Mr Charles Seaton (Librarian, the *Spectator*), Mr David Sexton, Dr Keith Walker, Messrs Canon, Hitachi and XeroX.

I am equally grateful to those who supplied the original bait in the press (some of whom resurface here); and also to those who wrote directly to Graham Greene at the time: in quoting from these it sometimes seemed wisest to adopt such phrases as 'a man from Colchester'. They know who they are.

I am grateful to the following for permission to reproduce copyright material: Professor Walter Allen, Mr Nicholas Bagnall, Mr Anthony Burgess, Mr Alexander Chancellor, the Estate of Randolph Churchill, Mr Rupert Cornwell, the Estate of Sir Noël Coward, Mr Brian Crozier, Mrs Elisabeth Dennys, the Estate of F. H. R. Dix, the Estate of T. S. Eliot, *Express* Newspapers, Mr George Gale, the Estate of John Gordon, Dr Donald Gould, the Estate of Sir Hugh Greene, Mr Herb Greer, Lord Hailsham, Mr John Harriott, the Estate of John Hayward, Mr Peter Hebblethwaite, Mr Ronald Hingley, Mr Anthony Howard, Mr Derek Hudson, the *Independent*, Mr Brian Inglis, Lord Jay, the Estate of David Jones, Mr Francis King, the Estate of Sir Allen Lane, the Estate of Philip Larkin, Mr Nigel Lawson, Mr Bernard Levin, the Estate of Kingsley Martin, Mr Ernest Mehew, Lord Molson, Lord Monson, Mr Charles Mosley, the *New York Times*, Mr Simon Nowell-Smith, the Estate of Sir Herbert Read, Mr Piers Paul Read, Lady Redgrave, Sir John Rothenstein, Dr A. L. Rowse, Mr Colin Simpson, the Estate of Lord Snow, the Estate of John Sutro, the *Tablet*, Lord Thomas of Swynnerton, Mr Auberon Waugh, the Estate of Evelyn Waugh.

The letters of 21 September 1961, 20 July 1964 and 6 February 1976 are included by kind permission of the Harry Ransom Humanities Research Center, Austin, Texas.

Although efforts have been made to trace everybody quoted, this has now sometimes proved difficult; gratitude and apologies are offered, and amends will be made – it must be said, however, that this does not apply to G. E. Fanshaugh and his Eltham Laundry Supplies Ltd.

PROLOGUE

Horizon, the magazine edited by Cyril Connolly, had praised the recently deceased 'primitive' painter, Alfred Wallis, which prompted a letter from Evelyn Waugh in the issue for March 1943: 'Blue, decayed streaks of silliness are healthy in art as in cheese. I have the honour to offer a prize of ten pounds annually, as long as *Horizon* is published, for the silliest contribution, to be called "The Alfred Wallis Prize", and to be awarded by subscribers. All contributors will be eligible with preference for the old and famous rather than the young and contemporary. The work need not be complete in itself or in anything else.'

Graham Greene replied two issues later:

— May I record a vote that Mr Evelyn Waugh be awarded the first 'Alfred Wallis Prize' for his little castrated letter, which so admirably fulfils his last condition, that 'the work need not be complete in itself or in anything else'?

As Alfred Wallis is dead and is unlikely, therefore, to notice Mr Waugh's generous offer, I suggest that the prize might more suitably bear the name of the donor.

YOURS ETC.

Gill's Monkey

— It is frequently difficult for artists and writers to escape anti-clericalism for their professions as a rule bring them more closely in touch than other people with the lack of imagination and stupidity of those in official circles. The latest example of clerical ignorance and lack of taste, the disfigurement of one of Eric Gill's statues in Westminster Cathedral, will raise again an instinctive anti-clericalism in many of us. The monkey forming part of the St Thomas More statue, which apparently has offended one of our Church authorities, was not only justified aesthetically in Gill's statue, but it was obviously justified historically and psychologically, and it is indeed difficult to plumb the depths of ignorance and irresponsibility which must have been responsible for its removal.

At the foot of the letters page (7 March 1947) the Editor noted: 'a very large number of letters on this subject have been received. Some are unpublishable. Most are omitted because of space.'

On 7 February 'Art Critic' had described Gill's 'plaque representing the Crucifixion, with the figures of SS Thomas More and John Fisher, standing on either side of the Cross. It stands behind the altar of the shrouded English Martyrs' chapel, awaiting the last touches of the contractors before it is unveiled for the public.

'It was at Pigotts [Gill's home at Speen, near High Wycombe] that I first saw the work. It showed St Thomas accompanied by his pet monkey – but, alas, where is the monkey now? In

Westminster Cathedral a neat job of eliminating has been done, and the monkey is no longer visible beside his master.

'Could this absurd, mischievous, harmless and loving little companion of a saint be a cause of scandal? One thinks of the animals that have appeared in medieval church decoration, grotesque animals as well as naturalistic animals. The ox and the ass are allowed to attend the birth of Christ and proudly sit among the straw of our cribs today. Fishes, even, swim round the marble borders of St Andrew's Chapel in Westminster Cathedral itself. Why not a monkey?'

Among those whose letters were published was David Jones: 'I remember Mr Gill speaking to me of the monkey, and I should like to reinforce what Mr Tegetmeier [Gill's son-in-law] says concerning its symbolism ... Mr Gill had in mind far more than the inclusion of the characteristic pet of the Renaissance Chancellor: he seemed to be thinking also of the ape-ishness in man and, further, and more important still, of the whole animal creation suppliant at the Tree, the Tree to which all creation owes a kind of Latria ... the ape-made-stone turned out to be one of the more lively passages of the whole work. So that not only as to content, but as to form, a deprivation would seem to have been inflicted.'

*

Listener / 10 April 1947

Bare Yellow Skulls

— Mr Bradshaw is, of course, quite right. I meant 'atebrin', and 'atropin' was one of those slips of the brain that it would need a psycho-analyst to explain. But he is quite wrong in thinking that atebrin was not in fairly general use on the Coast before 1943. By the summer of 1942 quinine was already severely rationed. Nor can I imagine that any woman of sense would abandon atebrin for quinine (usually a much more harmful prophylactic for

(4)

women) for the sake of her complexion. After all, the white skin has a horrible albino out-of-place look in Africa whatever the shade of white.

In a talk, 'Heroes Are Made in Childhood' (an early version of 'The Lost Childhood', *Collected Essays*), printed in the *Listener* of 27 March, Greene had written of his young discovery of reading, in particular, of Haggard and *King Solomon's Mines*: 'If it had not been for that romantic tale of Allan Quatermain, Sir Henry Curtis, and, above all, the ancient witch Gagool, would I at nineteen have studied the appointments list of the Colonial Office and very nearly picked on the Nigerian Navy for a career? . . . Wasn't it the incurable fascination of Gagool with her bare yellow skull, the wrinkled scalp that moved and contracted like the hood of a cobra, that led me to work all through 1942 in a little stuffy office in Freetown, Sierra Leone? There is not much in common between the land of the Kukanas, behind the desert and the mountain range of Sheba's Breast, and a tin-roofed house on a bit of swamp where the buzzards moved like domestic turkeys and the piedogs kept me awake on moon-light nights with their wailing, and the white women yellowed by atropin drove by to the club; but the two belonged at any rate to the same continent, and, however distantly, to the same region of the imagination – the region of uncertainty, of not knowing the way about.'

S. Bradshaw of Liverpool commented (3 April): 'Mr Graham Greene is made to speak of the white women in Sierra Leone who were "yellowed by atropin". The time was 1942.

'Mr Greene, I take it, would not speak of their yellow "color". Why, then, of "atropin"? He must have meant "atropine". But did he? If the good ladies of Freetown were dosing themselves with belladonna, Mr Greene was well advised to stay inside his tin-roofed house on a bit of swamp and not to accompany them to the club. To them Gagool would have been a very Helen. Picture them: pupils dilated, eyes focused on infinity, their mouths dry, their gastric juices absent – maniacal, hallucinated creatures, breathing deeply and their hearts pounding like mad as, across Mr Greene's nystagmic field of vision, they reel like inco-ordinate harpies! Also, their temperatures would have been raised, and they'd have died of heat stroke, one by one, before sunset. Mr Greene might well have considered them fit companions for his buzzards and piedogs.

'Science, alas, will have none of it: atropine does not make people yellow. It may suffuse their gills with a delicate red colour. Colour blindness, then? To Greene, red was yellow? But the mania ... Perhaps these ladies were in fact polygamously married to the big bush devil of whom Mr Greene speaks, and had blinded him to all but their odd complexions.

'No, I think he meant "atebrin" (alias, "quinacrine" or "mepacrine"). Yet atebrin, if memory serves, was not in general use as an anti-malarial prophylactic on "The Coast" until 1943. Moreover, any lady to whom it gave the slightest yellow tinge very soon found she was allergic to it and simply had to use quinine instead.

'Then – was it, could it have been, that the Sierra Leonean ladies of 1942 were suffering from a toxic jaundice? And, did England make them so? Or had they been sampling too much Brighton rock on the voyage out?'

*

Daily Mirror / 9 January 1948

Knife Work

— I have read the somewhat violent attack by your critic [Reginald Whitley] with bewilderment. If he had said that the book [*Brighton Rock*] was 'false, cheap, nasty sensationalism', it would have been, to me, a quite possible personal point of view, but to praise the author of the book at the expense of the directors of the film is surely unbalanced.

As it happens, I am also the author of the film play, and I

can assure your critic that John Boulting (the director, while his twin brother Roy was producer) worked quite as hard as myself to retain the religious theme. And modifications of that theme are the responsibility of the British Film Censor, who objected to various passages in the dialogue of a specifically religious nature. Apparently one is allowed a certain latitude in using the name of God as an expletive, but any serious quotation from the Bible is not permissible on the English screen.

But in spite of this handicap I should have said that what your critic describes, almost too kindly, as 'the subtle religious theme' was as present in the film as in the book. Mr Whitley remarks that 'Hollywood has banned the production of gangster films because they give a false impression of life in America', but in fact Hollywood has not banned the production of gangster films but only the production of films that hold the gangster up to the sympathy of the audience. Obviously this has not been done in the case of Pinkie Brown, and your critic's disgust is an indication that one purpose of the film – the presentation of a character possessed by evil – has been successfully achieved.

Naturally, parents will not want their children to see it (must all films be made for the juvenile market?) nor would they be allowed to take their children to it without breaking the rules of the cinema, since the picture has been granted only an adult certificate.

The film, which in exchange for location work carried a disclaimer to the effect that the town no longer resembles its notorious pre-war days, was in fact given an 'A' certificate, which meant that it could be seen either by those over sixteen or with an adult.

*

Incident in Prague

— I have received a press cutting of 'John Bouverie's Journal' for 27 February and for pure curiosity I should like to know whether this Journal comes under the heading of fiction [the story also appeared in the *Daily Herald*'s 'Chanticleer' column]. Under the heading Czech-mate there is a paragraph dealing with me of which the only accurate statement is that I happened to be staying in the Alcron Hotel. As far as I know the Alcron did not pass from private into public ownership, I am certainly unaware of ever having been served by a Communist waiter who had been appointed national administrator, and I was not lecturing for the British Council. Do satisfy my curiosity about this Journal.

Bouverie had written, 'A guest in Prague's most ambitious hotel, the Alcron, when it passed yesterday from private into public ownership, was novelist Graham Greene, who is in Prague at the moment to lecture for the British Council. He looked for his Communist waiter. He had been appointed national administrator.'

This might have strayed from *Scoop*; but, then, so – at first – did the actual events, as related in *Ways of Escape*, where Greene is obliged to kip down in a room with an agency and a BBC reporter: 'In the basement we found that we were not the only ones in search of food. The Venezuelan Ambassador was there dancing ponderously with the fat cook . . . If this was really a revolution it seemed to me not so bad. The band played, everyone was happy, the beer flowed . . . who could have foretold on that fantastic night the Slansky trial, all the Stalin horrors, the brief spring, and then Dubček and Smrkovsky dragged as prisoners to Moscow?'

*

Week-end Competition No. 999

— Thank you for awarding a prize [one guinea] in your Competition the other day for Greene or Green openings to M. Wilkinson, who is – in the only too probable words of one of my characters – yours truly. I wish you had also given awards to D. R. Cook and M. Wilkinson, because prize money in these days is free of Income Tax.

The competition, set by Walter Allen, had invited parodies of opening pages from the numerous contemporary novelists called Green(e). First prize was taken by pastiche F. L. Green. Among the also-rans, from whom excerpts were quoted, was P. A. Larkin, not then well known for a novel, *Jill*, and a volume of poetry, *The North Ship*: 'Hatred moved in him like fatigue as, unsurprised, he recognized betrayal: he had never been weaned from it: the planted wallet, Norah's promise, the stolen rosary.'

'M. Wilkinson's' entry, 'The Stranger's Hand', was sub-titled 'an entertainment': 'The child had an air of taking everything in and giving nothing away. At the Rome airport he was led across the tarmac by his aunt, but he seemed to hear nothing of her advice to himself or of the information she produced for the air hostess. He was too busy with his eyes: the hangars had his attention, every plane on the field except his own – that could wait.

'"My nephew," she was saying, "yes, that's him on the list. Roger Court. You *will* look after him, won't you? He's never been quite on his own before," but when she made that statement the child's eyes moved back plane by plane with what looked like contempt, back to the large breasts and the fat legs and the over-responsible mouth: how *could* she have known, he might have been thinking, when I am alone, how often I am alone?'

A writer never lets anything go to waste. This sketch became a treatment for *The Stranger's Hand*, a 1954 film which, co-produced by Greene and directed by Mario Soldati, included both Trevor Howard and Alida Valli from *The Third Man*. 'It was my first appearance on screen, or rather, my hand's,' says Greene. 'It appeared in the film undoing the knot of the fireboat. Unfortunately, by the time the film was finished and ready to be shown, Tito had become a kind of white-headed boy of the West; he had split with Russia ... the film was about a Yugoslavian kidnapping of a British officer – in that sense, Tito would have been the villain of the piece – which didn't do the film any good.' (Quentin Falk, *Travels in Greeneland* [1984].)

Competitions have been a further spur to production. On 14 April 1961 Greene wrote to the *New Statesman*:

> — I'm sorry, but I've done it again. The prize you have awarded to a Mr Baxter for a fragment of my autobiography in verse should in fact be sent to me. If you feel I had an unfair advantage in knowing about that dog in the pram you are at liberty to send the guinea, to support a good cause, to the John Gordon Society, of which I happen to be President [see page 76ff].

As prose the entry became part of the first chapter of *A Sort of Life*.

> '*A dead dog I remember in my pram;*
> *It had a vulpine air even in death.*
> *I cried out to the squint-eyed nurse, but words*
> *Were still a miracle I had not learned.*
> *Only I knew the hour had struck for me –*
> *A business man went grumbling into dark,*
> *The District Officer I'd never be*
> *Soared from my pram for darkest Africa.*
> *I lay and watched that vulpine grin of death*
> *Until the squint-eyed nurse to comfort me*
> *Delved in her tomb-like bag and found interred,*
> *Long, slim and pink, a stick of Brighton Rock.*'

Competition 1850, set by L. W. Bailey in the *New Statesman* in August 1965, required an extract from the biography of a man by his namesake, such as Angus Wilson's account of Harold. Among the winners announced on 27 August was Sebastian Eleigh, who gave this sample of Sir Hugh Greene (Director-General of the BBC) by Graham: 'Hugh lost his faith the day I hit him on the head with a croquet mallet, and years later at his desk in Broadcasting House, arranging some series of talks by atheists, he would feel his mind darkened by the shadow of the falling mallet as by the wing of a great bird.

'I was twelve that summer and already conscious of God moving among the weeds between the raspberry canes. Hugh was six.

'The nursery maid of the day (our mother changed them with the frequency of young girls in a Gran Bassa brothel) crunched by on the gravel, her thighs sleek as a cat's. But it was in one of her plump calves that Hugh sank his teeth, through the acrid black stocking to the succulent flesh.

'I swung the mallet. Was it a foretaste of adult jealousy? I had known her for a week as an instrument of pleasure. Or was it that, as the blood spurted, I had some vague presentiment of my brother's future, the godless and orgiastic roads he was to follow, the too brilliant ascent, the sudden fall exactly fifty years later under the goads of the Puritans, the seedy and mysterious end.'

This was Hugh posing as Hugh by Graham, who, under the guise of Malcolm Collins, took second prize (a very welcome eight guineas): 'I begin this biography therefore in the year 1920 – on one of those long summer days at Berkhamsted, among the empty buildings of a school out-of-term, when my green gauge O clockwork train burst through a cordon of lead soldiers (in the uniforms of the South African war) and broke the siege of my headquarters. "I am betrayed by my own men," Hugh said, and climbed sadly the long stairway, past silent dormitories, to the room we shared.'

(The biography of Hugh Greene by Michael Tracey ran into

some trouble, appropriately enough in the form of Mary Whitehouse, who demanded that the page on which she appears be amended forthwith.)

The *Spectator* ran a competition (1111) in April 1980 which asked for an extract from an imaginary novel by Graham Greene. Among the winners was Mr Eleigh once again. He won first prize: 'As usual the Euston train was twenty minutes late by the time it reached Berkhamsted. Through Watford, King's Langley and Boxmoor Sergeant had picked thoughtfully at the sore place on his lower lip until the blood was running down his chin. What did the General want, he wondered with impatient affection? What could he want so many years since the mugging in Belize?

'At Berkhamsted station he walked rapidly along the tiled passage smelling of urine, like an elongated public lavatory, and came out into the misty Hertfordshire rain. Under the weeping willows on the canal bank a child was crying and a dog barked.

'Driver was waiting for him on the canal bridge. How much time, he thought, the General must have spent all those years ago on acquiring a sergeant called Driver and a driver called Sergeant. "Whom are we to kill this time?" he asked, almost cheerfully.'

Mr Eleigh was joined on this occasion by 'Katharine Onslow', Graham's sister Elisabeth Dennys, who, too, mailed her entry from a 'safe house': 'He lay on the fallen beech leaves at the edge of the Common as the sun disappeared behind the gorse bushes. Faintly he could hear the voices of the golfers at the seventeenth hole approaching nearer to their gins and tonics in the club-house bar. A beetle scraped its way through the skeleton leaves. They had always found him before, but he could persuade himself as the sky darkened that perhaps this time they would not notice. Even she might be tired of descending yet again from the nursery to the drawing-room with the news that he was missing. But would she tire? He pressed himself deeper into the

wet dark leaves as his mind peered down a reversed telescope of
time where she grew smaller and smaller, but from the evil and
the fear he would find no escape.'

In his 'Notebook' column a few weeks later (7 June), the
Spectator's editor, Alexander Chancellor, wrote: '. . . the family
acquitted itself remarkably well. But what of Graham? We felt
sure that he had entered. Our suspicions, for a number of good
reasons, came to rest upon an entry under the name of Colin
Bates, which, I am afraid, was not included among the five best
that we printed. It ran as follows:

'"I am a man approaching middle-age, but the only birthday I
can distinguish among all the others was my twelfth. It was on
that damp misty day in October that I met the Captain for the
first time. I remember the wetness of the gravel in the school
quad and the blown leaves which made the cloisters by the
chapel slippery as I ran to escape from my enemies between one
class and the next. I slithered and came to a halt and my pursuers
went whistling away, for there in the middle of the quad stood
our formidable headmaster talking to a tall man in a bowler hat
who carried his walking stick over his shoulder at the slope like a
rifle. I had no idea of course who he was or that he had won me
the previous night at backgammon from my father."'

This continued the pattern set in 1949, for, revised, the entry
became the opening page of *The Captain and the Enemy* (1988).

*

When *The Heart of the Matter* became a Book Society Choice in
America, Evelyn Waugh gave some advice gained from his
success there with *Brideshead Revisited*: '. . . this American coup
relieves you of work for fifteen years . . . my own experience is
that it is simply not worthwhile earning more than a gross
£5,000 a year nowadays. I get about £2,000 from English sales
and odd articles (your price for articles in the USA will now be
about five times what it was), so I take £3,000 a year from my
USA publishers in half-yearly sums of $6,000 each . . . You will
have the most ghastly post-bag for six weeks or so. Then quite

abruptly they lose all interest. I read all letters and answered a few rudely. I think this was bad policy . . . I should advise against going over to enjoy your –' Here the manuscript breaks off, and Greene's proposed visit ran into difficulties:

The Times / 21 June 1949

Dollars for Authors

— Writers are creeping up on industrialists as dollar earners, but one department of the Bank of England still appears to regard us as an inferior race, or at least as distinct outsiders. I have recently signed a contract with the well-known American theatrical producers Rogers and Hammerstein for a dramatic version of my last novel, *The Heart of the Matter*. This has to be written in New York in collaboration with the director, and the play has been scheduled to open on Broadway in the autumn. I asked the Bank of England for the usual business man's allowance of £10 a day to keep me in New York during the period of writing. Royalties had already been advanced to me by Rogers and Hammerstein to enable me to visit New York for the preliminary consultations last year, and it is unreasonable to expect further advances before the play is written.

Even if the play were unsuccessful, by the terms of the contract the dollars earned could not fail to equal the small amount the Bank of England was asked to sanction. If the play were a success, the dollars accruing to this country would be incalculable. The Bank of England, however, tells me that it cannot 'gamble on an unknown quantity to the extent of £350', the amount asked for. Are the odds so very much longer than when I went last year to America as a publisher, or when thousands of other business men have gone in the praiseworthy attempt to sell their goods for dollars? The Bank of England has offered to sanction a daily allowance of £4, on which it is impossible to live and work in New York under present conditions. I have, therefore, had to cancel my contract. One wonders how many other authors have been prevented in the same way from earning dollars for this country.

Questions were asked in Parliament, and, in reply, Stafford Cripps claimed that Greene 'did not state in his application . . . either that he had a contract or that the dramatic version had to be written in New York under the contract, or that royalties had already been advanced to him, or that even if the play were unsuccessful the dollars earned would reimburse his expenditure'. Greene wrote to *The Times* on 2 July:

— I had not expected when I wrote my first letter to you on the subject of 'dollars for authors' that the matter would go so far as it has done. I had no desire to have my personal case used as political propaganda but only to draw attention to what seemed a general attitude on the part of the Bank of England to people of my profession.

However, I would like with your permission to correct the impression conveyed by the Chancellor of the Exchequer in his reply to a question from Mr [Christopher] Hollis in the House of Commons last Tuesday. The Chancellor said that I had not stated in my original application for a dollar allotment that a contract had been signed for the dramatization of my book. In all but the omission of the word 'contract', Sir Stafford Cripps has been misinformed. My application stated definitely that I wished to visit New York by arrangement with Messrs Rogers and Hammerstein, the theatrical producers, in order to dramatize my book *The Heart of the Matter* for them. The Bank of England replied that they were only prepared to allow me a maximum amount of £4 a day when they were satisfied that the application was a genuine one. There was no question, whatever the terms of the arrangement, of their allowing a larger amount. It is true that the

Bank were unaware that the 'gamble of £350' was, by the terms of the contract, no gamble at all, but I persist in thinking that they should have allowed so small a gamble in the case of an author when they automatically gamble in the case of a business man.

Life commented that the Bank's deeming it too risky an enterprise to justify the money's leaving the country 'somehow, in view of the *South Pacific* take . . . strikes us almost speechless'.

The work was done in London and the adaptation eventually opened in Boston, but did not move to Broadway. 'I long to hear an account of your Boston disaster,' wrote Evelyn Waugh in March 1950. 'I never liked the idea of that play.'

The novel was filmed in 1953, with Trevor Howard, but was given an altered ending, which had none of the ambiguity of that demanded for *Brighton Rock* a few years earlier. Banned in Singapore, Hong Kong and Malaya, and censored in Ireland, most bizarre of all was the Italian version, which was dubbed and rewritten (not by Greene) so that it could go out under a title topical enough for events on the other side of Africa, *The Mau Mau Story*. Almost as dire was an internationally produced 1983 television 'mini-serial' which defied one to sit through it until whatever ending was chosen. All the players were of different nationalities and dubbed.

It is not perhaps well known that *Our Man in Havana*, as well as being filmed by Carol Reed with a Greene script (1959), was made into an opera in 1962 by the young Australian Malcolm Williamson, who had lived in England for ten years. His Mass in a 'beat' idiom was to have been heard the previous October at the church of St Anselm and St Cecilia, Kingsway, but the Roman Catholic authorities banned its performance there.

The libretto for the Greene opera was written by the veteran scriptwriter and producer, Sidney Gilliat. Greene had told the *Sunday Times* (9 June 1963), which pictured him amid the orchestra, that he did not wish to write one because 'writing for me is a cold act. I write against the grain. It's a cold war, not a hot one. I couldn't feel the passion.' Following the opera's première at Sadler's Wells, *The Times*'s anonymous music critic praised the enterprise of all concerned, including Eric Shilling's Hawthorne 'which almost obliterates happy memories of Mr Noël Coward in the film'. However, he went on to say that it 'is a poor opera, in certain respects a bad one, and as a representation of a great novel it is a travesty. . . One had not dared to hope that the depths and distances of Greene's novel would be retained, but one had expected some shape and consistency which does not show itself in this version.'

Greene wrote to the newspaper on 4 July 1963:

— As I had no hand in the opera of *Our Man in Havana* may I be allowed without vanity to disagree with your Critic? To me the opera was in no way a travesty of the novel and I admired the great skill with which the libretto had compressed the action and yet brought out every political point. Surely it is a little odd to write of 'the weak characterization of the head of the Secret Service', for he is a very minor character in the novel. Perhaps your Critic had in mind Sir Ralph Richardson's brilliant performance in the film. As the author of the film script may I say that I infinitely preferred Mr Gilliat's libretto?

I haven't spoken of the music only because it would be impertinent on my part perhaps to disagree with your Music Critic on his own ground. All the same to me it was very satisfactory and added a new dimension to the story.

*

The Times / 17 April 1951

Sharp Practices

— Sir Stanley Unwin writes that 'until comparatively recently agreements between author and publisher took the form of an agreement to divide any profit which might accrue from the publication of a book . . .' and he suggests that this system was mutually discontinued for a variety of reasons. In fact, authors had to fight hard for their right to a royalty. They learned from bitter experience that with certain publishers there never were any profits on their books. When the mysterious uncheckable 'overheads' had been deducted, as well as advertising costs at whatever figure the publisher chose to allot to the particular book (most advertising is general advertising and the author can hardly be expected to keep account of his half inches of space in each paper and catalogue), profits could easily become negligible. For the author this might mean starvation; for the publisher a profitable business. Sir Stanley Unwin may reply that there should be mutual trust between 'partners'. The author knows that in those black days trust was very one-sided, nor is he ready to call himself a partner in a business over which he has no control.

Sir Stanley Unwin does not exactly get down to figures, and his argument seems to belong to a different mathematical world from mine. 'If I pay on your new book the same high royalty as the last, the price must be X, since I must provide for an equally sharp increased payment to you on each copy sold. If, however, you choose to accept a slightly lower royalty, the price can be reduced to Y, producing for you a slightly, but not so sharply, increased return to you on each copy sold.' I receive, say, 15 per cent on a book previously sold at 10s (1s 6d royalty a copy). If he is forced to increase the price to 12s 6d he will have to pay me a royalty of 1s 10½d. If my royalty is reduced to 12½ per cent and he is enabled to publish my book at 12s, I shall receive 1s 6¾d! The price of the book has gone up 2s, the booksellers are receiving 8d more a copy sold, the publisher has 1s 4d more to put against his costs, and the man who wrote the book over the space of a year or more will be getting ¾d more.

The cost of living for the author has risen as well as for

the publisher and the bookseller. He has his raw materials, too, of food, lodging, paper, typing. Why is it always the middleman who seeks protection against rising costs? The author has in the past been able to live without publishers, but the publishers cannot live without authors. May I suggest a more equitable way of keeping down the price of books would be for publishers to make a substantial cut in their own salaries and directors' fees?

*

Spectator / 14 March 1952

Norman Douglas

— Mr Harold Nicolson's timid denigrations of Norman Douglas should not go unanswered. Unfortunately Mr Nicolson has himself supplied most of the phrases with which we should have liked to describe his article – 'moral cant', 'a certain primness', 'a middle-class shape of mind', 'more bourgeois than I like to suppose' – much as a man who has exhibited in battle great physical cowardice might try to disarm criticism of himself later by referring to 'a certain psychological timidity', 'a recurrent desire to escape my fellows'.

Mr Nicolson confesses that he only met Norman Douglas twice and one would think he might have left it to those who knew Douglas better to write a tribute to a great writer and a great man. Douglas died at the age of eighty-three, and those who knew him in his last years saw no sign of the boasting, the noisy drunkenness, to which Mr Nicolson, with gleeful deprecation, refers in a style rather reminiscent of a protocol officer discussing last night's dinner with his Minister. One knew Douglas as a man more loved by more people than is usually the lot of any of us: a man of great personal dignity and of great charity. I use the word charity in the theological sense. He had a love too great to be other than tolerant of the strange foibles of his fellow men. Even meanness he regarded charitably, and I have no doubt that this sudden laugh to which Mr Nicolson refers would have exploded at this obituary tribute with all its veiled depreciation. 'Oh yes, I met the man somewhere once,' he would have said and produced a valid and amusing reason for the strange ambiguous tone in which Mr Nicolson's article is written.

Towards the end of Douglas's life there were old peasant women who would come the length of Italy to spend a few hours in his company. He carried always in his pocket small change to give to those even poorer than himself. I doubt whether many apart from Mr Nicolson have seen Douglas 'noisily drunk' (one does not associate noise with him in any form), and if he had no sense of 'superior virtue', perhaps that too was only one more sign of his enormous tolerance. It may not have been 'what the French call *tenue*', but his friends may be allowed to call it charity.

Harold Nicolson had given over his 'Marginal Comment' column (22 February) to the death of Norman Douglas, and said, 'I certainly am liable to be shocked by people who, when past the age of seventy, openly avow indulgences which they ought to conceal'; his own long and rackety life has now been described in Nigel Nicolson's *Portrait of a Marriage*, two volumes of biography by James Lees-Milne, Victoria Glendinning's *Vita*, and, more circumspectly, three volumes of *Diary and Letters*. See also Greene's 'Poison Pen' (*London Magazine*, March 1966), an attack on Richard Aldington's *Pinorman*, which the magazine could not print in 1956.

*

The Western and Christian Side

— In your editorial on the Russian proposals for German unity you use a phrase which might once have seemed remarkable but which now seems to slip as smoothly through the mind as a cliché: 'the Western and Christian side'. Has Christianity really sunk to a political and geographical division? Or is it time to divide our patriotic and our political beliefs from our theological?

To write as you do, as though by building a better national air force we were contributing to the survival of Christianity, has a rather repulsive ring. It suggests that Christianity depends on strength. One begins to speculate on the moral values of Hiroshima. Let us by all means defend our country and prefer our own political institutions to those of Russia, as so many Catholics preferred the rule of Elizabeth to that of Philip, but need we pretend that our struggle has other than a fortuitous and temporary connexion with Christianity? If we are Catholics we believe that the Church will survive a Russian victory: we even believe that it will survive an American.

I would suggest that for Catholics it is necessary to reassert the difference between loyalty to Caesar and loyalty to the Church. In the West we have Caesars (but not always Christian Caesars) who allow the Church to exist in freedom and comfort. Whether the Church in its temporal form is better for that freedom and comfort than it was in the catacombs of Rome is at least a disputable point. To equate the two ideas – the West and Christianity – is as demonstrably absurd as to equate the ideas, the East and Atheism. We may be prepared to rearm and fight for our country and for Western Europe, however materialist Western ideology may be, but when we rearm and when we fight, don't let us deceive ourselves into believing that we are necessarily fighting for our Church. We have no right, nor have Mr Truman or Mr Taft the right, to wear the cross of the crusader.

*

Spectator / 20 June 1952

The Young Saki

— Miss Munro speaks of 'the extraordinary delusion that some writers on Saki have had, that he had "a miserable childhood"'. Miss Munro seems to look now through far more rosy spectacles at her brother's childhood and her own than she did when she wrote the short biography of Saki which was included in the collected short stories. If writers on Saki suffer from delusions, the delusions are all based on her own writing:

'We slept in rooms with windows shut and shuttered, with only the door open on to the landing to admit stale air. All hygienic ideas were to Aunt Augusta, the Autocrat, chot rot, a word of her own invention.'

'Our grandmother, a gentle, dignified old lady, was entirely over-ruled by her turbulent daughters, who hated each other with a ferocity and intensity worthy of a bigger cause.'

'The other aunt, Augusta, is the one who, more or less, is depicted in *Sredni Vashtar*. She was the autocrat of Broadgate – a woman of ungovernable temper, of fierce likes and dislikes, imperious, a moral coward, possessing no brains worth speaking of, and a primitive disposition. Naturally the last person who should have been in charge of children.'

'Well do I remember those "fearsome silences"! Nothing could be said, because it was certain to sound silly, in the vast gloom. With Aunt Tom alone we should have fared much better . . . but as we could not obey both aunts (I believe each gave us orders which she knew were contrary to those issued by the other), we found it better for ourselves, in the end, to obey Aunt Augusta.'

'We had early learnt to hide our feelings – to show enthusiasm or emotion were sure to bring an amused smile to Aunt Augusta's face. It was a hateful smile, and I cannot imagine why it hurt, but it did; among ourselves we called it "the meaning smile".'

'Both aunts were guilty of mental cruelty: we often longed for revenge with an intensity I suspect we inherited from our Highland ancestry.'

'Charlie really came off worst – Aunt Augusta never liked him, and positively used to enjoy whipping him.'

'I think Aunt Augusta must have mesmerized us – the look in her dark eyes, added to the fury of her voice, and the uncertainty as to the punishment, used to make me shiver.'

Derek Hudson had reviewed (30 May) Greene's edition of *The Best of Saki* (whose introduction is in *Collected Essays*) and commented that 'earlier commentators have related Munro's cruel strain to his own miserable childhood spent in the house of his maiden aunts . . . That there is an element of cruelty in much of his work must be clear to any dispassionate observer. His devoted sister denied it, but her biography of her brother . . . provides further evidence of it in a series of drawings by Saki, too many of which show people being savaged and slaughtered, in the jolliest possible way, by wild animals . . . Mr Greene might, indeed, have gone further and linked the cruel element, doubtless derived from childish repressions, with Munro's early and continuing interest in fighting . . . more seriously expounded in an article in the *Morning Post* in 1915. "Nearly every red-blooded human boy," he wrote in that article, "has had, in some shape or form, for his first love, war; if his blood has remained red, and he has kept some of his boyishness in after life, that first love will never have been forgotten."'

Saki's sister, E. M. Munro, protested (13 June) that they had 'enjoyed our childhood in our grandmother's house, and, being blessed with amazing vitality and love of mischief, rode over all storms with an appetite for the next! When forbidden visits were paid to the lumber-room, with knowledge of the punishment that would follow if found out, those visits were naturally intensely exciting, and exciting events were continually happening in that house. I should say that the stern discipline he had in early life, far from causing a "cruel element" in him, was enough to make him detest cruelty in any form but not enough to stop him from writing about it.'

She replied (27 June) to Greene's letter and denied that the phrases quoted were indicative of misery and that 'it is rather strange that only in the last two or three years has the theory of "miserable childhood" cropped up . . . Mr Greene quotes from that biography, "that we slept in rooms with windows shut and shuttered" – though unhygienic, this did not constitute a misery – and "our grandmother was entirely over-ruled by her turbulent daughters" – this was also no misery to us. A friend who has read the biography said she never noticed anything suggesting misery in it. Moreover Saki's remark to me (and his memory of our childhood was as distinct as mine), that in spite of a strict upbringing, and having no other children to play with, he was glad of it, as otherwise we should never have been original, is not what he would have said if he had had a miserable childhood.'

*

New Statesman / 27 September 1952

The Return of Charlie Chaplin

An Open Letter

Dear Mr Chaplin,
    — I hope you will forgive an open letter: otherwise I would have added to that great pyramid of friendly letters that must be awaiting you in London. This is a letter of

welcome not only to the screen's finest artist (the only man who writes, directs and acts his own pictures and even composes their music), but to one of the greatest liberals of our day. Your films have always been compassionate towards the weak and the under-privileged; they have always punctured the bully. To our pain and astonishment you paid the United States the highest compliment in your power by settling within her borders, and now we feel pain but not astonishment at the response – not from the American people in general, one is sure, but from those authorities who seem to take their orders from such men as McCarthy. When Russia was invaded you spoke out in her defence at a public meeting in San Francisco at the request of your President; it was not the occasion for saving clauses and double meanings, and your words were as plain as Churchill's and Roosevelt's. You even had the impudence, they say, to call your audience your comrades. That is their main accusation against you. I wonder what McCarthy was doing in those days?

Remembering the days of Titus Oates and the Terror in England, I would like to think that the Catholics of the United States, a powerful body, would give you their sympathy and support. Certainly one Catholic weekly in America is unlikely to be silent – I mean the *Common-weal*. But Cardinal Spellman? And the Hierarchy? I cannot help remembering an American flag that leant against a pulpit in an American Catholic church not far from your home, and I remember too that McCarthy is a Catholic. Have Catholics in the United States not yet suffered enough to stand firmly against this campaign of uncharity?

When you welcomed me the other day in your home, I suggested that Charlie should make one more appearance on the screen. In this would-be story Charlie lies neglected and forgotten in a New York attic. Suddenly he is summoned from obscurity to answer for his past before

the Un-American Activities Committee at Washington –
for that dubious occasion in a boxing ring, on the ice-
skating rink, for mistaking that Senator's bald head for an
ice pudding, for all the hidden significance of the dance
with the bread rolls. Solemnly the members of the Committee watch Charlie's early pictures and take their
damaging notes.

You laughed the suggestion away, and indeed I had
thought of no climax. The Attorney-General of the
United States has supplied that. For at the close of the
hearing Charlie could surely admit to being in truth un-
American and produce the passport of another country, a
country which, lying rather closer to danger, is free from
the ugly manifestations of fear.

The other day a set of Hollywood figures, some of them
rather out-moded (Mr Louis B. Mayer and Mr Adolf
Menjou were among the names) set up a fund to support
McCarthy's fight in Wisconsin – a form of Danegeld.
Now Hollywood uses English stories and English actors,
and I would like to see my fellow-countrymen refusing to
sell a story or to appear in a film sponsored by any
organization that includes these friends of the witch-
hunter. Our action would be an expression of opinion
only; it would not condemn them to the unemployment
and slow starvation to which McCarthy has condemned
some of their colleagues. They will say it is no business of
ours. But the disgrace of an ally is our disgrace, and in
attacking you the witch-hunters have emphasised that this
is no national matter. Intolerance in any country wounds
freedom throughout the world.

For an account of Chaplin's pursuit by the FBI, and other
American organizations, in the years between *Monsieur Verdoux*
and *Limelight* (première, Odeon Leicester Square 16 October),
see Charles Maland, *Chaplin and American Culture* (1989). 'The
FBI had spent a tremendous number of hours and massive

amounts of paper preparing long reports about Chaplin that
were based on shaky, distorted or even downright false information.'

*

The Times / 22 August 1953

Anglo-Texan Society

— May we beg the courtesy of your columns to
announce the formation of the Anglo-Texan Society? The
society has the general object of establishing cultural and
social links between this country and the state of Texas
which occupies a special historical position not only in
relation to the United States but also in relation to Great
Britain. It is hoped, when funds permit, to establish special
premises in London for welcoming visitors from Texas
and – if our ambitions are realized – of providing them
with a hospitality equal to that which Texas has traditionally given to English visitors. Those interested
are asked to communicate with the undersigned at
1, Montagu Square, London W1.

We are, Sir, yours, &c.,

Graham Greene, President,

John Sutro, Vice-President

In the *Daily Telegraph Magazine* (22 November 1974) an article
by Greene appeared – 'A Thorn on the Yellow Rose' – along
with a blown-up copy of the above letter and a photograph of
some of the 1,500 Texans who attended a barbeque at Denham
Film studios. It was sub-headed: 'With all the solemnity of a
letter to the Editor of *The Times* Graham Greene presided over
the birth of the Anglo-Texan Society. This flourishing group
may well be surprised to hear how the idea first occurred.'

— Once upon a time, I regret to say, I was addicted
to practical jokes. When I was an undergraduate there was

a lantern lecture I gave to the upper forms of Highgate School in the guise of an explorer of Outer Mongolia; there was a Mrs Montgomery who played havoc with the nerves of El Vino's proprietor and a Charing Cross Road bookseller and harassed the staff of Eyre and Spottiswoode. But I have learnt better now. I have learnt that nothing can be more difficult to stop than a practical joke which succeeds too well . . .

It all began on 22 August 1953, when a letter appeared in *The Times* under the heading 'Anglo-Texan Society'. So on 22 August this year the Society – which I had conceived in a mood of tipsy frivolity with John Sutro after a pint or two of Black Velvet in the Edinburgh to London Express – must have celebrated its coming of age. Was there a dinner at the House of Lords in the presence of Royalty? The Duke of Edinburgh a few years back *did* attend a cocktail party, for from the first day the joke jumped completely from my control and took wing into outer space, aided in its flight by the irresponsible genius of Sutro.

I was well out of the way on a trip to Kenya to report the Mau Mau rising for a Sunday paper by the time my letter to *The Times* appeared.

When I reached Nairobi a telegram was waiting for me from Sutro. 'Letter appeared. Sixty Enquiries on first day including Sir Hartley Shawcross, the Attorney General, and Samuel Guinness, the banker.' The Society was well and truly launched. If my mind had been less occupied with the Mau Mau I might have felt qualms. Was Sutro in my absence going too far? By the time I returned to London a month later he had already held a cocktail party, notepaper had been printed, and soon a second announcement appeared in *The Times*. 'The Society has by now been inaugurated. The officers include Mr Samuel Guinness and Sir Alfred Bossom, MP.' John Sutro had quietly slid into the office of Chairman. I remained President.

Not one cynical reader of *The Times* ever questioned

how a society could have been born with a self-elected president or wondered what exactly was the special historical position of Texas in relation to Great Britain or what kind of cultural links could possibly be formed with the Lone Star State. Americans regarded the letter more cynically, and the comments of the *New York Times* were shrewd: 'We could not believe our eyes. We remembered only too vividly Mr Greene's controlled but consuming anger towards us because of what he considered was a reactionary reign of terror over here ... We can feel scepticism, like a calcium deposit, residing right in our bones. Mr Greene may be on the side of God, but he has created some fascinating diabolisms and plenty of hells in his time, and we wonder whether Mr Greene doesn't have some insidious plot underfoot. Maybe like getting Texas, our richest, vastest, proudest state to secede from the Union.'

I would have liked to have written and told the *New York Times* the real reason why the Society was founded – how Sutro and I had passed an enchanting and innocent evening in Edinburgh with two delightful Texan girls whom we had picked up in the lounge of the Caledonian Hotel, and how under the influence of a happy memory and the Black Velvet, I remarked to Sutro, with some difficulty in getting my s's clear, as the Yorkshire moors spun backward through the [train] window: 'Le's found an Anglo-Texan Sh-Society.'

If it had not been for the Chairman, I doubt whether the Society would still be here to celebrate its 21st anniversary. The President, I'm afraid, tired of the joke rapidly and tried to disrupt the Society. For example there was a rather terrible meeting at which a member showed a home movie of her holiday in Texas with a running commentary, all happy exclamations and family jokes. I wrote with simulated indignation to the Chairman:

I hope you will regard what I have to say in this letter as something inspired only by the wish to further the aims of the Anglo-Texan Society of which you and I were the founders. An organization like this Society has to pass through its birth pains and we can only learn to direct its activities successfully if we are frank with each other about our failures. I cannot help feeling that the meeting last Friday was one of the failures which should not be repeated. It seemed to me that Mrs — 's address, with no intention on her part, was liable to cause a great deal of ill-feeling. It was patronizing and tactless in my view, and liable to do a good deal of harm to Anglo-American relations if any unsympathetic Americans had been present in the audience. Nor do I think the film served any good purpose . . . I do not think that members will be satisfied with a film of an American visit which however suitable for family consumption is certainly not suitable for general exhibition. I had understood that the film was about Texas but Texas occupied only a small portion of it, and I think it highly undesirable that members of the Anglo-Texan Society should be expected to sit through a succession of scenes featuring one of the members and her family . . . Nor do I think we should expect somebody in Sir Alfred Bossom's position to lend his house for a programme which would be more suitable in the privacy of a home.

I feel very strongly that this is a point of principle which should be cleared up, and I am quite ready to put my resignation as President in your hands if the Council so wish, but I personally am not ready to sit through another meeting in which so many remarks are made (however innocently) which must be offensive to any Texan or any American present in the audience. I think that I am as ready as anyone to criticize America in general terms, but I am not prepared to patronize America.

It was during one of my annual absences in Vietnam that John Sutro, free from my carping and inhibiting presence, really let his imagination soar, and with the aid of the American Air Force staged a giant barbecue at Denham Film Studios. Fifteen hundred Texans mingled with the members of the Anglo-Texan Society and their guests. The Houston Fat Stock Show dispatched four prize steers – 2,500 lbs of prime beef, three hillbilly bands played 'Beautiful Texas' and 'San Antonio Rose', 300 people rode to Denham in red London buses with destination signs, 'Texas from Piccadilly Circus', and the Governor of Texas sent a telegram to Mr Winthrop Aldrich, the United States Ambassador in London, commissioning him to act as Texas Ambassador for the day. Mr Aldrich handed over to John Sutro the flag of the Lone Star State, and I feel certain that at that moment of crowning triumph Sutro put out of memory the night in Edinburgh, the Black Velvet on the express, and the ignoble hilarity of two tipsy travellers when they plotted their little joke. The future of the Society was established, soon there would be a proper President from the House of Lords (Lord Bossom, as Sir Alfred had become) and the Society would entertain the Duke of Edinburgh at cocktails.

It was more than time for me to depart. I wasn't really of presidential timber, and perhaps I was a little frightened of what might happen next. There was a dinner one night for the head of the great Dallas store of Nieman Marcus, world famous for their luxurious Christmas catalogues, at Mr Samuel Guinness's house in Chelsea. I thought Mr Marcus seemed ill-at-ease, uncertain of why he was there with a table-load of strangers, so after dinner, walking with him in the garden, I unburdened my guilty conscience and told him the origin of the Society, swearing him to secrecy. At that moment I think he began to enjoy his evening.

On a suitable date, 1 April 1955, I wrote to Mr Guinness, resigning from the Presidency on the ground of my frequent absences abroad, and Sutro, my fellow conspirator, resigned from the Chairmanship, though he remained a member, an unsuspected skeleton in the Society's cupboard.

I received a very courteous letter from the new Chairman dated for some reason from the *Time* and *Life* building in New Bond Street. I hope I shall not seem conceited if I suggest that it provides the right valedictory note to the joke which went wrong:

Mr Guinness read your letter of resignation as President of this Society at the last meeting of the Council on 4th April. It was very regretfully received by us all as it arrived at the same time as Mr Sutro's resignation as Chairman. You and he were the Founders of the Society and did so much at its inception to get people together and to get things going. I am sure that I express the feelings not only of the Council but also of the members of the Society when I say how grateful we will always be to the two of you for what you did.

What indeed had we done? How little parents know of their children and my imagination boggles when I think of the long distinguished future which lies ahead for the Anglo-Texan Society.

*

The Times / 4 December 1953

A Nation's Conscience

— I spent the month of September in the Kikuyu areas of Kenya, and it was with small surprise that I read of what happened on the Nyeri–Mweiga road. Too many similar cases had already reached one's attention: three bodies exposed for days in the yard of a police station where every passer-by could see how little respect there was for a dead African: the honourable record of certain regiments like The Buffs matched by the dishonourable record of other trigger-happy units who fire first as soon as curfew falls and look at papers afterwards. (The papers, we are told, of these dead Africans were not in order. How many Africans' papers are in order? Four or five scraps of paper have to be carried around at one time – there is no proper system of passports to include all the necessary forms from tax receipts to travel permits.)

Those bodies at one police station were meant to impress whom? The real Mau Mau is in the forest: were they meant to terrorize our friends? There isn't a settler in this area whose life is not preserved by the loyalty of the Kikuyu, and the loyalty of Kikuyu who have taken the Mau Mau oath. The dead men at Nyeri had taken the oath. What of it? So have 90 per cent of the Home Guard. If this were ever to become a war between white and black, it would need more than three generals to wage the campaign. It is the Kikuyu who have suffered heavy casualties, not the white settler or the soldier (casualties from Mau Mau action are fewer than casualties from accidental shootings). There isn't even the excuse of a terrible and costly war to explain carelessness and nerves.

The pictures of the Lari massacre have had a wide circulation, and very terrible they are, but if photographs were available of the scene on the Nyeri road it would be seen that the Bren gun can produce a result as horrible as the panga. Many of us will find it hard to forget the story of the dying African trying to crawl under the wheels of advancing cars and crying, 'Is there no God?' One accepts the decision of the court martial, but I remember one of the older settlers saying, 'There's no room in Africa for those who do not love the Africans.'

H. D. Zirma, the *Daily Telegraph*'s correspondent in Mweiga, Kenya, wrote on 21 December: 'An Indian-run local weekly reproduces today (20th) a recent letter in the London Press [i.e. *The Times*] by Mr Graham Greene, the novelist. He suggests that Mau Mau corpses lie exposed for days outside police stations to terrorize Africans, and that the "real Mau Mau" are in the forest, so we terrorize our friends. Certainly bodies are sometimes seen briefly outside police stations, but only until they have been photographed, fingerprinted and identified. There are no mortuaries at small police posts, and nobody in this climate willingly leaves bodies in the sun. It is difficult to excuse this fantastic misunderstanding of a startling sight, but the writer's assumption that police, soldiers or settlers are unaware that most Kikuyu are our friends, if they dare be, is still more inexcusable. I have spoken to nobody who thinks otherwise. The difficulty is to be sure who is loyal and whom to protect.'

*

The Times / 25 March 1954

Dien Bien Phu

— In *The Times* of 15 March your Paris Correspondent in a long dispatch on the war in Indo-China continually refers to the town of Dien Bien Phu, now being attacked by the Vietminh. No town has ever existed at Dien Bien Phu: the village was completely erased months ago when the French began to build their fortress: not a house is left standing to afford cover. Like many of the delta fortifications, Dien Bien Phu has been dug in, and consists almost entirely of trenches and dugouts. To speak of a 'town' gives a very wrong impression of the battle.

*

New Statesman / 22 May 1954

Partition of Vietnam

— You write that 'the one immediately practicable solution, corresponding to military realities, seems to be the partition of Vietnam', along the 17th parallel. Practicable possibly, but I doubt whether morally defensible. Such a line would hand over to the Vietminh the real nationalists of Vietnam, those almost independent States of Bui Chu, Phat Diem and Thai Bin. Here the majority of the population are Christians; one village in Bui Chu, with no help from the French, resisted nine attacks of the Vietminh between August and 30 December 1953.

The Christians of Tongking are not 'colonial' Christians: they were converted by Spanish missionaries before France ever came into Indo-China, and the great grand-fathers of these men now fighting the Vietminh for their country and their religion with home-made mortars survived the persecution of the Emperor in the 1850s. In 1851 the Emperor issued his edict that 'Annamite priests, whether or not they have consented to tread on the crucifix, must be sawn in half. In this way the whole world will understand the severity of the law . . .'

The word 'partition' is now glibly used without any understanding of what it entails to human beings. No wonder that the present Government – which looks like being the first independent government of an independent Vietnam – resists the proposal to hand over to Communist control millions of the strongest supporters of a Vietnam free from European and Communist domination.

On 18 May Kingsley Martin, Editor of the *New Statesman*, wrote to Greene: 'The enclosed letter, with your proof, was awaiting my signature when I came out from a Board meeting, and heard . . . that you had rung [and] that you feel deeply concerned about the letter, and it shall, therefore, of course appear. I am still sending you the former letter to explain why, at the last minute, I held it over last week; it will also make clear that I was willing this week to publish it.'

He had written: 'I didn't print your letter . . . because, with some knowledge of the proceedings now at Geneva, it seemed so remote from the realities that I thought, on second thoughts, you would probably prefer it not published . . . The best information I have, which comes from British, American and

French sources, is that, without Allied intervention on a big scale, probably leading to the dropping of "unconventional" weapons on Chinese towns and starting a world war, the French can hold no part of Indo-China, except, perhaps, a precarious foothold in the ports. I am afraid our reference to the 17th Parallel was a piece of undue optimism; certainly it is as much as the British now negotiating hope for. Eden is desperately trying to persuade the Western Powers to make concessions which will lead to an armistice, and Molotov, equally afraid of war, is apparently trying to persuade the Communist Powers to a less triumphant and more compromising attitude. Molotov appears to have had some success in obtaining concessions from the Communists; Eden has, so far, not pulled off any promise of compromise from the West.

'If you really wish to say that you oppose some sort of partition, and that the Vietminh are the real nationalists, who should rule the whole country, then you must go on, under present circumstances, to say you think this is worth a full-scale war with China, and perhaps a world war. I don't believe that you can mean this, but the inevitable retort to your letter would be that you want, on the grounds that some villages are Catholic, to adopt the policy of the more extreme American group which is willing to start a war. Eden is trying – with full support from the *New Statesman and Nation*! – to prevent a war. The price which he realizes is to be paid is the loss of Indo-China to France. Do you think he is wrong?'

*

The Times / 5 June 1954

Prosecutions for Obscenity

— It is our pride as writers that we are a part of Europe: Rabelais, Villon, Flaubert, and Baudelaire are in our bloodstream, and it is hard to listen with patience to denunciations for obscenity which would be impossible

(36)

today in Europe, where literature is taken more lightly and a great deal more seriously in the same way that a man may risk his life, with a light heart and a serious intention.

All this has happened before, about ten years after a great war. Blake's drawings were impounded by police officers in a raid on a London art gallery (the fact that they had made a mistake did not make their action less absurd), copies of Joyce's *Ulysses* were seized by the Customs, the publishers of *The Well of Loneliness* were prosecuted and condemned. Must we have the whole nonsense over again? One is tempted to call it Manichaean nonsense, for it seems to condemn any description of man's sexual nature as though sex in itself were ugly. *Ulysses* is now openly published, *The Well of Loneliness* can be obtained in the uniform edition of Miss Radclyffe Hall's works. Is the whole dreary routine to be followed once more – books to be condemned and then resuscitated when a more reasonable official attitude prevails?

Expert evidence by fellow authors as to a book's literary merit (which must inevitably include the intention of the writer) has never been admitted in a court of law, but surely the opinions of such novelists as Arnold Bennett, H. G. Wells, and Virginia Woolf might in the case of *Ulysses* have prevented the law appearing foolish. It is with a sincere desire that our magistrates and judges should take no rash risk that one writes this letter.

There had recently been a series of court cases brought not only against the publishers T. Werner Laurie, Hutchinson and Secker, but also the proprietors of *Zest* and *Slick*, as well as a man who loaned typescripts from a suitcase beneath his market-stall. This letter provoked a correspondence which continued for most of the month. Among them was one (8 June) from Charles Porter of Galloway and Porter in Cambridge, who recalled 'walking into a bookshop some time back and seeing a very learned divine sitting at a table looking at a very handsome edition of Boccaccio – he knew I was able to see the book and said to me, "Mr Porter, to the pure all things are pure."' Herbert Van Thal mentioned that there had been a French commissioner of police who wanted to prosecute a contributor to *Le Paris* for a line of asterisks which he had deemed obscene.

On 10 June Stanley Unwin wrote: 'So much emotion and so little knowledge is displayed in connexion with this difficult problem of obscenity in literature that it was a relief to read Mr Graham Greene's letter on Saturday.

'The real question at issue is whether we ought to be satisfied with an *obiter dictum* of a Victorian Judge, delivered nearly a hundred years ago, under which much great literature could be prosecuted, or whether we should consider as more appropriate and intelligent the masterly judgement of the United States District Court, rendered 6 December 1933, by the Hon. John M. Woolsey, lifting the ban on *Ulysses*. He emphasized that a book must be read (and judged) in its entirety, and that it must first be determined whether the intent with which it was written was pornographic – that is, written for the purpose of exploiting obscenity. He used the expression "dirt for dirt's sake", a definition of obscenity which would, I imagine, be accepted by, and secure the wholehearted cooperation of all responsible publishers.

'Judge Woolsey's decision was upheld in the United States Court of Appeals on 7 August 1934, when Judge Augustus N. Hand confirmed that the question in each case is whether a publication "taken as a whole" has a libidinous effect. Over here judgement may be passed on brief extracts detached from their context, and the intent of the book dismissed as irrelevant.'

On the same day Simon Nowell-Smith of the London Library provided another perspective: 'It will be a happy day for lending librarians when all forms of censorship and all forms of obscurantism, both civil and ecclesiastical, are abolished. But Mr Graham Greene must not lightly assume that Great Britain is less enlightened in this matter than "Europe". There are books that the London Library cannot send to its members in

France lest they be impounded by the French customs authorities as obscene; yet we should have little fear of the same books being withheld from us by the British customs.

'Books may be refused entry into several countries, notably Spain, on either political or religious grounds; and there is often no knowing what will be stopped, or why. Only the Irish authorities are consistently helpful in that they issue lists of books prohibited under the Censorship of Publications Acts – Mr Greene himself has rubbed shoulders in these lists with such distinguished writers as Malinowski, Dr Stopes, James Joyce, and Miss Radclyffe Hall.' Dissent came from a woman who wondered whether Greene would 'think it wrong of me if, without breach of copyright, I made money, as I easily could do, by disseminating the passages in the epilogue to *Ulysses* in which the girl describes her various forms of experience with men?'

On the 16th Greene wrote:

> — One of your correspondents has drawn a comparison between the Roman Index and the prosecutions for obscenity in British courts. He considers that I as a Catholic cannot support the one without supporting the other. In common with many other Catholics I have little regard for the Index in the rare cases when it deals with imaginative writing. The Roman Index is not an infallible document and sometimes makes mistakes as absurd and regrettable as British judges, juries, and magistrates. However, it is mainly concerned not with questions of obscenity but points of theology and philosophy: it acts as a guide for the student by excluding from his curricula inexact expressions of Catholic belief. So far as imaginative literature is concerned (according to rumour both Tolstoy and Lewis Carroll have been condemned) most Catholic laymen follow their own consciences – they do not even know what books are on the Index, and they are not penalized by a fine or imprisonment if they write or publish a work condemned by the Holy Office.

*

A Propos des Obsèques de Colette

Lettre à son Éminence Le Cardinal-Archevêque de Paris

Eminence,

— Ceux qui aimaient Colette et ses œuvres se sont unis aujourd'hui pour l'honorer dans une cérémonie qui a dû paraître aux catholiques étrangement tronquée. Nous sommes habitués à prier pour nos morts. Dans notre foi, les morts ne sont jamais abandonnés. C'est le droit de toute personne baptisée catholique d'être accompagnée par un prêtre jusqu'à sa tombe. Ce droit, nous ne pouvons pas le perdre – ainsi qu'on perd la citoyenneté d'une patrie temporaire – par crime ou par délit, pour ceci qu'aucun être humain n'est capable d'en juger un autre, ni de décider où commencent ses fautes et s'achèvent ses mérites.

Mais aujourd'hui, par votre décision, aucun prêtre n'a offert de prières publiques aux obsèques de Colette. Vos raisons sont connues de nous tous. Mais auraient-elles été invoquées si Colette avait été moins illustre? Oubliez le grand écrivain et souvenez-vous d'une vieille dame de quatre-vingts ans qui, au temps où Votre Eminence n'avait pas encore reçu l'ordination, fit un mariage malheureux non par sa faute (à moins que l'innocence ne soit une faute) et dans la suite rompit la loi de l'Eglise par un second et un troisième mariage civil. Deux mariages civils sont-ils tellement impardonnables? La vie de certains de nos saints nous offre de pires exemples. Certes, ils se sont repentis. Mais se repentir signifie qu'on repense sa vie, et nul ne peut dire ce qui se passe dans les esprits entraînés à la lucidité lorsqu'ils sont confrontés au fait imminent de la mort. Vous avez condamné sur d'insuffisantes évidences, car vous n'étiez pas avec elle, ni aucun de vos desservants.

Votre Eminence a donné, à son insu, l'impression que

l'Eglise poursuivait la faute au-delà du lit de mort. Dans quel dessein Votre Eminence a-t-elle fait cet exemple? Est-ce pour avertir vos ouailles du danger de traiter la loi de mariage légèrement? Il aurait certainement mieux valu les avertir du danger de condamner les autres trop facilement et les préserver du manque de charité. Les autorités religieuses rappellent fréquemment aux écrivains leur responsabilité envers les âmes simples et les risques de scandale. Mais il existe aussi un autre risque qui est de scandaliser les esprits avertis. Votre Eminence n'a-t-elle pas considéré qu'un scandale de cette nature pouvait être causé par sa décision? Aux non-catholiques il pourra sembler que l'Eglise elle-même manque de charité; il semblera que l'Eglise elle-même puisse refuser ses prières au moment du plus grand besoin. Combien Gide mort fut autrement traité par l'Eglise protestante! (Votre Eminence pardonnera la chaleur de ces expressions en se rappelant qu'un écrivain dont nous aimons les livres nous devient un être cher. Ce n'est pas ici un cas abstrait tiré d'un recueil de théologie morale à l'usage des séminaires.)

Bien sûr, à la réflexion, les catholiques pourront estimer que la voix d'un archevêque n'est pas nécessairement la voix de l'Eglise; mais beaucoup de catholiques, non seulement en France, mais en Angleterre et en Amérique, où les œuvres de Colette étaient lues et aimées, ressentiront comme une blessure le fait que Votre Eminence, par une si stricte interprétation de la règle, semble dénier l'espoir de cette intervention finale de la grâce dont sûrement Votre Eminence et nous tous dépendons à notre heure dernière.

Avec mon humble respect pour la Pourpre Sacrée.

'Last week', reported *The Times* (20 August), '[*Le Figaro Littéraire*] published an "open letter" from Mr Greene to the Cardinal [Maurice Feltin], reproaching him with the decision not to allow any religious ceremony at the funeral of Colette . . . Cardinal Feltin replies this week . . . The Cardinal recalls the rules of the Roman Catholic Church about last rites. When a baptized person has voluntarily and freely left the Church, the Church does not wish to impose those rites. Nor did Colette show any sign of repentance before death . . . *Le Figaro Littéraire* of this week also prints a large selection of letters written either to Mr Greene and sent on by him to the paper or direct to the paper. The majority of the writers support the Cardinal's decision.'

The *Universe* commented, 'The Church has to be particularly careful to maintain her principles where the risk of scandal is particularly great,' a view with which François Mauriac agreed, writing in *L'Exprès*: 'The scandal . . . is that people who all their life have jeered at the Church should be treated . . . as if they were members of the flock.'

In writing to Nancy Mitford (15 September), Evelyn Waugh said, 'Graham Greene's letter was fatuous and impertinent. He was tipsy when he wrote it at luncheon [on the day of the funeral] with some frogs and left it to them to translate and despatch.' 'I was not tipsy with alcohol when I wrote the letter but tipsy with rage,' Greene told Mark Amory.

*

The Times / [31 January 1955]

The Formosa Crisis

— If, as we all hope, there is a prolonged breathing space in the Far East, say of thirty years, what exactly happens to Chiang Kai-Shek's army in Formosa? Will it consist of fifty-year-old privates and senior officers in wheel chairs, or is the army expected to add to its training the production of sufficient children, and men children at that, to replace the wastage of old age? I like to think that our children will see the wonderland of an old Formosa, like a scene from The Sleeping Beauty, with the long white beards, coiling round the out-of-date bayonets and

the heavy sleep of age fallen over the palace of Chiang
Kai-Shek.

*

Sunday Times / 8 May 1955

Denominations

— Mr Austin's opinion is of course that of all true
Buddhists. I quite realize that the Hoa Haos are not a
legitimate branch of Buddhism, but they claim to be
Buddhists, and I loosely described them as such just as one
might loosely describe a Unitarian church as Christian.

A Zen Buddhist priest, Jack Austin, had written (1 May) 'with all
due respect for Mr Greene's on-the-spot observation' in the
first of his reports from Indo-China (24 April), but complained
about the paragraph which said that 'the sects have always lent
the South an air of comic opera, but a comic opera written by a
cynic with a story of treachery. The most "respectable" of the
sects, I suppose, are the Caodaists with their Pope at Tay Ninh,
their female cardinals and the synthetic religion worked out by a
civil servant in the 1920s. The most savage but ill-armed are the
Hoa Haos, the Buddhist sect which boasts a woman's army
under the general's wife.'

The priest's long letter argued that Buddhists, except for
some in medieval Japan, have been a peaceable lot for 2,500
years and that the Hoa Haos were shady impostors.

*

(43)

The Times / [18 May 1955]

The Shepherdess

— As Mr Dix is so great an admirer of Mrs Meynell's odd lines

> *'Into that tender breast at night*
> *The chastest stars may peep'*

perhaps he can explain something which has always puzzled me. Which are the less chaste stars and are any stars definitely unchaste?

F. H. R. Dix, founder of the Catholic preparatory school at All Hallows, Cranmore Hall, Shepton Mallet, protested about Oliver Edwards's harshness towards the lines as printed in Quiller-Couch's *Oxford Book of English Verse*; of this revised version, Dix said it is 'a couplet which seems to me strikingly beautiful'.

*

New Statesman / 16 July 1955

Epstein and the Church

— Sir Herbert Read in his review of Epstein's *Autobiography* makes the rather puzzling statement that 'the campaign (against Epstein) has usually been conducted by a certain section of the press, supported if not instigated by bodies such as the National Vigilance Society and the Roman Catholic Church'. Is there some encyclical letter from the Pope directed against Sir Jacob? Somehow it has not reached England. Have there been any fulminations from the Vatican? We haven't heard them over here. All that we do know is that Sir Jacob's superb Mother and Child, which is one of his latest works, was commissioned by a Catholic Convent in Cavendish

Square. Perhaps some Bishop at some time somewhere has criticized Sir Jacob. To call that a campaign supported by the Roman Catholic Church is rather as though a criticism by you of the works of Karl Marx were heralded in Russia as 'campaign against Marx supported, if not instigated, by Great Britain, her Commonwealth and Colonies'.

'How careless of me to suggest that the Catholic scourgers of Sir Jacob Epstein, such as Father Bernard Vaughan, spoke with papal authority! They spoke as outraged individuals, no doubt; but judging from the kind of art the Church does generally encourage,' replied Greene's great friend Herbert Read the following week, 'they were representative enough. The Convent in Cavendish Square, and the chapel at Vence decorated by Matisse, are encouraging signs of enlightenment, but a recent papal pronouncement (I regret that the text is not at hand to refer to) was in effect a warning against such dangerous flirtations with the spirit of modernity. Not that churches theologically more modern in spirit are any better in this respect: it is generally a choice between bad art and no art at all.'

In *Time's Thievish Progress* (1970) John Rothenstein recalled that 'Graham tried to account for the elements of aridity and defensiveness in T. S. Eliot by relating them to his refusal to accept the logical consequences of his own religious belief, owing to a shrinking, social rather than doctrinal, from the many vulgar manifestations of present-day Catholicism. Unlike Eliot, Graham himself took them very much in his stride and even enjoyed them as he enjoyed much else that was shabby and vulgar – an expression of his own revulsion from the refinement whose absence made Catholicism unacceptable to Eliot, and from accepted "good taste" in general. I even heard him flatly declare himself satisfied with current Catholic art "even at its worst".'

*

Observer / 12 February 1956

Manners of Speaking

— It is sad to find that by Miss [Nancy] Mitford's exacting standard Henry James was frequently Non-U in his correspondence. Frequently he followed the 'unspeakable usage' of writing to someone as Dear XX. Many examples will be found in the last edition of his letters: 'Dear Walter Besant', 'Dear Auguste Monod' and surely most shocking of all to Miss Mitford 'Dear Margot Asquith'.

In *The End of the Affair* Bendrix goes further, and writes of 'note paper'.

*

The Times / 13 February 1956

Drinks at Airports

— I am surprised to see that no proud Scottish Member of Parliament pointed out in the debate on Tuesday that drinks were already available for oversea travellers at Prestwick Airport. The restrictions seem to apply only to England.

'Schiphol Airport [Amsterdam] is surely one of the most comfortable airports in the world,' wrote Greene in *Getting to Know the General*. 'On the ground floor there seems to be a sofa for every passenger . . . Thanks to General Torrijos I was travelling first class so that I had the use of the Van Gogh lounge with its deep armchairs and heavily laden buffet. Even several hours of waiting passed pleasantly in those surroundings, and by the time I got on the plane I felt unusually happy, especially as I prefer Bols to any other gin. "Young or old Bols?" an air hostess asked me as soon as we had taken to the air. "Which is best?" "I don't know, but my father – and he is as old as you are – prefers the young." I tried both and I disagreed with her father. I stuck to the old Bols all the way to Panama.'

*

Spectator / 13 July 1956

'A Coward's Way'

— Mr [Harold] Wilson in the House of Commons during the economic debate caused laughs and editorial footnotes by his references to a businessman's decision not to leave England permanently. 'That would have been the coward's way out.' There is a tradition in the House of Commons that a civil servant is not to be attacked by name, but an ordinary member of the public has no protection from a Minister against the misuse of Parliamentary privilege. We have seen during the TV debates the intensive jealousies among Members of Parliament: now we see those jealousies turned on an author and entertainer who is paid by the demand for his services and not paid, whether we will or no, by the ordinary taxpayer. Mr Wilson has tried to extend the meaning of the word 'cowardice' to include a writer's conduct in preferring another part of the British Commonwealth [Bermuda] to England as a place of residence, but surely 'a coward's way' might be better applied to a Member of Parliament who attacks one of the public under the protection of privilege instead of making his charge of cowardice openly in such columns as yours.

Relations between Noël Coward and Greene had not begun on so sympathetic a note. Of *Australia Visited 1940* Greene wrote (*Spectator* 23 May 1941), 'Patriotism is not enough: he had to talk about England at war, and he had not seen England at war. If he had experienced the daily autumn blitz it is doubtful whether he would have said so easily: "During the last two months, in America, I have often felt how infinitely preferable it would be to be kept awake by bombs and syrens than by the clamour of my own thoughts"... it would have been well to have waited to make the comparison until he had experienced both'. Two months later, he reviewed *Blithe Spirit* (11 July 1941) and said that Cecil Parker, Fay Compton and Kay Hammond were 'acted off the stage by the character who had the fewest words to betray the author with – Miss Ruth Reeves as Edith (a maid)'.

Coward, incensed by these reviews, wrote 'The Ballad of Graham Greene', posthumously published in his *Collected Verse* (1984). In 1947 he recorded in his *Diary*, 'really Mr Greene has a most unpleasant mind'; two years on, he 'met Graham Greene at long last and belaboured him for being vile about me in the past. Actually he was rather nice.' By 1953, 'his beastliness to me in the past I have forgiven but not forgotten', and, at the end of the decade, the prospect of a swift £20,000 found him in the film of *Our Man in Havana*.

*

The Times / 3 September 1956

The Naga Hills

— I address my letter to you as one of the few editors who has printed any account of what is, or is not, going on in the Naga Hills of Assam. The mystery must be attributed to the Indian Government.

I have just asked the Indian High Commissioner's Office in London whether I can obtain permission to visit the Naga Hills (it may seem curious that 'permission' should be required). My purpose was relatively innocent. I wished to investigate the activities of a namesake of mine who seems at the moment to be in gaol in that region, and I hoped incidentally to see something of the Assam tea gardens. An official at the High Commissioner's Office in

London has informed me that no permits to this area have been allowed for many months past and that there is no chance at the moment of my receiving a permit. I suggested that an Indian writer would not be forbidden access to Cyprus, and his reply was that the case was different – Cyprus was 'colonial territory', a new definition of colonialism, an area open to world opinion.

There have been grave questions addressed in the Indian Parliament to Mr Nehru concerning the situation in the Naga Hills. Is this ban on foreign correspondents due, as suggested to me, to the fact that foreigners, including missionaries, have been 'stirring up trouble', or is it due to an unwillingness on the part of the Indian Government to have their actions in that area exposed to world opinion?

I have for some time wanted to know what has happened to my namesake, Mr Graham Greene, and now I begin to want to know what is happening in the Naga Hills.

Greene's wish to visit the Naga Hills is explained by earlier speculation in the *Sunday Times* (29 July): 'There are conflicting reports about the fate of Mr Graham Greene in Assam. One dispatch says that he has been killed within half an hour of his release from the local prison. Another report says that he was rearrested there after trying to flee from the authorities.

'I wonder if this particular Graham Greene is the same peripatetic gentleman whose reported career has included a brush with the Paris police? "He has been in my hair for a long time," Graham Greene tells me. "Recently I got a letter from a French editor asking me to do a piece for him, and complimenting me on my tennis game. I haven't played tennis since I left school. When I was in Paris a girl kept ringing me up. We finally met in a bar in Rome and it turned out that she had come across this other Greene chap in Arabia."

'Now the writing Greene is considering a flying visit to Assam to discover the fate and the facts of his namesake.'

M. Moulik, Public Relations Officer at India House, wrote on the 5th: 'Mr Graham Greene's letter, published in your columns today, ascribes to the Indian High Commission certain statements which are misleading. Mr Greene did not make any official request for permission to visit the Naga Hills, nor did the Government of India refuse such permission. He wished to have an itinerary from Suchar to Sibsagar in Assam, which was supplied to him, and he was informed that he could go there at any time he wished. At the same time he inquired if he would need a permit to visit the Naga Hills. It was pointed out to Mr Greene that there still existed a problem of security in that area and that it was not considered safe for tourists to visit the Naga Hills at the present time, and the Government of India was therefore, naturally reluctant to take avoidable risks in regard to their safety.

'May I be permitted to add that there is no "mystery" about the Naga Hills, as suggested by Mr Greene. This problem, as admitted by Mr Greene himself, has been openly discussed and debated in the Indian Parliament and Press. India, since independence, has been an open book to all foreigners, even to those who choose to malign her. There is no ban on foreign correspondents in India and the actions of the Government of India in every field and every sphere are "exposed" to world opinion.

'Mr Greene has referred to other issues like Cyprus. I do not wish to enter into a controversy as to whether permission is required for Indian correspondents to visit certain security-risk areas in Cyprus. I also wonder whether Mr Greene, or any foreign correspondent, would be allowed to visit all areas in some of the British territories where there is physical insecurity as a result of violent opposition to authority.'

Greene replied the following day:

— Dr Moulik is correct in saying that I had not yet applied for permission to visit the Naga Hills when he rang me up to say that such an application would be useless. I did not understand him to give as his reason the security of visitors (a somewhat feeble reason, for a correspondent in an area at war does not expect security or protection). He referred instead to the trouble which had been caused by foreigners, including missionaries, in that area (it will be remembered that the leader of the Nagas is a Christian).

There is, of course, no point in his writing, 'There is no ban on foreign correspondents in India and the actions of the Government of India in every field and every sphere are "exposed to world opinion".' The Naga Hills are part of India, or why are Indian troops operating there? And I challenge Dr Moulik to name the foreign correspondents who are allowed to work in that area, and to name an area of British territory to which an accredited British correspondent would be forbidden access.

And Ronald Beale of Weybridge reported: 'I am interested to read the letter from Mr Graham Greene in your issue of 3 September since I was fortunate in being permitted to visit the Naga Hills with two European friends in February last. My purpose was to see Kohima and the war cemetery there and to take cinematograph films of those and of Naga tribal types. Some effort was necessary to obtain the requisite permits from the various authorities involved, but apart from one incident when we were sent back from a road control at Nichugard to Dimapur – a distance of nine miles – in order to have our permits stamped again, we encountered no difficulty.

'Our treatment by the military authorities whom we encountered at several points was extremely courteous and I can assure Mr Greene that the journey is well worth while, even though it involved in our case twenty-six miles each way over very rough roads for which we chose a utility vehicle. There have been trouble makers who have suggested that the rifles found in the possession of certain Naga tribesmen have been supplied by the British or the Americans on account of the markings on them, but in fact it can safely be taken that they were the remnants of materials dropped to aid in the defence of Burma against the Japanese.

'Incidentally if Mr Greene wishes to visit some of the Assam tea gardens he does not need to go in the direction of the Naga Hills.'

The other Graham Greene, who once wrote to the *Listener*, has yet to be waylaid: the efforts to do so are described in the Epilogue to *Ways of Escape*.

Not guilty, however, was Graham J. Graham Green, Chairman of the Catholic Marriage Advisory Council, who surfaced, and caused a moment's perplexity, on the letters page of the *Catholic Herald* in 1947.

*

The Times / 3 December 1956

Pygmalion

— The news that the Public Trustee and the Society of Authors – Bernard Shaw's literary executors – have agreed to ban *Pygmalion*, one of his major works, from the stage for a period of years in order to make room for an American musical, *My Fair Lady*, will come as a disagreeable surprise to members like myself of the Society of Authors who forget that the society is not run solely in defence of their legal and moral rights but as a literary agency in competition with other literary agencies.

No effective measures can be taken against the Public Trustee (who is probably an innocent in the case), but a sanction does exist against the Society of Authors. May I appeal to all members who feel it deplorable that a dead author's work should be so casually banned from the stage to which he devoted his life to express their feelings in action, by resigning from the society? Otherwise we become accomplices in the affair.

On 1 December *The Times* had reported: 'The Shaw Society stated last night that *Pygmalion* had been banned – with the free consent of the Public Trustee and the Society of Authors – for some time ahead (ten years, according to some reports), from stage, film, radio, and television representation. This had been done, the society said, so that *My Fair Lady*, an American musical adaptation, which was not scheduled to arrive in England for a year or more, might have a clear run.

'The society asked whether a great writer had ever been so treated by those appointed to safeguard his literary reputation.

' "For them to make the concession they have to the Tennent interests – even though they now express themselves as 'slightly pained at the efficiency with which Tennent's took them at their word' – is little short of disgraceful. In fact, they have (as the Shaw Society of America has pointed out in its vigorous protests) been 'party to a new type of censorship' – a 'commercial dictatorship' that is certainly contrary to the spirit of Shaw's last will and testament." '

The following day an article was published on the news pages, which included a statement from the Society of Authors: 'In the case of professional performances the sensational success of *Pygmalion* in its musical form is merely an important additional factor in a situation which is always complicated whenever a particular play is in general demand. Some form of traffic control is necessary in such circumstances if congestion and collisions are to be avoided. Professional companies applying for licences will receive exactly the same consideration as in the past. There is no ban.'

Beneath was an account of the developments which followed the original incident: 'The Shaw Society stated on Friday that *Pygmalion* had been banned, with the consent of the Public Trustee and the Society of Authors, so that *My Fair Lady*, an American musical version of the play which is not due to be performed in England for a year or even longer, might have a clear run. Because of this, the statement continued, the Pitlochry Festival company, which had intended to make

Pygmalion the centre of its season next year, had had to abandon the idea. On Saturday, however, the day the statement appeared, the Pitlochry company received permission from the Society of Authors to give a limited number of performances until 1 August if it still wished. But the society had already rearranged its repertory, and in any case had wanted to retain the Shaw play for the whole season, which is to continue until 5 October.'

In the same issue was a letter from D. Kilham-Roberts, Secretary-General of the Society of Authors, which was at some odds with earlier statements: 'There is no truth in reports that *Pygmalion* has been banned from our stage and an official statement to this effect has been issued to the Press by the Society of Authors. It is astonishing that Mr Graham Greene, as a member of the Society's Council, should have written his letter before ascertaining the facts from the Society.'

Allen Lane, founder and director of Penguin Books, wrote: 'I have been publishing Shaw's works in cheap editions for twenty years. During his lifetime Shaw on many occasions expressed his approval of what I was doing to give the widest possible diffusion to his ideas. He consistently refused to give any publisher exclusive rights in his work because he wanted his message to reach several different segments – and price-levels – of society. I am certain that he would never have sanctioned the action which his literary executors appear to have taken over the production of *My Fair Lady*.'

Greene replied on 5 December:

— Mr Kilham Roberts finds it 'astonishing', in his letter today, that I, as a member of the Authors' Society Council, should have written my letter before ascertaining the facts of 'the ban' from the Society. Perhaps it is even more astonishing that I knew nothing about it. True, I have been abroad, but I have received no minutes of any council meeting held to discuss the matter. Presumably if I had applied to the Society I should have received the same

(54)

'facts' as are contained in the statement to the Press. This is in complete contradiction to the experience of the Pitlochry management and the action taken by Mr Hugh Beaumont [of Tennent's, forbidding the production].

Surely the compiler of the statement is writing (if I may alter Mr Aneurin Bevan's famous phrase) with a twisted nib when he tries to explain away the ban by referring to it as a form of traffic control. Perhaps one is expected to remember that red lights flash automatically on empty roads, for it seems unlikely that *My Fair Lady*, which has not yet been produced in London, will be blocking the routes around Pitlochry next autumn.

There is nothing in this statement which is likely to make those of us who have resigned from the Society reconsider our decision.

Letters followed from, among others, Stephen Spender, E. M. Forster, Margaret Kennedy and A. D. Peters; there was a dull *Times* Third Leader on the subject, and it was left to the onlie begetter of *Cats* to sum up: 'My only excuse for adding one more letter to the correspondence in your columns about *Pygmalion* is that none of your previous correspondents appears to have enjoyed the advantage which I enjoy of having seen *My Fair Lady* in New York. This musical comedy has had great success in New York, and should have great success in London. Any suggestion that its success would be jeopardized by the simultaneous production of *Pygmalion* in the West End (to say nothing of productions outside London) would seem to me ludicrous. West End managers might hesitate to launch a new production of *Pygmalion*: but that decision, surely, could be left to their discretion, and need not be imposed upon them by the Society of Authors? I am, Sir, your obedient servant, T. S. ELIOT.'

*

Case of *The Quiet American*

— Your report of 9 January from Saigon has only just overtaken me [at the Hotel Algonquin, New York]. It is certainly true that if a story is sold to Hollywood the author retains no control over the adaptation. But perhaps a Machiavellian policy is justified – one can trust Hollywood to overbid its hand. If such changes as your Correspondent describes have been made in the film of *The Quiet American* they will make only the more obvious the discrepancy between what the State Department would like the world to believe and what in fact happened in Vietnam. In that case, I can imagine some happy evenings of laughter not only in Paris but in the cinemas of Saigon.

'Hollywood's version will be a safe one – that of the triumphant emergence of the democratic forces in the young and independent state of Vietnam backed by the United States, accompanied by the downfall of British and French imperialists,' *The Times*'s correspondent had written. 'Though some commentators here [Saigon] are mildly shocked that Mr Greene should permit this travesty of his work, others are saying "it serves him right for writing such an anti-American book". There is quite a controversy about it.'

'I try to explain to my friends,' Greene had told Alan Brien (*Evening Standard*, 25 January 1957), 'that once you sell a book to a company, it's out of your control. You can't spend all your life in film studios trying to keep your work intact.' And, in an interview with Thomas Wiseman (*Evening Standard*, 24 August 1956), he said: 'I don't suppose they can film it in the way it is written. They'll probably make it so that it looks as if the American was being bamboozled all the time by the Communists or somebody.' Wasn't it unfair to Americans? 'Oh, I don't know. Some of those bombs that went off in Vietnam, it was generally thought that the Americans were behind that. It's very dangerous writing in the first-person. Everybody thinks I am Fowler – well, I share some of his views about the Americans. But I'm not as bitter about them as he is. I didn't have my girl stolen by an American.'

One of the film's cast, Michael Redgrave, wrote to *The Times*; his letter was printed below the author's, and said that the report was speculation: 'Most of these differences can safely be left, so far as I am concerned, to other arbiters, when the film is completed and released, which is after all the normal time for such assessment; but as the only English member of the cast I would like to assure the many admirers of the novel, and a great many more people as well, that in no way is the "downfall of French and British imperialists" injected into the film-translation of Mr Greene's novel.

'People may travel half-way round the world and still get things wrong, but a film-unit and cast which do so are not content merely to "take views of Saigon and the surrounding countryside", as your Correspondent condescendingly puts it, and move on "when sufficient local colour has been gathered". They may surely be credited, at least for the time being, with a desire to get things right. It does not ease a difficult task to know that before the start so many people have been assured by "the man on the spot" that the whole conception is a "travesty".'

Greene would later regard the film, adapted, produced and directed by Joseph Mankiewicz, as 'a complete travesty' and 'that film was a real piece of political dishonesty. The film makes the American very wise and the Englishman completely the fool of the Communists. And the casting was appalling. The Vietnamese girl Phuong was played by an Italian.' In an essay the following year, he wrote: 'One could believe that the film was made deliberately to attack the book and its author. But the book was based on a closer knowledge of the Indo-China war than the American possessed and I am vain enough to believe that the book will survive a few years longer than Mr Mankiewicz's incoherent picture.'

*

Spectator / 8 February 1957

Eleven Minus

— Do the weekly verses contributed by the Minister of Education [Lord Hailsham] to your columns indicate that the works of Wilhelmina Stitch are to be made compulsory reading in English secondary schools?

Lord Hailsham meted out punishment in the following week's letters page:

> '*Alas, what ails you, Graham Greene,*
> *And why, and when this prurient itch*
> *To see the infant class at Sheen*
> *Reciting Wilhelmina Stitch?*
>
> *The End of the Affair will be,*
> *For you, poor Greene, a fatal shock,*
> *That I'll prescribe for G.C.E.*
> *A stick of (censored) Brighton Rock.*'

The *Spectator* continued to employ him to write verse, which generally addressed the meaning of life, and a collection of it, *The Devil's Own Song*, was published in 1968.

*

New Statesman / 9 March 1957

Dickens and Dostoevski

— Mr [C.P.] Snow writes that 'if Dostoevski had been an Englishman with the gallows as much in his mind as it was in Dickens's, he would have ruined the best parts of both novels'. Surely the gallows was rather more in Dostoevski's mind than in that of Dickens, since he underwent the ordeal of being condemned to death and was only reprieved at the last moment. It was hardly the accident of the Russian legal code that saved him from 'a sadistic miasma' which would otherwise have seeped through into 'Raskolnikov's confession of the trial of Dimitri Karamazov'.

On 16 March C. P. Snow wrote: 'I must have made my point about Dostoievski [the *New Statesman*'s style of spelling in the days when it was consistently copy-edited] and capital punishment more obscurely than I intended or else Mr Greene would not have misunderstood me. Of course capital punishment existed in 19th-century Russia, but only for political offences; of course Dostoievski was sentenced to death for his part in the Petrashevski group, and was reprieved while in sight of the firing squad; of course this left a mark on him – more humdrum men than Dostoievski would have found the circumstances disturbing – and there are traces of it scattered through his work, not only in the famous reflection in *The Idiot*.

'My point was, however, something quite different. It was that there was no capital punishment for murder in Russia in Dostoievski's time. The normal punishment for murder was penal servitude, often for terms as short as eight years. Murder to a 19th-century Russian did not carry the shadow of the gallows. Dostoievski could therefore write about it and the emotions of murderers awaiting arrest, trial and verdict with surprising calmness, with none of the sadistic excitation of the nerves that he showed on so many other topics. I compared him in this respect with Dickens, who, as excitable as Dostoievski and morbidly aware of the hanging to which murderers were sent by the English penal code, wrote such scenes as Fagin's last night on earth.'

Ten years went by, and the matter was not entirely forgotten: the *Evening Standard*'s 'Londoner's Diary' reported: 'Is Mr

Graham Greene, the novelist, engaging in a mild literary feud with his fellow author Lord Snow? Sharp-eyed readers of Mr Greene's last two books will have noticed references to Lord Snow that are anything but complimentary.

'In his new collection of stories, *May We Borrow Your Husband?* the narrator comments scathingly on the heroine: "She had, it seemed, a nostalgia for Dornford Yates, had graduated in the sixth form as far as Hugh Walpole and now she talked respectfully about Sir Charles Snow, whom she obviously thought had been knighted like Sir Hugh for his services to literature. I must have been deeply in love or I would have found her innocence almost unbearable – or perhaps I was a little tight as well." The sarcasm is thinly concealed.

'In *The Comedians*, the reference to Lord Snow's last book is more subtle but just as pointed: "I tried to read a novel but the heavy foreseeable progress of its characters down the uninteresting corridors of power made me drowsy, and when the book fell upon the deck, I did not bother to retrieve it."

'The final allusion may of course be unintentional but cannot pass by unmentioned. In a poem recently submitted to the New Statesman, Mr Greene wrote in his last verse:

> *It's exceedingly windy*
> *In the spring,*
> *And children go to the beaches*
> *To fly kites.*
> *The climate is bright, dry and invigorating;*
> SNOW IS UNKNOWN.

'A firm reaction from Lord Snow yesterday: "I feel an utter lack of response." Ah well.'

*

Time / 18 March 1957

Hollywood Abroad

— Why do American moviemen require pith hel-
mets, salt tablets, quinine pills to visit the Cao Dai capital,
Tayninh [to film *The Quiet American* – TIME, 25 Feb.].
The climate is somewhat similar to a Washington summer. Perhaps the inhabitants were mystified by their
strange attire and eccentric diet.

The Editor commented at the foot of this letter: 'American
moviemen take about the same precautions in Washington.'

*

New Statesman / [20 September 1957]

Freedom and Justice in Ghana

— What an *Alice Through the Looking Glass* world
we enter when we read the political sections of the *New
Statesman*. In your anonymous leader, under the above
title, you write 'nothing can atone for the British record in
West Africa, where people still recall the unparalleled
horrors of the slave trade'. From this one would imagine
that the British had entered West Africa in order to
enslave the population, when, of course, the exact opposite
is true. Our Colonies in West Africa were established to
stop the slave trade, carried on between successful warring
chiefs and the Arabs from the East, and whatever we may
feel of the British record in East Africa the worst that can
be said of our record in the West was that the human
element may sometimes have failed. There was never any
planter problem: no white man has ever been allowed to
own land in West Africa, and even though Lord Lurgan's
policy of indirect rule through the native chiefs may have

retarded independence (not necessarily unwisely), it was a noble experiment.

*

New Statesman / 14 September 1957

Greene and Shaw

— Your film critic writes that I was brought in to de-Protestantize Shaw's *St Joan* – a rather offensive suggestion. Such a role was never proposed to me nor would I have accepted it. I suspect that your reviewer remembers little of Shaw's play and knows less about Catholic doctrine. There is nothing in Shaw's play offensive to Catholics, although there are a number of historical inaccuracies. The play of course had to be cut for film purposes, but these cuts were mainly drawn from the long discussions on the growth of nationality and the decay of feudalism which would hardly have been understood by film audiences. No line was altered for the purpose of watering down Shaw's Protestantism or instilling a Catholic tone. Even the 'miracle' which your film critic in his notice attributed to my influence he could have found in the original play if he had been familiar with it. Perhaps the most intelligent appreciation of Shaw's play and the best defence of Shaw against ignorant Catholic criticism was written in the *Month* by Father Thurston, the distinguished Jesuit, at the time the play was produced.

Unaware that the playwright had written a screen version of *St Joan* in the thirties (published in 1968), Otto Preminger had commissioned Greene to prepare one, and gave him six weeks in which to do so.

In an essay on Samuel Butler (1934) Greene wrote of 'the smartness which makes *Erewhon* so insignificant beside *Gulliver*, [the] many superficial half-truths in the form of paradoxes which have become aggravatingly familiar in the plays of his disciple'. After Greene had reviewed Mrs Cecil Chesterton's *The Chestertons*, they were in dispute in the *Spectator* (25 July 1941). In 1956 he told Thomas Wiseman (*Evening Standard*, 24 August): 'It [*St Joan*] is one of the few Shaw plays that I like. I'm in sympathy with what he says. I shan't change any of his ideas. I don't like his other plays very much, except *Heartbreak House*. I've never been able to get through *Man and Superman*. *Candida*? That's a bore, isn't it?'

William Whitebait, the *New Statesman*'s film reviewer, had referred to *St Joan* while remarking of the film version of *The Crucible* that 'Sartre is brought in to add the Party line to Arthur Miller'.

Henry Adler (21 September) wrote to blame Greene for the film's being 'a vulgar travesty of Shaw's intention', even if some of it 'must be shared by Preminger's ham-fisted sentimentalism in direction . . . and by Miss [Jean] Seberg who makes Joan a clean-living co-ed sassying her elders . . . the film shows Joan as the crudest kind of miracle worker . . . And why was the epilogue cut and the Gentleman from Rome not allowed to appear? Its retention would not much have lengthened the film. Did Shaw's remarks on the attitude of the Church and people to saints prove embarrassingly to strike near home?'

Greene replied:

New Statesman / 28 September 1957

— Really Mr Adler should stick to the point. I was not defending the film version of *Saint Joan*, or even my part in it, I was replying to the offensive statement that I had been brought into the film in order to Catholicize it. However, if Mr Adler will look again at Shaw's play he will find the incident of the hens laying is left unchanged in the film – except for the exclamation 'Christ in Heaven!' which no censor would pass. What, of course, happened is that in place of a curtain, which gives the audience time to laugh happily at Baudricourt's reaction, there is a 'fade': a curtain lasts ten minutes, a 'fade' as many seconds: a film has to go on. This kills the laugh and I don't see how the killing could have been avoided without recourse to a drastic rewriting of Shaw's text.

Personally I have always found the incident of the wind changing in Shaw's play sentimental and unconvincing and it remains sentimental and unconvincing in the film. Personally I would have liked to omit the scene altogether, but then what would Shaw's admirers have said? None of the three so-called miracles in Shaw's *Saint Joan* has been omitted, but none of them has been made to look any more authentic than in the original play. The criticism of the third 'miracle' is left, as Shaw wrote it, in the mouth of the archbishop. I have a haunting impression that it is a long time since your correspondent read Shaw's play.

Certainly there were cuts in the epilogue, but rather less cuts perhaps than in the rest of the play. I doubt whether Mr Adler's reverence for Shaw would have stood up to a film of three and a half hours. There is a very simple reason why the Gentleman from Rome was cut. When the play was first produced the canonization of Saint Joan was still a recent event and the dialogue of the Gentleman from Rome had a lively contemporary flavour. Now to the vast majority of any film audience Saint Joan's canonization has faded into past history; it is no longer an issue, and surely they would have been mystified by the sudden appearance of a gentleman in a top hat, announcing something which they had known all their lives, in a costume they could not easily identify.

Mr [John] Hobbs makes a great song-and-dance about what Mr Christopher Hollis once wrote about Shaw's play [in the *Dublin Review* of 1928]. With all due respect to Mr Hollis I can hardly accept him as the voice of the Church. The best critical appreciation of Shaw's *Saint Joan*, as I wrote before, is that by Father Herbert Thurston, SJ, which appeared at the time of the first production in the pages of *The Month*. Of course Shaw was critical of many things that Catholics believe, but does Mr Hobbs really expect Catholics to find criticism offensive? What a strange angry young life he must live if he finds any opposition to his ideas 'repugnant' and 'offensive'.

See also Greene's review of the Catholic J. P. Hackett's *Shaw: George versus Bernard* (*London Mercury*, September 1937): 'Mr Hackett seems to have read Father D'Arcy's magnificent essay, *The Nature of Belief*, but it has had no effect on his style or the commonplaceness of his thought. Mr Hackett, indeed, is too great an admirer of Mr Shaw to be a fair critic; you have to hate the man a little to give a just estimate of his importance. The "eternal sewing machine" of Yeats's metaphor has clicked to some purpose, and it is one of the awful enigmas of human life that the Vestryman for St Pancras, the absurd Jaeger suit, the little ugly rationalistic volumes, should be connected so intimately with the firing squads practising across Europe, the genuine physical agony. Mr Sassoon once wrote a poem about the jokes in music halls which "mock the riddled corpses round Bapaume", and when the stalls rock to Mr Shaw's slapstick, there is the same ugly taste in the mouth when we remember men slain in Italy, Germany, Russia, and Spain in order that the Life Force shall have a high old time. The trouble is that this unpassionate puritan is disastrously free from that sense of chaos and lunacy which opens dreadfully before most men at periods of moral indiscipline. He has never had to accept constraint for the sake of sanity.

'There was a time, the time of his admirable and angry preface on the subject of public school education, when Mr Shaw seemed the champion of the young against the inhumanities of age. Now that he is old himself we have to look for him in the camp of the physical force men, of Lenin and Mussolini. "Try how wicked you can be; it is precisely the same experiment as trying how good you can be." Only an essentially innocent man, a man quite ignorant of the nature of evil, could write that: a worthy man, an ethical man, of course, but the ethical is much further from the good than evil is.'

*

The Times / [25 February 1958]

Sites for Rockets

— We are assured by the Minister of Defence that rocket missiles 'will not be launched except by a joint positive decision of both the British and US governments'. What happens when a surprise attack is designed to coincide with one of the President's quail shoots and a British weekend?

*

Daily Telegraph / 12 April 1958

Author in the Box

— I would like to join Mr A. S. Frere [Greene's publisher at Heinemann] in objecting to the report of the Select Committee on Obscene Publications on the ground of hypocrisy.

It is, one must admit, a cunning hypocrisy. A great many people will think that the suggestion of allowing an author to give evidence in favour of his book is an advance. But how few writers have the forensic talent of Oscar Wilde, and even Oscar Wilde failed in the long run under Carson's cross-examination. One can picture the scene:

Mr Blank, QC: Mr Doe, if I understand you aright, you defend your book on artistic grounds. One of your characters remarks on page 83: 'This is a — mess.' Do you feel that the use of this adjective really adds to the artistic quality of your novel?

Mr Doe: That is a natural expression for my character to use.

Mr Blank, QC: And you feel the artistic nature of a novel depends on the use of realistic language, however offensive?

Mr Doe (weakening): Well, I don't know that I would go as far as that.

Mr Blank, QC: As far as what, Mr Doe? You have already in your book gone as far as 'This is a — mess.' Would you say that realistic language is allowable only so long as you are the author of the novel in which it appears?

It seems unlikely that any more justice will be done in police prosecutions by admitting the evidence of authors inexperienced in the law, inexperienced in cross-examination, and unprepared for the offensiveness of counsel.

I agree with Mr Frere that the labours of the Authors' Society and of the Select Committee have left us exactly where we were. In spite of Mr Justice Stable, every writer is still at the mercy of a policeman and a Director of Public Prosecutions whose tastes in obscenity are no better or worse than that of the most ignorant juryman.

After further letters from Frere and an increasingly outraged A. P. Herbert, Greene added (1 May):

— I have received a letter couched in rather offensive terms inviting my attendance on certain conditions at a meeting of the self-designated Herbert Committee.

As the invitation is issued by the Society of Authors, I have paid no attention to it. I resigned from the society rather more than a year ago, as it no longer seemed to me a suitable body to represent the interests of writers after an attempt had been made, with the consent of the society, to ban *Pygmalion* from the English stage for ten years to make room for the American musical, *My Fair Lady*.

The changes in the law concerning obscenity are illustrated by two letters about Greene's biography of Lord Rochester. When he was planning the book in 1931, John Hayward wrote to him: 'Undoubtedly Messrs Heinemann will have inserted a clause in your contract relating to what publishers commonly call "scandalous matter", so that I presume that you will have to use your discretion in deciding what you may safely quote. I mention this because the Nonesuch edition [made by Hayward] could not have been published except as a limited edition, and would indeed have been issued "to subscribers only" if the whole issue had not been taken up by the booksellers before publication. Even so the American copies were "destroyed" by the New York Customs. I must ask you therefore to bear in mind that a charge of obscenity brought against you might possibly be extended to include me and my publishers!'

The book could not be published at the time that it was written, for these reasons. It eventually appeared in 1974 under the title *Lord Rochester's Monkey*, in an illustrated edition prepared by George Rainbird Ltd, whose Deputy Chairman, John Hadfield, wrote to Greene (2 November 1973): 'I think we still require a few more pornographic lines, merely to exemplify the "scandalous" reputation Rochester has always had ... I feel we want one or two examples of *really* shocking verse, as illustrations of the cruder aspect of Rochester's mind.'

*

Spectator / 23 May 1958

Justice

— One is inclined to write letters after a good meal, and after a good meal one has the desire to carry an idea a little farther. Mr Levin's interesting article for me supported by implication the belief I have always held – that

Lord Jeffreys has suffered posthumously from injustice. At the culmination of a dangerous rebellion he allowed himself phrases which surely have been equalled and surpassed for their inhumanity and stupidity by many of his successors as Lord Chief Justice, but his successors have not had his excuse of an armed revolt against the existing order. I would like Mr Levin, who knows far more than I do on this subject (for I have 'come up against' only one Chief Justice, Lord Hewart), to answer this question: have we ever had a Lord Chief Justice superior in law and human understanding to Lord Jeffreys? This is not a very high standard to demand.

Bernard Levin (16 May) had reviewed *Lord Goddard: His Career and Cases* by Eric Grimshaw and Glyn Jones. He commented in the course of this: 'Still, it would be idle, even if agreeable, to maintain that Lord Goddard is, as far as general opinion goes, anything but typical. Muddled, narrow, overwhelmingly emotional, with a belief, the roots of which he is a thousand light-years from understanding, in retributive punishment and the causing of physical pain to those who have caused it to others – in all this he represents only too well the attitudes of most people in the country whose judiciary he heads. Perhaps every country gets the Lord Chief Justice it deserves.'

*

Spectator / 30 May 1958

What Are the Facts?

— Mr Randolph Churchill has written a stirring article on the lack of truth in popular journalism. It is a pity that last week in his report from Algiers to the Beaverbrook press he should have suggested that General Salan was held responsible by many of the parachutists who had served in Indo-China for the defeat of Dien Bien Phu. General Salan had left Indo-China before the occupation of Dien Bien Phu. The decision to occupy the village, to establish the armed camp there for the defence of Laos and to hold it at all costs was made by General Salan's successor, General Navarre. I doubt whether the French parachutists are so ignorant of the facts as Mr Churchill makes out, and it is a pity that Mr Churchill should have attempted to slur General Salan's admirable record with this 'battle dishonour'.

Randolph Churchill, son of the Prime Minister and butt of Evelyn Waugh's humour, was being assaulted on two fronts. In the same issue was a letter from the *News Chronicle*'s religious correspondent, who cast doubts on the truth of his report about a meeting between Princess Margaret and the Archbishop of Canterbury at Lambeth Palace three years before: 'If Mr Churchill is really concerned to establish the right of the individual to privacy, I suggest in all seriousness that he should not himself circulate tittle-tattle.'

Churchill objected (6 June), and went on: '. . . May I, sir, at the same time, so as not to trespass unduly on your space, deal with the allegation of Mr Graham Greene in the same issue that I "should have attempted to slur General Salan's admirable record with this 'battle dishonour'"?

'Of course, I did no such thing. Unlike Mr Greene I am not a novelist or a moralist. I am a reporter and I seek to report faithfully what I see and hear, instead of depending on my imagination, which is limited. When I wrote of *Dien Bien Phu* I was not thinking of the houses that constitute that village any more than when one writes the word Munich one is thinking of the particular conglomeration of buildings which constitute that town. I was referring, of course, to the policy and decisions which resulted in the French evacuation of South-East Asia. I know very little about this and would not presume to form a judgment as to whether what was done was right or wrong. I confined myself to reporting the view, widely expressed, rightly or wrongly, in Algeria during the last few weeks.'

The following week, the *News Chronicle*'s religious correspondent was moved to comment in the *Spectator*, 'I ask him to go farther and admit that it is not within his competence to lend any sort of authority to the story', and on 13 June Greene added to his side of the two-pronged debate:

— The infallibility of a journalist is not, like the infallibility of the Pope, limited by conditions. A journalist is never wrong. I would have had an increased respect for Mr Churchill if, unlike his fellows, he had been ready to admit for once that he had been mistaken and that he had obviously misunderstood a conversation overheard in Algiers. Instead of that he attempts to cover up his mistake in a flurry of phony indignation. I simply do not believe that 'When I wrote of Dien Bien Phu I was not thinking of the houses that constitute that village any more than when one writes the word Munich one is thinking of the particular conglomeration of buildings which constitute that town. I was referring of course [*sic*], to the policy and decisions which resulted in the French evacuation of South-East Asia.' Would he, if he had referred to the Fall of Tobruk, 'of course' have been referring not to a 'conglomeration of houses' but to Britain's whole strategic and political policy in North Africa? In any case, General Salan, unlike his predecessor Marshal de Lattre, was never responsible for general policy, but only, for a short period, for military operations. He had left Indo-China some time before the series of events – military and political – began which culminated in Dien Bien Phu. Surely a reporter before going to a scene of action should make himself acquainted with the background and not put himself in the rather ignominious position of having to write, 'I know very little about this.' It seems more than probable that Mr Churchill's parachutists were talking of quite another general than General Salan and quite another place than Dien Bien Phu, but perhaps they were talking French too fast for Mr Churchill.

*

New Statesman / 31 May 1958

'I Grow Old, I Grow Old'

— Critic's [i.e. Kingsley Martin, *aetat* 61] attack on age in your last number seems a little ungenerous — Cocteau 'an arthritic old bore of 64', de Gaulle with 'sagging face, protruding stomach, stoop'. Many of us stoop: to some of us arthritis is a painful ailment for whose victim we feel sympathy. 'Bore?' That is a subjective term which those who find excitement and interest in M. Cocteau's works would be more inclined to apply to that love of cats and fear of the H-bomb expressed rather too frequently by one weekly journalist. I happened to be at General de Gaulle's press conference and I feel that there were many of his opponents who found his speech and replies impressive in delivery, in timing and in the sense of relaxed humour. Certainly his voice towards the close did turn a little uncertain. Age comes to all of us, and there are rumours in London that Critic himself has passed sixty, has white hair and has been known to recite limericks of a dubious kind after dinner. 'Boring?' Not necessarily, but a sign of age rather than youth, and more controllable than arthritis.

'Hurray! Just read my Staggers [*New Statesman*],' wrote Janet Adam Smith to Greene. 'It needed saying.'
  Kingsley Martin took a different view. On 1 June he wrote on an ancient typewriter, '. . . the letter by you which we published last week has, perhaps naturally, led to inquiries [*sic*] about your motives and intentions in writing it. I can't myself explain its

(72)

rudeness which would seem to imply some sense of grievance or animosity on your part. As far as I knew we were on perfectly good terms. If you can let me know either privately or for publication what has led you to write like this I'd be grateful.'

'The explanation of my letter is a very simple one and I think if you will re-read Critic's paragraph you will understand it,' replied Greene. '"An arthritic old bore of 64" – most people would agree that Critic's rudeness had far outdistanced mine, and he who lives by the sword must perish by the sword. Let our good terms survive the strange observations of Critic!'

Kingsley Martin did not accept the explanation. He wrote back: 'De Gaulle – whom we may or may not have been fair to – is a public figure and the dictator of France and we said nothing of his private life. His public qualities – even his ailments – are of public importance. But what would you – or anyone else – have thought of me if I'd written what I know of your private habits and interests? My capacity for knowing – on suitable occasions reciting – indecent limericks is to me a matter of pride and pleasure, so it is not from pique that I wrote.'

'I agree', replied Greene the following day, 'that de Gaulle is a public figure and his ailments are of interest, though whether "sagging face and protruding stomach" can be classed as ailments is more doubtful. Don't you find a certain vulgarity in the description? What really made me write my letter was your reference to Cocteau who is no more a public figure than any other author or critic himself. This correspondence looks like turning into a pamphlet published by the Turnstile Press!'

'Agreed. Enough said,' replied Martin the next day, and went on: 'Perhaps I should tell you that I was prompted to write because two people, both in the writing world, have asked me, à propos your *New Statesman* and other published letters, if I could explain why anyone so successful and creative as you, should have become so "bitter, rude and disgruntled". And though I was rude myself, I still don't know the answer in your case, which I regret because I have a high regard for you.'

In June 1978 Greene wrote to Alexander Chancellor (then

editing the *Spectator*), 'The *New Statesman* is certainly a horror now. I am glad to think that it helps you.' And, in December 1979, 'The *New Statesman* becomes more and more unreadable . . . it seems grossly unfair that you are not increasing your sales as quickly as the *New Statesman* must be losing theirs. Even in its best days the *New Statesman* was read mainly for the second half of the paper, but now the second half of the paper is as drearily humourless as the first part. Not a laugh in an issue.' Later sent some recent copies by the *New Statesman* in the hope of an encomium, Greene replied: 'I look back with nostalgia to the old days when Raymond Mortimer was the literary editor and the boring part was confined to Kingsley Martin's end.'

The 'Staggers' has now lurched into a merger with *New Society*.

*

The Times / 3 January 1959

Cuba's Civil War

— The welcome success of Dr Fidel Castro in overthrowing the dictatorship of Batista reminds us again of the extraordinary ignorance of Cuban affairs shown by the British Government. If it had not been for the intervention of Mr Hugh Delargy, MP, this country would have gone on happily supplying the dictator with arms. When Mr Delargy first raised the question in the House of Commons Mr Selwyn Lloyd replied that, when the export permits were granted, the Government had no evidence of a civil war in Cuba. Yet at that very period the province of Oriente was already dominated by Dr Castro and a military reign of terror existed in Santiago.

Any visitor to Cuba could have given her Majesty's Government more information about conditions in the island than was apparently supplied by our official representatives: the mutilations and torture practised by leading police officers, the killing of hostages, such incidents as the arrest in November 1957, in Santiago of three small girls aged between 11 and 13 who were taken to the military headquarters in their night clothes to be held as hostages for their father (unlike most incidents at that period, this had a happy ending: a strike by all the school children of Santiago forced the military commander to surrender the girls). I have myself spoken to a girl whose brother had been blinded and fiancé mutilated in the prison in Havana. This was the situation *before* the British Government granted export licences for turbo-jets and tanks.

What kind of information, we may well ask, was the Foreign Office receiving from its representatives in Cuba? I was myself told quite untruly before visiting Santiago in November 1957, that Dr Castro was a Communist. It is strange that our officials in Havana had not learnt that Dr Castro was supported by the head of Catholic Action in Santiago and by the representatives there of the Protestant Churches.

One reads with distress of the bombing by Batista's forces of the beautiful seventeenth-century town of Trinidad – with more distress because the planes and the rockets used were very likely British, planes supplied because the Foreign Office acknowledge that they were unaware that there was such a thing as a civil war in Cuba.

The Times / 6 January 1959

— Your Diplomatic Correspondent writes in your issue of today that 'It was reported unofficially in October that the Batista régime was in complete control of Cuba except for a small mountainous area in the east.' If this be the case the mystery of who was informing the Foreign Office of what deepens.

I arrived in Cuba on 12 October, my first visit since November 1957, and the deterioration of Batista's position was obvious. In November 1957, the island had been still under Batista's control except (a very big exception) for the large province of Oriente where Santiago was only held by military force and terror and the troops were unable to penetrate into the mountains or even control the roads effectively at night. Still, at that period I could hire a car to drive me over large areas of the island – to Santa Clara, Trinidad, and Cienfuegos – and only once were we stopped by a military check on the outskirts of Havana itself. In October 1958 it was impossible to find a driver willing to take me either to Trinidad or Cienfuegos (the naval port) for fear of ambush. Indeed no driver would venture farther than the fashionable beach resort of Varadero, about eighty miles along the main highway from Havana.

In England we had heard only of the failure of Dr Castro's general strike earlier in the year. Batista's censorship had apparently not only prevented the newspaper reader from knowing that three-quarters of the island by *October* had passed from under his effective control, he had also succeeded in preventing that information from reaching the Foreign Office.

*

New Statesman / 24 January 1959

John Gordon

– I have undertaken to write a biography, as yet unauthorized, *The Private Life of John Gordon*, and I should be grateful to any of your readers for any unpublished letters or anecdotes that they can supply. Any letters will be carefully copied and returned.

This letter appeared in various journals.

John Gordon was a journalist, once a household name. His views and style are perhaps characterized by his describing the Wolfenden Report as a 'Pansies' Charter' and by the fact that his *Sunday Express* column was written for him during his dying weeks at the end of 1974 by John Junor without anybody realizing it. He was Beaverbrook's favourite editor, or, as George Gale said (*Spectator*, 4 January 1975), 'certainly the one who shared the largest number of his master's prejudices ... [he was] ill-tempered and very mean about money ... the sort of thing that pleased John Gordon was when the Beaverbrook press gave him a new Rolls-Royce for his 80th birthday.'

To return to 1959, Gordon replied the following week: 'I am thrilled that Mr Graham Greene has decided to become my Boswell. To have the promise of immortality from a writer of such distinction is the most wonderful thing that has happened to me in all my humdrum life.

'Of course, I realize that such a task involving so much research can be tedious and burdensome. Would it be immodest of me to offer Mr Graham Greene my help?

'If he will choose a day convenient to him, I'll be delighted to have him to dinner at which in quietness and comfort we can bare our souls and share our secrets.'

Greene wrote a few weeks later, in reply to a similar offer of help in the *Spectator*:

— I fear that my address will explain why I cannot accept Mr Gordon's invitation to dinner. Perhaps he will accept my invitation to a quiet dinner at the Savoy or Horseshoe on my return, though I doubt whether Mr Gordon can himself provide the best material on his life. (*PB 1028, Coquilhatville, Belgian Congo.*)

In the *Spectator* for 29 September 1984, John Sutro (whom Gordon called Greene's 'Jiminy Cricket' and 'ventriloquist's doll') recalled how this curious putative work came about: 'Now for the John Gordon Society, an absurd affair which ultimately made Vladimir Nabokov famous. For Christmas 1955 Graham was asked by the *Sunday Times*, as were other distinguished writers, to give his choice of the three best books of the year. He slipped in Nabokov's *Lolita*, one of those green-covered volumes of the Traveller's Companion series "not to be sold in the USA or UK" and eagerly purchased by book-lovers because of their doubtful moral contents. In fact the works were of a high literary quality. After publication of Graham's choice, not a murmur from the London press about *Lolita* until one bright journalist on the *Sunday Express* got hold of a copy which he gave to read to his Editor-in-Chief Mr John Gordon. From that moment the uproar commenced. Ian Gilmour and his *Spectator* were to play an important part in the foundation of the Society when John Gordon in the *Sunday Express* started off his campaign denouncing Graham and the *Sunday Times* for recommending to the public what he considered was a pornographic book. [Gordon called it (29 January) "the filthiest book I have ever read. Sheer unrestrained pornography . . . the entire book is devoted to an exhaustive, uninhibited, and utterly disgusting description of his (Humbert's) pursuits and successes."] After reading John Gordon's condemnation of *Lolita* and its sponsors Graham took up the cudgels together with the *Spectator*. Then came the idea of forming the John Gordon Society "against pornography", inspired by Graham, tongue in cheek – another chance to use his genius for practical jokes. We were all amused and excited, Ian Gilmour and I staunchly supporting the plan, Ian letting Graham reply to John Gordon in the *Spectator*.'

> — In recognition of the struggle he has maintained for so many years against the insidious menace of pornography, in defence of our hearths and homes and the purity of public life, the signatories propose to form the John Gordon Society if sufficient support is forthcoming.

The main object of the Society will be to represent the ideals of Mr Gordon in active form, in the presentation of family films, the publication of family books, and in lectures which will fearlessly attack the social evils of our time, and to form a body of competent censors, unaffected by commercial considerations, to examine and if necessary to condemn all offensive books, plays, films, strip cartoons, musical compositions, paintings, sculptures and ceramics. – Yours faithfully,

GRAHAM GREENE, President
JOHN SUTRO, Vice-president
[We will gladly forward applications. – Editor, *Spectator*.]

It is difficult now to decide whether or not a later correspondent, B. A. Young of Fulham, was being flippant (2 March 1956): 'Before your clever readers bust themselves with laughing at Mr John Gordon, may I be allowed a humble and, I fear, old-fashioned word in his defence?

'In an age when books and newspapers are available not only to the adult population of all classes but also to kiddies, it is not a bad thing to have at least one responsible journalist on the side of decent thinking and moral living. Mr Greene and his sycophants may sneer as they will; but John Gordon's column in the *Sunday Express* is courageous, Christian, and almost always accurate. To make fun of it is the act of a snob and a cad.'

In the same issue Greene commented upon Gordon's admitting to having imported material from Paris for research purposes:

— Since the publication of Mr John Gordon's confession that he has several times 'shamefacedly' smuggled pornographic books into this country in his suitcase, I have received several letters (including three from a doctor, a lawyer and a clergyman of the Church of England) protesting that our Society cannot under the circumstances continue with its present name. An alternative title

(79)

suggested by one correspondent is the Joynson Hicks Society to commemorate that great Home Secretary who purged our youthful shelves.

Personally (and I feel sure I speak for Mr Sutro too) I honour Mr Gordon all the more for his public confession, startling though it may have seemed to those who have for years admired his stand against the prevailing looseness of morals. It is so much easier to admit a spectacular and major sin than to plead guilty, as he has done, to a 'shamefaced' misdemeanour more common among schoolboys than men of maturer years. None the less certain members feel that the title of the Society will have to be subject to debate at the first General Meeting on 6 March, and therefore we are unable to invite the attendance of Mr Gordon himself on that occasion. I have little doubt that the point at issue will be honourably settled ('he that is without sin among you cast the first stone'), and that members, already numbering half a century, will continue to pursue their great objectives under the proud and unstained title of the John Gordon Society.

Sutro's recollection continued: 'On Tuesday, 6 March 1956, a private meeting was held at 6.30 pm at Albany to discuss the formation of a society provisionally called the John Gordon Society. The host was Graham. The minutes of the meeting give a list of the names, which include Mr A. S. Frere (Heinemann), Mr Ian Gilmour and Lady Caroline Gilmour, Mr Peter Brook, Lord Kinross, Venetia Murray (*Picture Post*), Mr Birch (editor of *Picture Post*), Lady Bridget Parsons, Baroness Budberg, Mr Angus Wilson representing Stephen Spender, Mr T. O'Keefe (Hutchinson's), Lady Juliet Duff, Professor A. J. Ayer, Mr Christopher Chataway (Independent Television News), Mr Janes (*Spectator*), Mr David Farrer (Martin Secker & Warburg), Miss Helen Winick (*Books & Careers*), Mr Christopher Isherwood, etc. About sixty people were present. These are the minutes of the meeting:

'*Mr Greene* was elected President of the Society: *Mr John Sutro* Chairman: *Mr Janes* Treasurer: and *Mr Gilmour* Vice-President. *Mr Sutro* then took the Chair.

Mr Greene read two letters of regret – one from the Home Secretary, who had been invited but regretted that he was unable to accept: the other from the Director of Public Prosecutions, who had also been invited and had very courteously replied thanking the Society for its letter (undated) and regretting his inability to attend.

The Chairman then proceeded with the Agenda, the first item being the question of the name of the Society. He said: 'Many of you may be readers of the *Spectator* and you will have seen that it was wondered, in view of a certain article in the *Sunday Express*, whether the name 'The John Gordon Society' should be retained. I will ask the President to give us his views about that.'

The President: 'Personally, as I think I have already written in the *Spectator*, I feel Mr Gordon very courageously and honestly confessed to having smuggled pornographic books into this country on several occasions (as indeed many of us have). In the circumstances this should not be held against him and I would like to propose that the Society should remain "The John Gordon Society"'. This resolution was duly seconded, put to the vote and carried unanimously.

The Chairman then raised the question of the Objects of the Society. The President said he hoped one of the publishers present might have some suggestions to make, and referred to Mr Frere in particular. The President suggested that the manufacturers of the game *Scrabble* should be asked to include a pledge for purchasers to sign that no words not used in the *Oxford Concise Dictionary* should be used.

Mr Frere: 'Publishers as a whole – most publishers, particularly of fiction – could very well be invited by the Society to submit proofs to them, or even bound books or review copies, and if the Society felt so inclined they might form a committee to read these books, on "John Gordon" lines and, if they condemned a book, the publisher might put a band round the book saying – not "The John Gordon Society recommends", but "Banned by the John Gordon Society".

The Chairman said that now that the question of the name of the Society had been settled, it was felt that at the next meeting it might be well for members to hear in more detail Mr Gordon's views and a John Gordon lecture should be delivered, preferably by Mr Gordon himself, to members of the Society and their guests. A sub-committee (to be called 'The Theatre Hours Committee') should consider whether this meeting should be in or out of theatre hours.

The question of a suitable emblem (or badge) was discussed. Someone – a lady member – suggested a safety pin. The President announced that one duty of the Committee had been performed in advance – the telegraphic address of the Society was 'POGO, LONDON' – to help members on the Continent.

The Chairman proceeded to the question of the subscription. This, it was felt, should be kept as low as possible, with possibly a small charge at meetings for comestibles (Ovaltine and biscuits?).

Question from a member: 'Is it proposed to take up Mr John Gordon's offer to defray the expense of the first meeting, which will now be the second meeting?'

The President felt that Mr Gordon was being somewhat over-generous in view of the large number likely to attend.

Reverting to the question of the subscription, half-a-guinea and two guineas were suggested. Ten-and-sixpence was proposed, seconded and approved.

Question from a member of Jesus College: 'Since the aim of the Society is to stop the rot before it begins, should there not be a special rate for school-children?'

The President thought this an excellent suggestion and suggested members under 16 might pay 2/6d per head.

The Chairman asked the meeting whether 6.30 pm was a convenient time for the next meeting and this was approved. He

(82)

asked whether there were any further suggestions from the floor.

Question: 'Would it not be fitting that the Chairman should send us away with "A Thought"?'

While the President was looking for a suitable 'Thought', someone else asked whether the title 'Vice-Chairman' was suitable and it was agreed that this might be changed to 'Second Chairman' or 'Deputy Chairman'.

The Chairman then read 'The Thought', being a quotation from a work by Mr John Styles in 1806 condemning William Shakespeare . . .

The Meeting was then adjourned.

'The farce continued. Letters poured in from everywhere, either inquiring about or applying to join the John Gordon Society. Many were sent to a fictitious secretary, "Miss Christine Thompson" at 32 Westbourne Terrace. My office was deluged with correspondence, cables to POGO LONDON and stamped addressed envelopes were strewn around like autumn leaves.

'On 5 May 1956, John Gordon wrote a most courteous letter to Miss Thompson, thanking the Society for its invitation. He was looking forward ardently to a meeting with us all, so he was delighted to take the opportunity we offered. But he thought we should change the subject on which we wished him to speak. We had proposed "The necessity of censorship". As he was opposed to censorship, he could hardly make a speech defending it. He proposed, instead, that we make the subject "Pornography", which was the original, and he presumed still the main, interest of our Society. He suggested that instead of a lecture we make the function a debate. He suggested that our distinguished President, Mr Graham Greene, should undertake to defend pornography in books and newspapers while he would oppose it. As the subject was of wide public interest and, he was sure we would agree, of considerable importance to the community, he thought attendance at the debate should not be restricted to

(83)

members of the Society but should be open to all who wished to participate.

'On 23 May 1956, another letter to Miss Thompson was sent by John Gordon. He wanted to know where we proposed to hold the meeting. If space was limited he would be happy, as he had said before, to provide us with adequate accommodation. He was sure we would agree that it would be a pity to spoil the evening by limiting the audience. Of course we should invite the press. The more publicity we got the better. After all the real object was publicity. As for the subject to be discussed, he thought we need not worry about any possible differences of opinion between our President and himself regarding what pornography was. He felt sure that they both knew exactly what it was.

'On the day, we all arrived early at the Horseshoe Hotel feeling rather worried that perhaps John Gordon might not come. Our backs to the door, we never heard it open when, also before time, a tall figure slipped in. Everything about him was grey, hair, face and suit. "Am I in the right room for the John Gordon Society dinner?" he asked. "Yes," we said. "I am John Gordon."'

In the *Daily Express* (26 July) William Barkeley reported: 'The John Gordon Society made a splendid start in the Horseshoe Hotel, Tottenham Court-road, last night – and probably a glorious finish . . .

'Hundreds of the public crowded in to what was to be a private society meeting to discuss standards of morality in newspapers and books . . .

'There he [John Gordon] was last night – with Mr Graham Greene sitting at his right side.

'Said John Gordon: "It was a book so dirty it was printed in Paris. No publisher in this country is ever likely to print it. It is the story of a man who devoted his life to seducing young girls. Let me read you this description . . ."

'Loud cheers went up from the crowded audience as Mr Gordon read the passage in a solemn voice.

'"More, more," shouted the audience. "Give us it at dictation speed."

'This did not embarrass John Gordon. He was not the chairman, but he took the chairman's gavel and banged for order.

'He then said this led him to probe back into Mr Graham Greene's past, and he found that eighteen years ago Mr Graham Greene wrote a review of a Shirley Temple film in a London magazine when Miss Temple was nine years old. That review, said John Gordon, showed that Mr Greene's mind moved like that of the author of this book. In court £2,000 damages was awarded to Shirley Temple, and other money to film companies, plus costs.

'Lord Hewart, the Lord Chief Justice, had described Mr Greene's reflection on the child as a gross outrage. Was Mr Greene in court? Not at all.

'"With wisdom and discretion he had buried himself in Mexico, leaving his publishers and printers to take the rap. If I were Mr Graham Greene, after that salutary experience I would not get myself mixed up with this sort of thing again."

'At this stage Mr Randolph Churchill, who had been interrupting a great deal at the back of the hall, moved forward. He went on interrupting – and being interrupted by members of the audience.

'One voice shouted: "Is he being paid for the number of interruptions he makes?"

'John Gordon wound up: "I hope what I have said will give food for reflection to people who began this thing as a joke, and will bring some of them to the penitent's stool."

'Someone shouted: "You should go to a psychiatrist."

'John Gordon said he was ready to go to one along with Mr Graham Greene.

'Mr Graham Greene announced: "I visited one at the age of sixteen."

'Randolph Churchill went on bouncing up.

'John Gordon: "I happen to be a shareholder [in the Beaver-brook press]" (loud shouts and laughter) "whose money has to be spent on Randolph Churchill in very large sums over many years. A majority of us in the organization would be glad to see the payments stopped."

'Loud was the laughter when Randolph Churchill shouted back: "Sell your shares."

'Mr Graham Greene then rose to recount what he recalled of the pre-war libel case concerning Shirley Temple.

'He said that as he remembered it, his solicitor described his film criticism as in no way libellous. But the Twentieth Century-Fox Film Company decided for the sake of publicity to bring a libel action.

'And his counsel, Valentine Holmes, said to him: "No jury would decide for you against this pretty child."

'Mr Greene went on: "Publishing standards are very queer in all countries. People like Mr Gordon have made it difficult for publishers to publish any book of an adult kind at all."

'Many people shouted: "Not at all, nonsense."

'Someone then asked if the *Daily Express* carried on a scurrilous attack on Burgess and Maclean because they were homosexuals.

' "It is because they are traitors," retorted John Gordon, amid great cheers.

'Amid uproar it became suddenly revealed that Randolph Churchill was not just a public visitor but a fully paid-up member of the John Gordon Society.

'John Gordon was disgusted to hear this. He said: "It is the first time anybody got any money out of him."

'Randolph Churchill then protested that the whole object of the society was being ruined because the saint around whom it had been built had said he would not favour a censorship of books.

' "This is heresy from the man whom we have all gathered to support. We should dissolve the society," he proclaimed.

'Amid loud laughter, the chairman, Mr John Sutro,

announced that the committee would carefully consider the point raised by Randolph Churchill.'

In the *Sunday Express* of 29 July 1956 John Gordon wrote: 'My greatest help through the hilarious evening was Mr Randolph Churchill, who presented himself to me as a stooge. I can never adequately express my thanks to him. He strode up and down the centre aisle of the packed hall, looking for all the world like a pompous ducal butler laying down the law to the peasants in "the local".'

On 1 March 1957 Greene wrote to the *Spectator*:

The HO and 'Lolita'

— In spite of Mr John Gordon's public confession to having smuggled pornographic books on occasions into this country, the John Gordon Society at its first meeting decided that it could still bear the name of its hero. We must be prepared for the vagaries of genius. Now Mr Butler – the best Home Secretary we have got – has come to the support of Mr Gordon in his condemnation of *Lolita*, the distinguished novel by Professor Vladimir Nabokov of Cornell University. The Home Office seems to have brought pressure to bear on the French authorities and induced them to suppress the series in which *Lolita* happens to appear from publication in English in France. Perhaps this was part of the price exacted for our support over Suez? As President of the John Gordon Society I feel the Society should follow loyally in Mr Gordon's footsteps, and at the next meeting of the Society I shall have pleasure in proposing that Mr Butler be elected an Honorary Vice-President. Whatever differences of opinion we may have about his action, we cannot but admire his temerity in extending the control exercised by his Ministry across the Channel. In the days when Baudelaire's poems were condemned by a French court there was no British Home Secretary with the courage to work behind the scenes in defence of our tourists' morality. The Society looks forward to the day when the Minister of the Interior in Paris will reciprocate Mr Butler's activities and arrange the suppression in London of any French books liable to excite the passions of Monsieur Dupont or Monsieur Jean Gordon on holiday. The Society might do a very useful work in compiling such a list and keeping an eye on that danger spot for Parisians, Messrs Hachette's bookshop in Regent Street.

*

Daily Telegraph / 19 August 1959

Getting to America

— Now that Mr Khruschev is visiting the United States, may those of us who are victims of the absurdities of the McCarran Act appeal to him to intercede on our behalf?

For any member of the Soviet Government a welcome is assured in America – perhaps a welcome of curiosity as we might welcome a visitor from Mars.

But for anyone who like myself was for four weeks at the age of nineteen a probationary member of the Communist party (a fact I disclosed, when the Act was passed, to an American newspaper man – it was not cleverly dug out by the FBI), there are always long delays at Idlewild while the strange handwritten symbols in the visa, 212(d)(3): (28), are interpreted, and then the necessity for reporting in advance all one's international flight movements *if* one happens to be in transit through one of America's overseas colonies; there is always the possibility of deportation – as happened to me a few years ago in Puerto Rico, although I was travelling with the knowledge of the American authorities at my point of departure.

I realize that this is not the fault of the State Department, but of a slow-moving obstinate bureaucracy whose faults are probably common to all countries – England and Russia not excepted.

My obsessive nightmare is that the junior civil servant should come to control the world. Compared with that the hydrogen bomb is a minor danger.

After all we don't have to continue living after an explosion, but the bureaucrats will offer us health services, pensions, and perhaps one day an almost indefinite prolongation of life. Our existence is important to them so that they can remain in full employment. They need us – so let us make sure they know that we don't need them.

*

Spectator / 21 August 1959

John Oliver Hobbes

— Mr Kermode asks, 'Who now reads John Oliver Hobbes?' [in an article on Vincent O'Sullivan's memoir of Nineties acquaintances (7 August)]. I certainly do, and I recommend in particular *Love and the Soul Hunters* (a bad title which disguises a witty book), *The Dream and the Business* (with its charming coloured Aubrey Beardsley decoration on the cover) and *The Gods, Some Mortals and Lord Wiekenham*. I even before the war contemplated a biography of this woman whose intimacy with Lord Curzon so angered George Moore that he kicked her bottom in Hyde Park. Perhaps I was influenced by the enchanting photograph at the beginning of her official biography: the young, absorbed, sad face with dark hair straying over one ear under the silly, elegant, feathered hat which seems to represent the wit and daring that lay on the surface of her serious work. But the official biography is painstaking and respectable (no kicks in Hyde Park), with an introduction by a bishop, though it is still worth reading if only for some passages in her letters to George Moore. Here is one I marked twenty years ago: 'I cannot face the loneliness of a crowded drawing-room: the host of mere acquaintances, the solitariness of the returns.'

Alas, if the introductory photograph might well be that of a Gaiety girl in love, the later photographs have the handsome false dignity of a distinguished woman of letters.

'Thank you for your letter on John Oliver Hobbes,' wrote Brian Inglis, Editor of the *Spectator* and presenter of *All Our Yesterdays*. 'We have had an indignant cry from her son, a Lieutenant-Colonel, who also felt that she had been unfairly treated.'

'I think I met John Oliver Hobbes's son when I was planning the biography, and I'm afraid he won't be very pleased by my letter,' replied Greene. 'He'll probably want to come and horse-whip me.'

*

Daily Telegraph / 2 September 1959

A Walk in the West End

— Having been away from London for two months and having read much about Mr Butler's New Look, I took a walk the other night. It was a sad walk.

I have never seen so many police in the streets even in a so-called Police State. They were a poor substitute for the decorative figures of the past.

As they snooped around in groups they wore a hang-dog air; perhaps they felt that they would have been better employed in the Notting Hill Gate area than in these peaceful empty streets; perhaps their look of despair came from the knowledge that one means of proving their chance of promotion had perished.

However, in Soho affairs remain much the same as ever. So long as a girl can afford a room with a door on the street she can linger at the foot of a staircase however many bedraggled policemen pass.

I noted the novel formula: 'Come and have a drink dear, and meet some nice girls.' London will defeat Mr Butler yet and in the cause of human free will I hope to God she does.

The Street Offences Act had been rushed through Parliament as a reaction to the swelling complaints made by Church, Police and local Councils in various parts of the capital.

It was a subject which now provoked a flurry of excitement among *Telegraph* readers.

Two days later there was a letter from Colm Brogan, who had intended to write about the newspaper's cricket coverage but, instead, 'I am driven to write about Mr Graham Greene . . . May I say that I did not find the street prostitutes decorative, but so offensive that there were certain streets in my own area where I would not walk at night. These immobile, pout-mouthed, sullen-looking women standing in nearly every shop entrance like functionless caryatids drove me away from the streets they haunted . . . they were women who would submit to inconceivable indecencies and indignities and even run the risk of murder rather than do an honest day's work . . . Mr Greene seems to hope that God will assist Londoners in putting them back on the streets. I do not share his pious aspiration. As a member of Mr Greene's own religious communion, I would like to be able to say that Mr Greene's letter surprised me. But nothing that Mr Greene writes can surprise me any more.'

One man had written to Greene himself: '. . . every man with a spark of manliness in him will agree in particular with your concluding sentence. But *you* have the intellectual honesty to speak out.' And another wrote 'to thank you for your [letter] in the *Daily Telegraph*, because I believe I understood its meaning'.

'I expect you saw Colm Brogan's silly little piece,' Greene replied to one of them. 'The *Telegraph* has refused me permission to reply.' Meanwhile a letter from Amersham was printed: '. . . by that token one could argue that we should get rid of all laws and of all policemen. London would then look even stranger, and perhaps more interesting, than Mr Greene found it; though, of course, most of his books would be so démodé as to be unreadable. Still, who would want to be reading at such a time, when he could be exercising his free will as never before?'

Nicholas Bagnall, Acting Correspondence Editor, had told Greene that he had received his reply to Brogan and 'I showed it to the Editor. I'm afraid it's a little too personal for us. I am sorry. But I think you will agree that, on the two letters already published, the honours are if anything on your side.' Greene replied: 'I have never yet in my experience heard that the writer of the original letter was not allowed to reply to one of his critics – especially when the criticism was vouched as personally as Mr Brogan's. If it is the custom of the *Telegraph* to forbid this I will refrain from any further letters.'

'The *Telegraph* has relented under pressure,' Greene informed one of his correspondents:

— Mr Colm Brogan writes: 'Nothing that Mr Greene writes can surprise me any more.' I remain – perhaps charitably – surprised, whenever Mr Brogan taps his typewriter, by the number of clichés he deposits on the page.

A cliché is not merely distressing to the sense of style; it is the mark of a muddled mind grasping for security at what has been often said before.

How the clichés bloom in Mr Brogan's latest letter: 'May I say that . . . ?' 'inconceivable indecencies' (if the indecencies are inconceivable how can they be practised?), 'obscene spectacle', 'human degradation', 'honest day's work' (recommended to the prostitute: at £6 a week presumably, rising, by annual increments of 5s, to £8 minus income tax), 'pious aspirations'.

Mr Brogan writes that he is a member of my own religious communion. So were Savonarola and Torquemada. They may well have been as holy and humorless as Mr Brogan, but I feel sure they must have had a better prose style.

Colm Brogan was not one to take a blow without flinching. He wrote on 14 September, again not about E. W. Swanton and cricket: 'The spectacle of Mr Graham Greene accusing anybody else in the whole world of having a muddled mind fills me with immense satisfaction and a kind of holy awe. However, I would not like to be outdone by Mr Greene in charity, and I will respect his allergy to clichés and turn to offer some remarks to your two other and more serious correspondents.

'If Mr John Muriel imagines that call-girls were unknown before the Vice Bill or that no prostitutes had protectors he imagines a vain thing (cliché). On the other hand, I wish to make it clear that I said nothing to suggest that I believed that the total effect of the Bill would be good.

'The long-term result (cliché) may prove to be that sweeping vice under the carpet (cliché) was a remedy worse than the disease (cliché). But who can deny that the disappearance of the public spectacle of the degradation of womanhood (cliché) is *in itself* good, even though this relief, for which I give much thanks (cliché) may turn out to have been bought at too high a price?

'If this proves to be so I shall be resigned to the return of those decorative young creatures with the possibility that even our bedraggled police may be furbished up to compete with their charms. But I shall once again find certain streets so offensive that I shall avoid them.

'P.S. I know nothing of the prose style of Torquemada, if he had any. But Savonarola's prose style was nothing to write home about (cliché). Savonarola believed that he had a singular access to the mind of God. If all Christendom were against him, then all Christendom must be wrong – because it was against Savonarola. He reminds me of someone.'

(Perhaps it was the presiding over this debate that set in the Acting Correspondence Editor's subconscious the work that later appeared as *In Defence of the Cliché* [1985].)

On 17 September Derek Avis wondered whether Mr Brogan had 'strolled through Gerrard Street since the "Vice Bill" (*sic*) came into force. Surely he would find the present scene much more offensive. Instead of the "public spectacle of street girls", he would be looking at a line of male touts, some in peaked caps, in many cases accompanied by the "white slave" inmates of their "clubs". He would also notice that although the police crouch in the shadows outside street-girls' flats in some parts of Soho, they completely ignore touting by the club "hostesses" and touts, especially the latter.' And a man from Cambridge asked, 'Why should removing prostitutes from the streets be likened to sweeping dust under the carpet? It is more akin to putting dirt in a dust bin. Mr Graham Greene *et al* are at perfect liberty to remove the lid if they so desire.'

One man had sent Greene quotations in his favour from Shakespeare and Pierre Louÿs, and another, a long extract from Flaubert's letters: 'My heart has never failed to miss a beat at the sight of one of those provocatively dressed women walking in the rain under the gas-lamps, just as the sight of monks in their robes and knotted girdles touches some ascetic, hidden corner of my soul.'

In all this, Lord Butler has been forgotten. As Anthony Howard relates in *Rab* (1987): 'Somewhat to his chagrin, Rab was even asked to resign from the Association of Moral and Social Hygiene – the high-minded Victorian rescue organization founded some eighty years earlier by his great-aunt, the penal reformer Josephine Butler; and he also had to endure an upbraiding from a formidable feminist deputation of protest, representing twenty separate organizations, which he bravely received in person at the Home Office.'

*

The Times / 19 October 1959

Arms for Cuba

— There is a saying that justice should not only be done but be seen to be done. There will surely be little visible justice if the British Government refuses the replacement of jet fighters to Castro in time of peace (even though an uneasy peace) when it supplied jet fighters to Batista in the middle of a civil war.

Surely your Washington Correspondent's suggestion that Castro might employ his jet fighters against Miami, that is to say, the United States, shows a certain sense of unreality.

*

New Statesman / 7 November 1959

The Man Who Built a Cathedral

— Although Father Fitzgerald built a fine church he seems to have neglected to teach the young Paul Johnson that a Bishop does not appoint a Monsignor and a Monsignor does not have a hat (perhaps Mr Johnson is thinking of stockings).

Paul Johnson wrote at the foot of this: 'Like other converts, Mr Greene likes to teach his fellow-Catholics their business. I wrote "offer", not "appoint" – in the sense that Mr Macmillan might '"offer" Mr Greene a "K"'. The phrase "a monsignor's hat" is, of course, figurative; how else would Mr Greene put it?'

*

'Pirated' Books

— It seems that I am one of the writers whose books have been withdrawn from the Soviet Book Exhibition on the ground that the translations are 'pirated'. In my case this accusation is completely untrue. Royalties have been scrupulously paid on all my books published: the blocking of royalties is no new practice, even in the West.

*

Bernard Levin in Moscow

— As I am about to leave tonight to visit for the fourth time the city so strangely described by Mr Bernard Levin I feel a great interest in his account. What has happened to all those coffee houses – or ice cream parlours – which I saw in Moscow on my last visit, for Mr Levin says there are none? What has happened to the attractive 'bar' with stand-up tables on one leg where one drank and ate so cheaply? (Mr Levin says there are no bars.) What has happened to all the friends of mine who have written to me for books and who have acknowledged their receipt? (Mr Levin says it is dangerous to receive books from the West.)

It is probably only a happy accident, or my ignorance of the Russian language, which has prevented me being accosted by the currency touts in Moscow as I have been so often accosted in Paris, Rome and Saigon. From the surprise Mr Levin shows at his encounter with these characters I get the impression that Moscow must have been the first foreign city Mr Levin has ever visited.

In spite of my dislike of lettuce, which seems to insinuate itself in a limp tired form as in Scandinavia under all kinds of cold British dishes, I hope to use some of the next few days in chasing it down, though I rather hope I don't succeed. I don't expect to find pasta either, thank God, though I look forward to the delicious Georgian dish of cold turkey with a nut sauce, and to drinking again a dry Georgian white wine.

How odd it is that when a journalist describes a city he makes it seem so different from the one others have encountered as ordinary travellers with no need to melodramatize their impressions. The Beaverbrook press, I was once told by an editor of the *Daily Mail*, teaches its young apprentices, of whom Mr Levin is one, that a story must 'stand up'. Mr Levin's story certainly does – as monumentally as a Cos lettuce.

Beneath this letter was an immediate reply from Bernard Levin: 'What has happened to the bars is that they have been closed in the anti-drunkenness drive. There is a tiny counter in one of the big stores at which it is possible to buy a glass of wine. Here, again, "the attractive bar with stand-up tables . . . where one drank and ate so cheaply" is another example of distance lending enchantment to the view. There are no tables in it, only a kind of ledge, and no seats, and it isn't attractive, and it isn't cheap. There is also a coffee-house, but the only time I tried to get into it there was a queue so long that I gave up. Mr Greene must not pretend to be even more naïve than he is; some people in the Soviet Union are allowed to receive books and letters from outside without anything unpleasant happening to them until the next twist in the line, when they are apt to be rounded up and shot. But outside the ranks of this *élite* it is dangerous to correspond with the West even while the line stays still. As for Mr Greene's reference to my work for Lord Beaverbrook's papers, I would be grateful if he could park his somewhat over-obtrusive artistic virginity in his new-found Wardour Street cloakroom for five minutes and give me some tips on how to keep the cash and let the discredit go.'

(Mr Levin also had to address himself to a complaint on the

same page from William Douglas Home, who asked 'Why is everybody being so horrid to Bernard Levin? He has written some dear little "Roedeaniana" in both your columns and the *Express* about going abroad, one assumes, for the first time. We all did in our youth. Why shouldn't he? Admittedly, we didn't try to publish them.')

*

Le Monde / 22 June 1960

Une Lettre Ouverte de Graham Greene à M. André Malraux

Cher maître.

— Comptant parmi les milliers de personnes qui, en Angleterre, ont admiré vos romans, et tout particulièrement *La Condition humaine* et *L'Espoir*, je vous demande de me pardonner si je vous donne ce titre plutôt que celui de monsieur le ministre. Peut-être vous rappellerez-vous que nous nous sommes rencontrés naguère, en tant que membres d'un jury littéraire qui, chaque année, attribuait un prix en souvenir d'une héroïque Française morte au camp de Mauthausen pour la défense des libertés françaises. Si quelqu'un le peut, vous pourrez certainement nous expliquer le sens de ce récent procès d'Alger qui a laissé ceux qui aiment la France moins animés d'un esprit critique que malheureux et perplexes. Nous ne pouvons croire que les victimes de tortures aient reçu un enseignement de leurs tortionnaires et que le nom de Mauthausen ne soit plus synonyme d'honneur pour les Français et de honte pour les Allemands. A Paris, en ce moment, les cinémas affichent *Le Dialogue des carmélites* d'après un scénario de Bernanos. Dans ce film, les religieuses persécutées prient pour les membres des deux partis qui meurent au service d'idéaux opposés au cours de la guerre civile que fut la Révolution. Mais il n'est pas aussi aisé d'inclure les tortionnaires dans nos prières, surtout lorsqu'ils prétendent qu'ils torturent dans notre intérêt. Tom Paine a écrit: 'Il nous faut protéger jusqu'à nos ennemis contre l'injustice.' Ce qui m'a poussé à vous écrire c'est un passage d'un journal anglais. En voici quelques phrases dont la lecture est pénible à ceux d'entre nous qui aiment la France et qui éprouvent un profond respect pour le chef de votre gouvernement.

'Parmi les accusés se trouve M. Henri Alleg, qui fut expulsé du banc des prévenus par la force, pour avoir accusé de meurtre ceux qui l'avaient arrêté.

'A la fin de 1957, déclara M. Matarasso, quatre intellectuels: M. Sartre, M. Mauriac, M. Martin du Gard et M. Malraux (actuellement ministre de la culture) demandèrent que toute la lumière fût faite au sujet de la torture, impartialement et avec la plus grande publicité. Il fallait absolument mettre fin aux activités de ceux qui torturèrent Alleg et assassinèrent Audin, ajoutait-il, parce que d'autres êtres continuaient d'être soumis aux mêmes supplices.

'A ce moment, le procureur de la République se leva et l'interrompit: "La défense vient de m'insulter. J'exige que l'avocat de la défense comparaisse devant la cour."

'Vint le tour des accusés de parler. L'un d'eux, critiquant la proposition d'un huis clos, déclara: "Dans cette même salle de tribunal, j'ai été condamné à mort par une cour de Vichy. A ce moment-là les débats étaient publics."'

Qu'un accusé soit chassé du banc des prévenus, qu'un procureur requière la comparution d'un avocat de la défense devant la cour et qu'un inculpé puisse citer Vichy comme exemple de justice rendue au grand jour, de tels incidents fournissent le sujet d'une tragi-comédie d'un insupportable cynisme. Il est difficile de croire que semblable tribunal puisse exister alors que le chef de la France libre est à la tête du gouvernement et que l'auteur de *La Condition humaine* est l'un de ses ministres. Les citations que je viens de faire ne sont pas tirées d'un journal comme le *Daily Worker* qu'on peut accuser de propagande communiste, mais du *Times* de Londres, qui, vous en conviendrez, ne s'inspire guère de l'idéologie communiste.

En tant qu'ami de la France, j'en appelle au ministre, à l'auteur de *La Condition humaine*, de *L'Espoir* et des *Noyers de l'Allenburg*. 'L'individu tué n'a aucune importance? Mais après, il arrive une chose, "Inattendue", tout est changé, les choses les plus simples, les rues, par exemple, les chiens . . .' Vous avez écrit cela, monsieur le ministre, et il n'est pas de mot écrit par vous qui puisse s'effacer aisément de la mémoire.

A vous en admiration et respect . . .

The Times (23 June) gave an account of this letter about the secret trial of M. Henri Alleg held shortly before in Algiers, when he was sentenced to ten years' imprisonment; Greene's account of the trial derived from earlier reports in *The Times*, 'which you will agree is hardly inspired by communist ideology'.

An unusual construction was put upon this, as Greene recalled (interview with Gaia Servadio, *Evening Standard*, 9 January 1978): 'Evelyn Waugh was one of my dearest friends. He was a rebel. Politically he couldn't stand anybody, the Tories included. It is a mistake to label him a right-wing writer. He did not reason in political terms. To give you an example: one evening we went to see Ionesco's *Rhinocéros* with Laurence Olivier [in it – at the Royal Court]. On the following day a letter of mine appeared in *The Times* [this item] in which I denounced tortures in Algeria. And then I got a little note from Evelyn: "I see that you send letters to *The Times* about tortures in Africa. Why don't you mention the torture inflicted upon us by Laurence Olivier last night?"'

*

Haggard Rides Again

– Is it only loyalty to an author who enchanted one as a boy that makes me regret that a critic of Mr Pritchett's integrity should make the mistake of writing a full New-Statesmanlike article on a novelist of whose large output he has read only two books – *King Solomon's Mines* and *She* – and chose two only to enable him to review with an appearance of authority a biography of Haggard? What would Mr Pritchett think of a reviewer who read for the first time a couple of Stevenson's novels so that he might give an impression of criticizing a new biography?

Many of Haggard's admirers will not place *She* very high among his works. (I would even prefer, with all its *longueurs*, *Allan Quatermain*, or *Ayesha*, the sequel to *She*.) But how can one write of Haggard without having read *Nada the Lily* (which has left, with me at any rate, an indelible impression of the tragic Zulu history from Chaka to Cetewayo) and *Eric Brighteyes*, a magnificent pastiche of an Icelandic saga, with a memorable villain, Earl Attlee? And still in the background remain *Montezuma's Daughter*, a novel of the conquest of Mexico, and *The Wanderer's Necklace*, a far from despicable novel of Byzantium.

Far more than Scott, Haggard gave us a sense of history, but Mr Pritchett has read two novels and made his critical decision.

*

Mr K. on TV

– I wonder how many of those who watched in England and America the televised interview between Mr Khruschev and Mr David Susskind will feel as I do that Mr

Susskind rendered a poor service to his country and to the West.

Mr Khruschev depended upon an interpreter, and this gave Mr Susskind an opportunity – like a small boy dealing with a new French master before his approving classmates – to interpolate little snide remarks unintelligible to the master. Cocking a snook has seldom been regarded as a sign of strength, but of course these particular interjections will undoubtedly save Mr Susskind from appearing at some future date before the Committee on Un-American Activities, in spite of his hand-clasps with the Soviet leader.

Another unsympathetic characteristic of an embarrassing broadcast: whenever Mr Khruschev mentioned the words 'U-2', Mr Susskind gave a histrionic gesture of despair and, as though he were confronting a peculiarly stupid guest, would repeat 'But that is *history*' – indicating like Henry Ford before him that 'history is bunk'.

Moreover, Mr Susskind and his sponsors obviously believe that 'history' is anything that has happened more than four months ago, so quickly time flies in the New World. In the antique trade I believe that 100 years still has to pass before an old object becomes an antique.

*

The Times / 23 December 1960

Censorship by ITA

— At this moment attractive prizes are being offered by Associated Television Ltd for new plays. Perhaps it would be as well to remind authors who consider submitting their plays that the Independent Television Authority exerts a censorship far more stringent than that old bugbear of the theatre, the Lord Chamberlain.

A play of mine called *The Complaisant Lover* was to have

been produced by ATV but I have before me the copy of a letter to the company from a Mr Noel Stevenson, whoever he may be, which demands nine cuts, seven more than the two slight ones demanded by the Lord Chamberlain. Mr Stevenson writes: 'Probably all of these would have been excised from the script by you when you came to them, but we felt strongly enough about them to feel it necessary to draw your attention to them in case they slipped through unnoticed.' Apparently Mr Stevenson does not yet know enough to realize that it is for the author, and not the company, to cut a script.

Presumably ITA defends censorship on the grounds that television reaches a larger audience than the theatre, and that the hour of performance and the parents' control are not sufficient to guard the young from corruption. But a mystery remains, when we remember the violence and crime almost daily shown on independent television. What in the eyes of ITA is corrupting? In my particular play a speech by Victor Root, the dentist, played in the theatre by Sir Ralph Richardson, which indicates his love for his wife, is forbidden by ITA. It is a key speech, and its omission would change the nature of the play into a rather dubious farce and the character of the husband into a comic cuckold hardly suitable for the nursery. Apparently it is not sex in itself which ITA objects to (a bedroom scene between husband, wife and lover passes uncut), but the expression of tenderness in connexion with the sexual act. What strange mentors for youth these censors – appointed by whom? – must be.

A dramatist may sometimes feel prepared to fight the venerable and entrenched authority represented by the Lord Chamberlain (whose officers, to do them justice, are always prepared to discuss their demands with the author), but who is going to bother to fight an unknown Mr Stevenson of ITA? Much easier to withdraw the play. It is for these reasons I would advise any would-be prize winners in the ATV competitions to consider whether television is yet regarded by the commercial companies as an entertainment for adults.

The next day a news item reported: 'At the Knightsbridge offices of the ITA the secretary of Mr Noel Stevenson, programme administration officer, confirmed that he was the Mr Stevenson named in Mr Greene's letter, but he was not available for comment, as he was indisposed.

'Later an ITA spokesman said: "Mr Stevenson is no more responsible in this case than any other civil servant. We are on a par with civil servants here. The decision taken and the advice given in this matter were those of the authority."

'The BBC stated yesterday that it had been asked to comment on Mr Greene's letter. In a statement it said: "BBC Television has for a long time wanted to put *The Complaisant Lover* on its screen, and several weeks ago it had made an offer for a ninety-minute version, to be cut by the author for length only, which is the normal practice of the BBC when producing the works of playwrights of distinction."'

*

The Times / 4 January 1961

Lessons That Were Not Learnt

– They are not worth much, the buildings of Vientiane, and the people who inhabit that shabby administrative centre had little to live for and less to die for. One hopes that Luang Prabang will have a better fate. This is one of the most beautiful towns in the world, with a royal palace the size of a very small country house, and almost every four buildings a temple – in one of them the footmark of Buddha: a town of bells and peace.

One cannot believe, now that the French have gone,

that the people of Laos are much concerned with either of the warring parties; there is not the fervent common enthusiasm, which made the war in Vietnam a national war, and it is tragic to think that it is a western Power which has brought war back. Wasn't Dien Bien Phu a sufficient lesson?

The dream of a neutral Laos was a good one, but it is idle to think that neutrality can fail to have a certain colouring when the neutral country lies on the borders of two conflicting systems. Would Sweden be more secure if Finland were maintained by American arms and money as a neutral state with a western tinge? If full-scale war develops in Laos we shall have a heavy load on our conscience, even though the load may have been imposed by an ally and not by our own Government. For four winters in Vietnam I was an unhappy witness of the disintegration caused by the intrigues of American under-cover agencies in the cause of an unrealizable dream – the dream of a Third Force: nobody with any knowledge of Laos is likely to deny that Prince Souvanna's Government had been undermined by the aid given from the United States to right wing forces. At least the Russian aid at the beginning of this mad competition was given to the legal government of the country.

One is painfully reminded of the Spanish Civil War. America has taken on the role played then by Germany and Italy, and they are American weapons which have helped to destroy Vientiane; one can only hope that England will not play again her former pusillanimous part by aiding, with her ambiguous diplomacy, the forces of the right. Can any sane person believe that a right-wing government would ever be allowed to exist, contrary to the agreement of Geneva, on the borders of China and the Democratic Republic of Vietnam any more than Guatemala was allowed to keep a government under communist influence?

'Now I see a damn fool letter in this morning's paper from Graham about Laos. He seems in a shocking bad way,' Evelyn Waugh told Elizabeth Pakenham.

'I was very pleased to have your support for the views which I expressed concerning American policy in Laos,' wrote Greene on 5 February to a Pierre-François Dupont-Gonin in France. 'Since then, as you will have seen, Prince Boum Oum has admitted the absence of any foreign communist personnel in Laos. One can only hope that under the new régime of Kennedy the undercover activities of American agencies in the Far East will be modified.'

A Friedmann Schuster wrote from Frankfurt to say that he had reason to believe Greene correct, but could not say whence his information derived. There had been enormous headlines in the German newspapers that a second Korea was imminent and that the Reds would march into Laos. Many people reacted straight away and a new hate had arisen. What would happen the day there was 'news' of the Reds on the march to Hamburg and it was too late to check the truth of this? 'Eine einzige Lüge kann heute die ganze Menschheit vernichten.' 'I can only say', replied Greene, 'that my information about Laos was partly based on private information I had received from Vientiane and partly from a long experience during the Indo-China war of American activities in Vietnam. Since I wrote the letter Prince Boum Oum's government have admitted that the story of communist forces having crossed the frontier from Vietnam and China was fallacious.'

*

New Statesman / 28 April 1961

Lines on the Liberation of Cuba

Prince of Las Vegas, Cuba calls!
Your seat's reserved on the gangster plane,
Fruit machines back in Hilton halls
And in the Blue Moon girls again.

'At 6 a.m. [15 April] two B26s with Cuban markings flew over the headquarters, dropping bombs,' wrote Hugh Thomas in *Cuba*. 'Six other B26s bombed three other Cuban airfields . . . The B26s were, of course, US aeroplanes, painted by the CIA,' the first stage in the Battle of Cochinos Bay two days later: 'in allowing it to continue, though with his heart not in it, [Kennedy] showed himself less a man of destiny than a Hamlet, a prince whose courtiers were out of control.'

*

Observer / 23 July 1961

Moving Writers

—I have been out of England or I would have commented sooner on Pendennis's remarks concerning the varying loyalty of writers to the firms who publish their books, since he named me specifically. I published my first novel with Heinemann more than thirty-two years ago, and although, as Pendennis says, I have for long now been a working publisher, neither of the firms with which I have been connected ever tried to induce me to join it as author. But a publishing house, too, has a debt of loyalty to the author. Loyalty is no one-way traffic. That debt in my case was paid by an individual publisher who risked his reputation by supporting through the lean years a writer whom his colleagues would perhaps have been happy to shed.

The character of a publishing house can very quickly change. A whole list can veer suddenly towards vulgarity ('Enterprise', the new leader may call it, but some of the old authors may feel a little lonely among the new accents). The sense of trust between author and publisher may vanish in a season. Perhaps this change happens more frequently now when the City has begun to move in.

(107)

Authors are not factory hands, nor are books to be compared as commodities with tobacco, beer, motor-cars and automatic machines. A novelist ought certainly to hesitate long before he deserts a publisher who has helped him when help was most needed, in the long years of poor sales, but does he owe loyalty to a board which changes from year to year and may, in this new phase, include directors with no experience of publishing and with little interest in books save as a 'quality' commodity less liable than others to depreciate in value at a period of economic depression?

Pendennis (2 July) had remarked upon Greene's leaving Heinemann for the Bodley Head, where he 'is very much a working director. It is he who has introduced Charles Chaplin to the Bodley Head. An old fan of Chaplin's, he encouraged him to write his autobiography, and has recently been looking over the manuscript. It will be published next year.'

*

The Times / [21 September 1961]

Pet Theory

— I quote a report from your Malta correspondent in *The Times* of September 21. 'John Azzopardi, aged 46, was fined £80 yesterday for spitting *or making signs of spitting* through the gauze wire on a window in his house at Archbishop Gonzi during a demonstration in the Archbishop's honour. Another charge that Azzopardi also sought to bring the Archbishop into contempt by calling his dog "Mike Gonzi" was not proven.' (The italics are mine.)

Some questions come to mind. Malta is a poor island: what is the equivalent value of £80 here? Who instituted the prosecution? Surely not the Archbishop, who would be aware of Christ's injunction to turn the other cheek. Are there any comparable laws in this country? I have no dog and my only pets are a colony of ants, but I am perfectly prepared to fight a test-case by naming one of them after my Archbishop.

The case being *sub judice*, the *Daily Telegraph*, too, declined to print a letter from him (which offered a contribution towards the fine and stated that the ant had now been christened).

The appeal was due the following January, but in the meanwhile (27 October) the 76-year-old Archbishop underwent an operation for acute appendicitis; convalescence was perhaps aided by news that Azzopardi's appeal had failed; indeed, Gonzi died, aged 98, on 22 January 1984, by which time his campaign against the religion-baiting Malta Labour Party and Dom Mintoff was long over.

*

The Times / 21 February 1962

Dr Castro's Cuba

—Your excellent leading article criticizing the American suggestion that Nato countries should aid in the suppression of Dr Castro's Cuba will, I feel sure, be welcomed in Brazil and Argentina (I don't speak of governments), and in Europe by all who saw something of the regime which Dr Castro overthrew.

President Batista's police state, addicted like most police states to the practice of torture, was supported not only by the American Government of the time, not only by the more influential racketeers of Las Vegas, who controlled the gambling concessions and brothels of Havana, but also, in a blinkered way by the present British Government.

You, Sir, may remember some correspondence in your

pages which dealt with the sale of fighter planes to President Batista, even after the export of arms had been stopped by the United States Government. You may remember too the rather weak excuse of the Foreign Secretary in the House of Commons that the Government had no evidence that a state of civil war existed in Cuba. This was said a fortnight before Dr Castro entered Havana.

With this past happily behind us let us be sure, before we support the policy of the State Department, that Dr Castro's regime is really regarded by the population of Cuba as despotic and unjust. Many businessmen, who supported Dr Castro secretly in his struggle, have certainly fled from Cuba to Miami. But for myself I cannot help remembering a morning in Santiago, then under the military discipline of President Batista, when the streets were full of young children, who had gone on strike from their schools, as a protest against the midnight kidnapping of three girls, the oldest thirteen, who were held as hostages in the military barracks because their father had fled to the mountains.

Government departments live at a great distance from events; papers in files marked 'for attention' fail to stir the imagination. But is it unreasonable that I, like any other passer-by that day in Santiago, should be distressed at the idea that the measures the Government failed to apply against President Batista should now be employed against Dr Castro? (Let us remember, not as a romantic fable but as a piece of evidence bearing on the question whether or not Dr Castro represents his country, that he began his conquest with twelve men.)

One man, from Hollywood Lane, Hollywood (in Worcestershire) objected: Greene 'misses the crux of the problem, which is the international problem posed by a Communist Cuba on the doorstep of the United States. The fact that the Cubans are now enjoying comparative bliss under Marxism is cold comfort for the residents of Florida.'

Donald Bruce, who had recently returned from his second visit to Cuba in six months and who had made a close study of Cuban affairs, joined Greene in his support for *The Times*'s leading article's view that Britain should have no part in any suppression of Castro. 'For the first time, the poorer section of the population are getting a fairer share of the basic necessities of life in terms of both food and clothing . . . a real decline in the consumer standards enjoyed by the middle class has resulted, understandably, in a volume of bitter criticism which is aired quite openly in the more expensive hotels and restaurants in Havana despite the fact that the essence of such criticism is that it is not possible under "the police state" to utter it in safety . . . But [among Cubans] there was a fierce pride in what they were seeking to do and of which, indeed, there is abundant evidence for those who care to see – notably in housing, education and employment . . . Live and let live can, of course, always be interpreted as appeasement, but in the context of the modern world it is more likely to avoid the mutual mass extinction which corporate interference seems hell-bent on accomplishing.'

*

The Times Literary Supplement / 26 March 1964

Cuban Itch

— As a Catholic and a recent visitor to Cuba I wish your reviewer would enlarge on his curious statement that Castro 'has dispatched' the Church. Odd then that I could attend Mass: odd that Castro could be the guest of the Papal Nuncio when he celebrated the coronation of Pope Paul. Perhaps your reviewer has been misled by a misguided broadcast by Bishop Sheen.

*

Fair Pay for Postmen

— I think if Mr [R.] Smith [General Secretary of the Postal Workers] were to ask the public to contribute to the strike funds of the Post Office Union he would be surprised and gratified by the response. There is no evidence at all that public goodwill towards postmen has been in the least affected by the present strike: another suggestion for Mr Smith, on the next occasion why not arrange the strike to coincide with the despatch of income-tax demands? This would ensure a loss to the Government by the delay in payments and a gain to the public even more substantial than they have enjoyed in this strike. How grateful many of us already are for a delightful freedom from having to read or write letters. One knows from experience that a high proportion of letters, after they have been delayed a few weeks, will not require an answer.

*

Daily Telegraph / 20 August 1964

Moral Issues of Train Robbery

Punitive Comparisons

— Am I one of a minority in feeling admiration for the skill and courage behind the Great Train Robbery? More important, am I in a minority in being shocked by the savagery of the sentences – thirty years for a successful theft as compared with a life sentence (twelve years at most in practice) for the rape and murder of a child?

If our legal system sentences a man to thirty years for an offence against property, it is not surprising if some of us feel sympathy for the prisoner who escapes, again with skill and courage, from such a sentence.

A great deal is written about prison life in Communist countries. Now we learn that in our own out-of-date, overcrowded prisons a man can suffer solitary confinement for an indefinite time, except for a brief period each day when he is distinguished from his fellow-prisoners by a distinctive dress, that he sleeps, if he can, in a cell with an ever-burning light, observed by warders every fifteen minutes.

Is it intended that this treatment should continue over thirty years if the prisoner does not break down and disclose where the money stolen from the Midland and other banks is hidden?

This is very close to torture for the purpose of eliciting information – torture on behalf of our banks is even less sympathetic than torture with an ideological motive.

'Mr Graham Greene is a distinguished novelist. His views attract attention. It is all the more unfortunate that sometimes his views are bizarre,' said the *Daily Express*. The letter was picked up by the *Evening Standard* later that day. Its 'Londoner's Diary' asked the opinion of various authors. Angus Wilson: 'I consider any penal measures approaching torture absolutely baraborous [*sic*]. You might say that a man uses skill and courage in snitching and raping a child. I don't believe in sentences which are passed just to satisfy the public and make it feel good.' Stephen Spender: 'I would agree with Mr Greene about the sentences, but to admire the robbers is irrelevant. It is a romantic, sentimental admiration. It is not necessary to admire the robbers in order to object to the severity of the sentences.' Anthony Powell: 'I have a hearty dislike of criminals. And in my own small experience of them I have found them boring and tiresome people. It is illogical to say that the defence of property carries the severest sentences when these robbers obviously prefer to serve thirty years in prison rather than give up the money. One can't think of these things hysterically, and I am against writing-up these people as romantic characters.'

Greene's publisher, A. S. Frere, by now retired, commented: '. . . the whole penal code urgently needs revision. Try to raise this vital question with either party at the coming election and be prepared for an evasive answer. I am willing to wager odds that the first "urgent" legislation likely to occupy the new Government, be it Conservative or Labour, will be increased pay for MPs.' Major G. E. Howard of Surrey said that it was Greene's sort of thinking and teaching that 'is largely responsible for the present crime rate being the highest ever, and his deplorable hero-worship of squalid, cowardly criminals is a major cause of the current appalling level of juvenile delinquency'.

*

Daily Telegraph / 6 November 1964

Western Approval of Torture

— In the past few weeks photographs have appeared in the British Press showing the tortures inflicted on Vietcong prisoners by troops of the Vietnam army.

In the long, frustrating war – now nearly twenty years old – in Indo-China there has, of course, always been a practice of torture – torture by Vietminh, torture by Vietnamese, torture by the French – but at least in the old days of the long, long war hypocrisy paid a tribute to virtue by hushing up the torture inflicted by its own soldiers and condemning the torture inflicted by the other side.

The strange new feature about the photographs of torture now appearing in the British and American Press is that they have been taken with the approval of the torturers and are published over captions that contain no hint of condemnation. They might have come out of a book on insect life. 'The white ant takes certain measures against the red ant after a successful foray.'

But these, after all, are not ants but men. The long, slow slide into barbarism of the western world seems to have quickened. For these photographs are of torturers belonging to an army which could not exist without American aid and counsel.

Does this mean that the American authorities sanction torture as a means of interrogation? The photographs certainly are a mark of honesty, a sign that the authorities do not shut their eyes to what is going on, but I wonder whether this kind of honesty without conscience is really to be preferred to the old hypocrisy.

This letter brought a number of letters, including one from a lecturer in economics at the College of Advanced Technology in Birmingham, who wondered whether some further protest could be made. 'I feel that I have shot my bolt over this affair of the tortures and it is up to others to take it a stage further,' replied Greene. 'I don't quite see that it is a subject for the Press Council. Nor have the Red Cross ever been able properly to control the treatment of prisoners. I once spoke to a Swiss Red Cross representative who was in Korea and who was present at a particularly disgusting piece of torture taking place in the presence of an American colonel. He reported the affair to MacArthur who simply refused to believe it.'

*

The Times / 26 April 1965

Teachers' Pay

— As the son of a schoolmaster who succeeded (but with who can tell what anxieties?) in bringing up a family of six children on the old Burnham scale, I feel great sympathy with the National Association of Schoolmasters who are seeking to raise the scale of salaries which at present rises from a minimum of £630 a year to £1,250 after fifteen years. As a young sub-editor employed on *The Times* in 1930 I received the minimum salary of £468 a year – the equivalent today can be hardly less than £1,000, but was I doing a job so much more valuable than a schoolmaster?

It would be interesting to take other comparisons. A refuse-collector employed by the Westminster City Council earns a minimum of £646 a year. In addition salvage from the refuse brings him in, on an average, £5 a week free of income tax. (This salvage doesn't consist of lucky finds: the greater part consists of newspapers and cardboard and old clothes – the paper-merchants send a lorry to the depot to pick up the salvage and the refuse-collector has only the labour of separating the clean salvage from the dirty.) The refuse-collector, who has also the enviable benefit of an open-air life, gains a minimum equivalent to about £1,000 a year compared with a school-master's £630.

In the same issue the Chairman of the Cape Asbestos Company Ltd of Park Lane commented that the demands from, and settlements with, the Post Office workers, the miners, railwaymen and Underground staff caused 'deep misgiving' and 'grave concern . . . Until any government will take a really firm stand on wages and face the consequences, private industry will always be struggling to achieve the impossible.'

One teacher wrote to thank Greene for pointing to this low rate of pay given those 'who prepare others for numerous profitable careers . . . I hope that all MPs, with their greatly increased pay, will realize that a loaf of bread is the same price to teachers as to MPs, that many teachers have a liking for "good" food, the same as many MPs, but have to control their appetites.'

It is a sentiment with which George Limburn, Assistant

Secretary of the National Association of Schoolmasters, doubtless agreed, but restrained himself from saying so in *The Times*: '. . . the concern of Mr Graham Greene for the plight of the schoolmaster is greatly appreciated and his sympathy . . . well placed. I would point out with deference, however, that his figures are not correct. The £468 a year which he says he earned as a sub-editor for *The Times* in 1930 would be worth nearer £2,000 today and not £1,000 as he stated. The Association is striving, not only to achieve the pre-war schoolmaster's standard of living for schoolmasters of today, but to obtain a share of the nation's increased prosperity for him as well.'

*

The Times / 12 May 1965

Pin-Pricks

— One small point has not yet, I think, been made concerning the motives behind the American intervention in the Dominican Republic. The so-called 'insurgents' are said by the State Department to be infiltrated by communists and the supporters of Dr Castro. This, of course, may be so, but 'pull devil pull baker'.

During the Government of Dr Reid Cabral (whose father was honoured by an OBE last New Year) the Dominican Republic provided a useful base for tip-and-run raids mounted by refugees against Cuba. Presumably they had the tacit support of American agencies after Florida had become an embarrassing base.

I remember seeing last January, before making a holiday excursion down the Dominican and Haitian border, one such Cuban boat temporarily laid up in a creek at the northern point of the republic near Monte Cristi. An American company owned the estate which bordered the creek.

These were not important operations, they were pin-pricks, but they were pin-pricks threatened by the re-establishment of a liberal government under Dr Bosch. Perhaps a giant forbidden the use of his club resents the loss even of a pin.

*

South-East Asia in Turmoil

In the *New Statesman* of 19 March 1965, Greene reviewed Brian Crozier's Penguin Special of this title.

— To write in less than 180 pages a clear account, unclogged by detail, of the revolutions and counter-revolutions since 1941 in Malaya, Siam, Burma, Korea, Indo-China and Indonesia would have been an extraordinary achievement, even if the result had been a dull textbook. Mr Crozier is never dull. One may disagree with his point of view, but he is fair enough to supply the material on which to base one's disagreement. He sup-ports the formation of Malaysia, but his facts are so justly selected that I found it possible for the first time to doubt its wisdom and to feel some sympathy for President Sukarno's policy. His account of post-war Burma is perhaps the least adequate, but then Burma of late years has closed the door on foreign observers (happy indeed is the country which is unaided and unobserved).

In South Vietnam he skips too perfunctorily, in my view, the period of Diem's rule: I would like to know more of what happened to those million Catholic peasants from the north who were scared into flight by their bishops and priests. How many now have turned to the Vietcong? I was there at the time of the great exodus, I saw them flocking onto the liners at Haiphong, and again I saw them in their waterless camps outside Saigon. Already they were home-sick, dissatisfied, rebellious, and afraid: in the north they had lived in Catholic villages, Catholic towns: now they were surrounded by people of an alien faith: it wasn't the security which they had been promised and even in the first months they began to react with spasmodic violence. The religious question is very much a political question in Vietnam, and I would have liked a longer and more penetrating account of it.

Mr Crozier, though he accepts the presence of America in South Vietnam, is blessedly free from semantic confusion. He never pretends, like some of Lyndon Johnson's advisers, that America is there to protect the 'freedom' of the Vietnamese. Freedom for what and from what? America has not brought freedom from war or from hunger: she has certainly not brought freedom to choose a government. Diem and all his successors (we begin to lose count of them now) have all been imposed on the people. Mr Crozier very fairly gives us facts; he seldom gives opinions.

I would have liked to ask this intelligent observer whether he sees any favourable future, save communism, for South-East Asia. It is naive to ask whether we have the 'right' to oppose it with Western weapons, whether indeed we have the 'right' to be there at all, for right is the first casualty in a struggle for power. But a more important question is, are we wise to be there? Mr Crozier writes: 'In Vietnam and Korea, the facts of power dictate an American presence, until such time as the Communist governments of East Asia have lost interest in subversion. This could well take more than a man's lifetime.' But the war in South-East Asia has already lasted a man's lifetime – if we take the chances of life there today – and it looks like turning into a hundred years' war. A temporary power-struggle is becoming a kind of religious war with the Capitalist the Good side and the Communist the Evil side. 'The facts of power' assume the existence of a monolithic Communism which is no more true of the East than of the

West, and Mr Crozier (honest inconsistency is a great merit of his book) has already criticized this conception.

'For years, Ho Chi Minh managed to keep his party out of the Sino-Soviet dispute. But when the partial Test Ban Treaty was signed in Moscow in the summer of 1963, it had to choose and opted for China – the giant on the doorstep. This must have been deeply distasteful to Ho, both as a Vietnamese Nationalist and as a politician who knows the value of playing off one side against the other ... It is quite wrong to assume, as many people have, that China calls the tune in Indo-China. Paradoxically, although the Chinese would like to get the Americans out of Laos and Vietnam and doubtless approve of North Vietnamese efforts to this end, they would probably not be too happy if Ho Chi Minh fulfilled all his original ambitions, bringing most of Indo-China under Vietnamese leadership and making Vietnam economically independent of China.'

Surely Mr Crozier has flinched away from the proper conclusion of his own argument – that it is the American presence which alone makes it likely that Vietnam will become a satellite of China.

Daily Telegraph / 23 June 1965

'Tactical Error' on Vietcong

— Surely the refusal of the United States to negotiate with the Vietcong who control the greater part of South Vietnam is a tactical error of the worst kind. What is to prevent the National Front of Liberation declaring themselves the legal Government of South Vietnam, possibly with Mr Nguyen Huu Tho as President, Mr Huyn Tan Phat as Prime Minister, and even Mr Huynh Minh, who was responsible for the brilliantly successful attack on Bien Hoa airfield, as Minister of National Defence?

At one stroke the anonymous Vietcong could become a Government with leaders whose names would soon be as familiar in the West as those of Gen. Giap and Mr Pham Van Dong. Their Government would presumably be recognized by the Soviet Union, China, the Democratic Republics of Eastern Europe, Cuba and even possibly France.

Their claim to be the *de facto* Government of South Vietnam would be difficult to dispute seeing that there is no legal basis whatever for the weary succession of Governments which have been imposed on Saigon since the assassination of Diem.

As junta succeeds junta in Saigon the claim of the Vietcong leaders to represent a *de facto* Government becomes stronger. To refuse to negotiate with them is to refuse to negotiate with the future and to repeat the unhappy mistakes of the past. But is there another off-shore island available for a Vietnamese Chiang Kai-shek?

On 2 July, Brian Crozier wrote: 'Mr Graham Greene's arguments (29 June) are singularly inappropriate. The Vietcong has not set up a "government" because this would mean finding an administration and garrisons for the towns it would then have to hold. In this event it would lose one of its main advantages.

'At present holding and terrorizing the villages, it is able to attack – and if necessary capture – towns, then retreat; and it is the Government that is forced to disperse its inadequate personnel in administrative garrison duties.

'Incidentally the Americans have now made it clear that they would be prepared to negotiate with the Vietcong if the latter were represented on Hanoi's negotiating team. This is as it should be, for the political arm of the Vietcong, the so-called National Front for the Liberation of South Vietnam, is merely a branch office of the Lao Dong party which rules North Vietnam.

'Why negotiate with a branch office when there is a head office that gives the orders?'

Daily Telegraph / 7 July 1965

Policy in Vietnam

— Since Mr Brian Crozier's answer to my letter of 23 June only appeared on 2 July you will forgive my own tardy reply. I have been away from England. Mr Crozier, except perhaps for Prof. Honey, is the most talented and informed British champion of the State Department's policy in South Vietnam. (The Foreign Secretary unfortunately has no personal knowledge of the country and is badly briefed.) Yet I find Mr Crozier's letter disingenuous. Has he any right to assume that for *de facto* recognition an administration must hold *towns*?

He is unable anyway to claim any legal basis for the present Saigon government (I am uncertain, after several days' absence from the British newspapers, who at this moment is President of South Vietnam). Even Mr Diem's right to rule depended on the medieval notion that he had been appointed by an Emperor – whom he soon afterwards disclaimed.

Under the circumstances it is wiser in Vietnam to abandon the idea of *de jure* government altogether. The Government of South Vietnam can claim *de facto* to represent a few principal towns; the *de facto* Government of the Vietcong can claim to administer three-quarters of the countryside. American – and not Vietnamese – air-power sees to it that the Vietcong administration works from deep shelters and not from conventional offices.

Would Mr Crozier argue that, if German air-power had been sufficient in 1940 to establish a German base and a collaborating government in London and to drive the resistance into shelters and trenches near Edgware, Epping, East Grinstead and Colchester, a resistance which none the less made it impossible for the government conscripts to control the countryside around London, General This and Air Marshal That and a Mr Jones could have legally declared themselves to be the *de facto* government of Great Britain? What Herculean laughter would have arisen at any such claim from a deep shelter in the Surrey hills where Someone who shall be nameless would have been cocking his snook at the German bombers as they destroyed a village in the Chilterns and an 'important' bridge at Bourton-on-Water.

Mr Crozier need not remind me that the geographical differences are very great – we both of us know Vietnam. The moral parallel is not so far astray.

As for his argument that the National Front for the Liberation of South Vietnam is merely a 'branch office' of the Lao Dong, and unworthy of separate negotiations, what is to prevent a 'branch office' repudiating any agreements made on its behalf by 'head office' and continuing the guerrilla war – which it has proved itself capable of doing? In such a situation all excuse for the bombing of the North would be removed. In any case Mr Crozier's argument is really an argument against negotiations with any local Communist government and for negotiation only with the Soviet Union or China. Thus the monolithic nature of Communism would be firmly established by our own actions.

Crozier wrote again on the 9th: 'While I thank Mr Graham Greene for his initial compliment, I suggest that it is he, not I, who is being disingenuous.

'He compares the Vietcong – a terrorist movement which brutalized the villagers of South Vietnam into co-operation, by torture and executions – with a hypothetical British Resistance movement against Hitler. Does he really suppose that "Someone who shall be nameless" would have had to torture or murder the people of Edgware, Epping, East Grinstead and Colchester into resisting the Germans?

'Mr Greene, by the way, misinterprets my argument about negotiating with the Vietcong's head office. This is in Hanoi, not in Peking or Moscow. The hard core of the National Front for the Liberation of South Vietnam is the People's Revolutionary party which is merely an extension of the ruling Lao Dong (Workers' *i.e.* Communist) party of North Vietnam.

'If Hanoi gave a cease-fire order – which it may do when the monsoon ends without an American Dien Bien Phu – the Vietcong would lay down its arms.'

And, on the 12th, Lord Monson, who has often been published in the *Telegraph* letter columns: 'The parallel that Mr Graham Greene seeks to draw between the struggle of South Vietnam and her allies against Communist aggression today, and an imagined German occupation of Britain in 1940, is only tenable if one also supposes that well over a million people from Scotland and the North of England would have fled eagerly from the "resistance"-dominated northern half of the country to the "collaborationist" German-occupied parts of the south, in the same way as more than one million Vietnamese have fled from the Communist North to South Vietnam.

'Such an hypothesis is about as ludicrous and fantastic as Mr Greene's implied comparison of President Johnson with Adolf Hitler.'

Daily Telegraph / 16 July 1965

Flight to the South in Vietnam

— Yes, as Lord Monson writes, one million Roman Catholics fled from North Vietnam after the defeat of the French. They followed their 'fighting' bishops, the Bishop of Phut-Diem who had organized his own private army and the Bishop of Bui-Chu, and there is some evidence that their priests told them that they were following our Lady who had also fled to the south.

Unlike Lord Monson I was a witness to their flight and I visited the waterless cantonments in the south where President Diem installed them. Already their unrest was taking a violent form. How many have in fact drifted back? How many would have gone back if the Diem terror had not taken the place of war?

There is much talk of the Vietcong terror, and I do not deny its existence, but the only photographs we have seen in your paper and others is of the torture inflicted by the South Vietnam Army.

*

The Times Literary Supplement / 16 September 1965

Last Post?

— The Bodley Head were following Ford's own wishes in publishing *Parade's End* as a trilogy and not as a tetralogy. In *The Letters of Ford Madox Ford* edited by Professor Ludwig will be found a letter written by Ford in 1930 to his agent Eric Pinker which is surely quite unequivocal.

'I strongly wish to omit the *Last Post* from the edition. I do not like the book and have never liked it and always intended the series to end with *A Man Could Stand Up*. Please consult Duckworth's about this. I am ready to be guided by them but should much prefer the above course.'

G. M. Gliddon, of the University Bookshop, Norwich, wrote (*TLS*, 23 September) to ask whether readers might not be able to judge matters for themselves: *Last Post* had once been available as a Penguin. 'My point is that publishers should be consistent, and should not heed the whims of authors.'

Greene replied the following week:

— Mr Gliddon's letter seems to express a glib impertinence towards writers. 'The whims of authors', he says, should not be regarded by their publishers. Mr Robert Graves, I suppose, should be refused the opportunity to eliminate poems from his various collections; I ought not to be allowed to suppress my second and third novels. Does Mr Gliddon really believe that an author has a less critical eye to his own work and a less clear idea of its merits and demerits than a bookseller? Luckily with the aid of a reliable literary executor and the protection of the copyright laws the whims of authors can usually be safeguarded, even after death.

This debate continued, regularly fuelled by a dissenting Anthony Burgess. Penguin now has the four novels available in one unwieldy volume. As well as his essays on Ford in the Bodley Head edition, Greene reviewed *Great Trade Route*, *Vive Le Roy* and *Provence* (*London Mercury*, February 1937; August 1937; December 1938).

*

Sunday Telegraph / 16 January 1966

Wrong Model

— Just for the record, your correspondent, Stephen Barber, in Washington is completely wrong in thinking that I took General Lansdale as the model for *The Quiet American*. Pyle was a younger, more innocent and more idealistic member of the CIA. I would never have chosen Colonel Lansdale, as he then was, to represent the danger of innocence.

On 7 January 1968 Greene wrote to the same newspaper:

— Your Washington correspondent Mr Stephen Barber again repeats the old story which I am getting tired of denying, that General Lansdale was the original of the quiet American of my novel. This story has no truth in it whatever. I left Vietnam for the last time without ever meeting General Lansdale or even knowing of his existence.

And, on 1 June 1975:

— I grow tired of denying that there is any connection between my character Pyle in *The Quiet American* and General Lansdale, the American counter-insurgency expert whom I have never had the misfortune to meet. Pyle was an innocent and an idealist. I doubt whether your correspondent Mr Beeston would so describe General Lansdale. He should not refer in this way to a book which he has obviously never read, but I hope at least he will read this letter. Other journalists please note.

*

Spectator / 13 May 1966

The Kremlin Talks to the Vatican

— I read with interest the serious article (29 April) by Dev Murarka, but there is a lighter side . . . In July 1963 I encountered Mr Adzhubei [Khrushchev's son-in-law] in the Tropicana music-hall in Havana. It was Cuba's national day, and the music-hall – unchanged since the days of Batista – was practically empty except for two ringside tables, one occupied by the Soviet Ambassador and his guests, the other by the British Chargé and his. Mr Adzhubei stole the most attractive member of our party for a dance, and as he two-stepped by I called out to him, 'How did you get on with Pope John?' He made a long nose at me as he passed.

Later with the Soviet Ambassador he joined our table, and I repeated my question. This time he replied with great gravity. 'The Pope told me we were following different paths to the same end' – surely a statement which not even the most ardent cold warrior could deny.

In a later version sent to the *Spectator* (13 March 1976), Greene recalled his own reply: 'Yes. To death, I suppose.'

'Nothing gave me greater pleasure than the accident by which I was able to publish your cruelly funny "The Invisible Japanese Gentleman" in my first issue as Editor,' Nigel Lawson said to Greene on 5 May 1966. (Under him, the *Spectator*'s circulation sank to an all-time low of 9,000, according to Charles Moore, in an interview with Steve Clarke, *Campaign*, 10 March 1989.)

The story was collected in *May We Borrow Your Husband?* Francis King reviewed it in the *Sunday Telegraph* (9 April 1967) and remarked of this and other stories: 'Mr Greene adopts the Jamesian device of the narrator whose powers of perception are so much heightened by the events going on around him that he can overhear every phrase of conversations conducted not merely at the next-door restaurant table but at the table one away. (To eavesdrop on a conversation in Bentley's Fish Restaurant – the locale of "The Invisible Japanese Gentleman" – suggests, as anyone who has dined there will know, not merely hyperaesthesia but actual ESP.)'

Greene wrote the following week:

— Francis King, I'm afraid, cannot know Bentley's very well or he would not have suggested in his review of my book that it was virtually impossible to eavesdrop there. (Perhaps he confuses it with another and noisier and equally famous fish restaurant.) I can assure him, as one who has dined there on the average probably once a week over several years – that between 8.15 p.m. and the closing of the theatres Bentley's is one of the quietest restaurants in London, and that is the reason I have always loved it . . . whether for eating, drinking, for reading, and, of course, for eavesdropping.

*

Daily Telegraph / 10 June 1966

Principles and Profits

— Pilate has no lesson to teach poor Mr Dwye Evans, the managing director of Heinemann's. I say 'poor' because he succeeded (a difficult thing to do) a great publisher, Mr A. S. Frere, whom he describes with studied vagueness as having been 'closely associated' with the company.

Mr Evans is a man with a principle – complete freedom of publication for the members of the Heinemann Group. Strange then that Mr Warburg didn't take advantage of that freedom to publish the sick Maugham's senile and scandalous work *Looking Back*, which Mr Frere refused to issue with the Heinemann imprint in spite of his long and close friendship with the author.

Mr Evans now writes: 'Judging by the large press it has received' (he refers to Mr Beverley Nichols's cheap little effusion [*A Case of Human Bondage*]) 'it must be inevitably considered a book of interest to many.' (Mr Evans's prose is rather ungrammatical.)

There is one point of justice for Mr Evans and Mr Warburg to consider when they return from their ritual washing of hands. The large profits made out of Maugham's books assisted the Heinemann Group to save several small publishing firms from disaster. Mr Warburg once wrote an autobiography called *An Occupation for Gentlemen*. No doubt he used the term 'gentleman' ironically, and perhaps it should now be redefined in that sense in the next edition of the Oxford English Dictionary.

In view of this 'principle' of freedom it is not surprising that an aging writer like myself should have thought it better to remove my books from the Heinemann list. Alas, only in so far as I can, since the firm clings to my old books like some divorced woman who fights over every chattel not for its intrinsic value but because she considers herself a wronged woman. I trust Heinemann's will never have accumulated sufficient profits from my work to make it worth while for one of the lesser hyenas of the group to wet its teeth in my dead bowels.

An Occupation for Gentlemen? Yes, it was that once, in the days when Mr C. S. Evans, Mr Dwye Evans's father, was 'closely associated' with the company. With him I began a relation with Heinemann's that lasted for thirty years. When Mr Frere left I considered it time to find another home. How right I was in view of the publication of *A Case of Human Bondage.*

The same day's 'Londoner's Diary' in the *Evening Standard* reported: 'Today Mr Evans was abroad on holiday; no one else at Heinemann's was prepared to comment. Nor was Mr Warburg available this morning.'

*

Commonweal / 24 June 1966

Haiti

— 'There is little the US can do except wash its hands of the mess' (Haiti editorial, 20 May). But can it? It was American military aid which armed the Tontons Macoute under the old excuse that it was defending the 'free' world against Communism. (I doubt whether there were fifty Communists in Haiti.) Not all the perfumes of Arabia are going to wash out that little stain.

You consider that 'the food and health programs . . .

should continue . . . even if much of the food is stolen and sold privately . . .' This is to imagine Haiti as a kind of corrupt Western country, but Haiti, apart from the governing class, is of an unimaginable poverty. There is no black market of food for the poor – they haven't the means to pay. American aid circulates in a closed ring of government auctioneers. Without it the poor will not starve any quicker, though the Tontons might begin to live less well and to have second thoughts.

To a foreigner like myself who knows a little of Haiti and of Vietnam, it seems inexplicable that America is willing to export billions of dollars in trying to prop a weak regime in Vietnam against the wishes of the people and not to spend the few hundred thousand necessary to put an end to a tyrant whose death, in comparison with Diem's, could be bought at a ten cent store. 'What would happen after?' Certainly nothing that was more horrifying than the present.

See Greene's 'Nightmare Republic' (*Sunday Telegraph*, 29 September 1963): 'There have been many reigns of terror in the course of history . . . surely never has terror base and ignoble an object as here – the protection of a few tough men's pockets, the pockets of Gracia Jacques, Colonel Athi, Colonel Desiré, the leaders of the Ton Ton Macoute, of the police and of the presidential guard – and in the centre of the ring, of course, in his black evening suit, his heavy glasses, his halting walk and halting speech, the cruel and absurd Doctor.'

*

New Statesman / 22 July 1966

The Case for a Siege Economy

— Mr Posner's suggestion that hire-purchase controls should be adjusted 'to produce the desired fall in demand – a fall which could be concentrated on TV sets, bigger motor-cars, refrigerators' appears a little oddly in your paper. Beware of the Trojan horse. Soak the underpaid and therefore unimportant is what he is really saying, with a hint of colonial paternalism. A kind Government who refuse to let our poor ignorant spenders run into debt. (The colonial spirit can easily be transplanted to home, and we may have yet district commissioners in Balham, leading us gradually – so gradually – towards self-government.)

I had the good fortune to begin my independent adult life in 1926 and for five years with an income that grew from £5 a week to nine guineas a week I was rich enough to avoid buying anything on hire purchase. At nine guineas a week (*The Times* paid, as Bond Street charges, in guineas) I was one of the privileged. Mr [Julian] Maclaren-Ross might trudge from door to door carrying his child vacuum cleaner in a gold bag, but at £500 a year I was not a potential customer [See 'Excursion in Greeneland', *Memoirs of the Forties*]. Today too the privileged – at rather more than £500 a year – will be unaffected by hire-purchase controls. The relatively well-to-do will always buy outright, TV sets and refrigerators. The badly off, of course, can always go to the cinema instead of watching TV – they can always eat cake. In the temperate climate of England they may possibly be able to do without a refrigerator if the housewife is ready to shop every day for those small quantities of milk, butter and meat which can be consumed the same day. A richer sister need only shop once a week and if she has a deep freeze large enough once a month.

Let's soak the underpaid!

*

'The Thunderer'

— All old boys of 'The Thunderer' will be encouraged, at this sad moment, that her affairs are in the hands of a Minister who is an old boy himself and does not depend for his knowledge of the press on the advice of civil servants. I well remember the evening when Mr Douglas Jay joined the Home subeditors' room in Printing House Square.

He was given the chair next to mine because I was on the point of a rash departure (my first novel had been published and was a dubious success – three years later when sales had fallen I tried in vain to retrieve the chair I had lost).

Perhaps George Anderson, the cynical chief subeditor who had yet published in his youth a translation of Baudelaire and had known Swinburne, thought that I might give Mr Jay a little advice, but I can't remember whether I ever did. In those days subeditors brought in books to read during the slack periods of the night.

I had with me, when Mr Jay took his seat, an early volume of Mr Cecil Day Lewis [Poet Laureate, 1968], *From Feathers to Iron.* He regarded it sceptically, even the poem I admired which compared sexual passion to a main line express. He was right and I was wrong. So I have trust in his judgment now, whatever my temporary and sentimental doubts.

On paper which carries the insignia of the Committee of Privy Council for Trade, Douglas Jay wrote (5 January) that he had just been shown the letter and that, much appreciate it though he did, Greene had probably been too kind. His memory of the poem in question was that it was by Stephen Spender; the line that came to mind was 'to run a city on, or drive a train' [*Poems*

1930, VII; *Poems* 1933 V], which he guessed to be Spender's, 'but I am probably thoroughly confused by now!'

'After a drink too many I'm always tempted to write a trivial letter to *The Times*!' replied Greene. 'I still believe that my memory was right and that the line was "So passion passes through" [*From Feathers to Iron* IV, 'Come on, the wind is whirling our summer away']. I was never a great admirer of Spender.'

Greene told Charles Douglas-Home in June 1984 that he spent 'happy years on *The Times* (which still haunt my dreams)'; in one, related in *A Sort of Life*, 'I would find an empty chair but not in my old place, and I would feel a sense of shame because I had been away so long and had returned only temporarily (the faces I saw around me were many of them by this time the faces of the dead). I would take Crockford down from the shelf over the coal-grate and check the name of an obscure vicar who had grown a prize vegetable marrow.'

*

Commonweal / 24 February 1967

Scriptural Nausea

— In full confidence I nominate as the Most Nauseating Catholic Advertisement of the year to come one which – alas! – appeared in *Commonweal*: 'Erica thought the rosary was as *passé* as the Italian hair-do. Then she discovered the Scriptural Rosary and says it's as sophisticated as straight hair.'

Only one more such advertisement appeared, which again included the explanatory paragraph, this time beneath a photograph of 'Lisa': 'The Scriptural Rosary is an updated version of the way the rosary was once prayed throughout Western Christendom in the Middle Ages. It provides ten short scriptural quotations for each decade of the rosary. You read, or recite, one quotation before each Hail Mary. These ten "points of meditation" tell the story of the mystery as you pray each decade.

'People who have prayed the Scriptural Rosary say the little mind-stirring quotations that you read before each Hail Mary make continuous meditation upon the mysteries much easier than ever before.

'Send for the 8op book ($1 postpaid). Or send for the Scriptural Rosary record set produced by The Catholic University of America (set of two records, $7 ppd.)'

*

The Times / 4 September 1967

The Writers Engage in Battle

— This letter should more properly be addressed to *Pravda* and *Izvestia*, but their failure to publish protests by Soviet citizens at the time of the Daniel–Sinyavsky trial makes it doubtful that mine would ever appear.

Like many other English writers I have royalties awaiting me in the Soviet Union, where most of my books have been published. I have written to the Secretary of the Union of Writers in Moscow that all sums due to me on these books should be paid over to Mrs Sinyavsky and Mrs Daniel to help in a small way their support during the imprisonment of their husbands. I can only hope that attention will be paid to my request, as this might encourage other writers with blocked royalties to follow suit. I have no desire to make use myself of my royalties by revisiting the Soviet Union so long as these authors remain in prison, however happy my memory of past visits.

There are many agencies, such as Radio Free Europe, which specialize in propaganda against the Soviet Union. I

(135)

would say to these agencies that this letter must in no way be regarded as an attack upon the Union. If I had to choose between life in the Soviet Union and life in the United States of America, I would certainly choose the Soviet Union, just as I would choose life in Cuba to life in those southern American republics, like Bolivia, dominated by their northern neighbour, or life in North Vietnam to life in South Vietnam. But the greater the affection one feels for any country the more one is driven to protest against any failure of justice there.

As Rupert Cornwell wrote in the *Independent* (2 January 1989), after Yuri Daniel's death on 20 December, he was at the time of the trial in February 1966 'an emerging author of satire and fiction, a noted member of the Soviet intelligentsia who six years before had served as a pall-bearer at the funeral of Boris Pasternak. Fatally, however, four of his most scathing short stories parodying the Soviet regime – "This is Moscow Speaking", "Hands", "The Man from MINAP" and "The Story of an Atonement" – had found their way to publication in the West, under the pseudonym of Nikolai Arzhak. The moment could not have been worse: the Krushchev thaw was ending, and what better way of bringing Soviet writers to heel than public condemnation of two of their number? In 1965 the KGB discovered the true identities of Nikolai Arzhak and Abram Terts, the name used to cover another errant writer, Andrei Sinyavsky . . . [The trial] in two important ways departed from previous practice: the intended victims pleaded not guilty, and for the very first time authors were tried explicitly for what they had written, not on vague generalities. Even Stalin had never dared that. An intriguing legal point arose too. The charge was of libelling the Soviet state. But could writers be found guilty for words and views expressed by fictional characters? In those bleak times, the answer was, "of course". Protest was of no avail. After a clumsy travesty of justice Sinyavsky received seven years of hard labour and Daniel five years. In 1970 he was freed, but forced to live in virtual exile at Kaluga before being permitted back to the capital in 1979.'

(In *The Times*, 17 January 1970, Daniel's eighteen-year-old son, Alexander, printed an 'open letter' to Greene about the worsening prison conditions as Daniel came towards the end of his sentence.)

The trial marks the point at which dissident literature published abroad became a flood, and, towards the end of Daniel's life, his work began to be published in Russia, among it, 'The Story of an Atonement'. Sinyavsky set foot in Russia for the first time in seventeen years the day after Daniel's funeral.

Greene's comment about preferring life in Russia was seized upon by many correspondents; only James Brazil, from Ilford, remarked that 'Mr Greene, like many people, finds it rather difficult to reconcile his admiration of the sociological improvements (the Soviet way of life) with the totalitarian form of government which made this possible. I believe his confusion is sincere. Dostoevsky once said: ". . . the human mind, if it accepts the idea of equality, almost invariably loses the concept of liberty. If it maintains the idea of liberty, it loses the conception of equality."'

Greene wrote on 9 September:

— How very odd! I thought that my letter (4 September) was about the unjust imprisonment of Mr Sinyavsky and Mr Daniel. All your correspondents seem to have forgotten these two men. I advise them to read *On Trial*, in which they will see how the process has been condemned by such devoted Communists as Monsieur Aragon and Mr John Gollan. This is not a simple matter of being Communist or anti-Communist.

In his 'Table Talk' column in the *Spectator*, D. W. Brogan addressed himself to the subject (15 September): 'I was struck by one implication of the protest which seems to have been ignored. I have no doubt that Mr Greene would refuse the description of being a "Catholic novelist". But he is a Catholic who is a novelist or a novelist who is a Catholic. If he settled in the Soviet Union, he would find it very difficult indeed, at any rate outside Moscow and Leningrad, to share in the sacramental life of his church. More than that, he would be a voluntary resident in a country in which millions of his co-religionists cannot share in that sacramental life.'

Greene replied on 22 September:

         – Professor Brogan, turning from scholarship to journalism, has mislaid accuracy. I never asserted that if I had to leave Britain I would rather live in the Soviet Union than in the United States. I *have* left Britain and I am living in France.

Certainly Professor Brogan knows the United States far better than I do, but I would like to make a single one-upmanship claim. *I* have been put under surveillance and deported from American territory – one of my most agreeable memories (I nearly drank a charming plain clothes officer under the table). Has Professor Brogan had that experience? To make the occasion even more memorable, they tried to deport me to Haiti, but I slipped into Havana instead.

As for Moscow I obviously know the place superficially rather better than Professor Brogan, and surely he is wrong in believing that before the revolution I would have been able without difficulty 'to share in the sacramental life' of my church. Russia never had a large Roman Catholic population. In any case Christianity is surely more important than Catholicism and there would be no great problem in finding an orthodox church for worship. In any case I would rather see my church honourably suppressed than corrupted within by such war propagandists as Cardinal Spellman and Bishop Sheehan.

On the 29th Ronald Hingley said that 'on the eve of the First World War there was hardly a large town in European Russia without its Catholic church or chapel, and Mr Greene's much-publicized spiritual needs could also have been catered for as far afield as Tashkent, Tomsk, Tobolsk, Irkutsk and Vladivostok. See Walter Kolarz, *Religion in the Soviet Union*, p. 180.'

Brogan wrote, too: 'I don't feel particularly distressed by learning that Mr Graham Greene now lives in France and not in England. I don't see how it affects my argument, although Mr Greene is more likely to suffer the horrors of deportation in France than in his native land.' Brogan went on to make an elaborate parallel with Lithuanian exiles in Scotland and then commented: 'I share Mr Greene's dislike of Cardinal Spellman. I may even dislike him more than Mr Greene does since I have had to read, "in the line of duty", the cardinal's dreadful sermons and more dreadful verse. On Cardinal Spellman we can agree. But why Bishop Sheehan? Who *is* Bishop Sheehan? Does Mr Greene mean Cardinal Sheehan? If so, I can't argue, as I know nothing about this cardinal if too much about the other. Can Mr Greene mean Monsignor Fulton Sheen, the former auxiliary Bishop in Cardinal Spellman's archdiocese? Monsignor Sheen is now Bishop of Rochester and one of the most vehement enemies of American Vietnam policy in the American hierarchy – a fact important because of the bishop's fame or notoriety as a TV performer. Or can it be Bishop Sheehan of the Catholic University, a cultural apparatchik?'

*

Sunday Telegraph / 6 October 1968

Padre Pio

— Mandrake writes: 'Pope John XXIII was very concerned over Padre Pio because a souvenir racket had developed around his Monastery; he had him removed to San Giovanni Rotondo for greater obscurity.' The truth, of course, is that Padre Pio had spent his whole life as a priest at San Giovanni, it was at San Giovanni that he received the stigmata, and it was at San Giovanni that a 'souvenir racket' began. Padre Pio was never removed anywhere by anyone.

Lionel Birch, former editor of *Picture Post*, who was responsible for the 'Mandrake' column, wrote to Greene that he was 'deeply mortified . . . and sorry for the inaccuracies . . . the fact that the piece came from an outside contributor who had edited a Sunday national newspaper – as, you would say, "newspaper" – only makes the whole thing worse. It is obviously no excuse; and, not being John Gordon, I do not offer it as one.' 'I am sorry you suffered my poison pen,' replied Greene. 'It always gives me a certain pleasure to pull the legs of the more respectable newspapers and I didn't realize that I was pulling your leg . . . I wonder whether your information came from a former editor connected with Intelligence? I am never surprised at misinformation from Intelligence sources.'

*

The Times / 5 July 1969

Tyrannies

— The days of ideals – and ideologies which are their political expression – are certainly over. The invasion of Czechoslovakia by the Soviet Union and her allies was an echo of the invasion of the Dominican Republic by the United States and her allies. Now your paper today prints a photograph of Governor Rockefeller presenting a letter from President Nixon to that monstrous dictator, President Duvalier of Haiti. Of course we cannot tell what the letter contains, but the public presentation will appear as an encouragement of tyranny to all those brave men who have been risking their lives in attempts to overthrow Papa Doc. The convenience of the major powers now is all and morality counts for nothing in international politics.

Let us remember that when the United States – or the Soviet Union – demand 'moral support' for their policies. Of course the two super powers do not need our support – they are allies in all but name.

*

The Times / 6 August 1969

Dilemma over Russia for Novelists

— Surely with Mr Kuznetsov's flight the crunch has finally come for those English novelists who like myself have been regularly published in the USSR. This is not a question of a cold war and of choosing a political side. (American policy towards Vietnam and Cuba, the Dominican Republic and Haiti may be partly responsible for that lack of a human face in what is still called Soviet 'communism'.)

But we have been unduly favoured (bribed our enemies might say) because unlike the Russian novelists our books have been published without alteration. We have been used, to give an impression of cultural freedom. 'It is not true that we publish nothing newer than Dickens. We publish Snow, Galsworthy, Murdoch, even the Roman Catholic Greene.'

I appeal to all my fellow novelists to refuse permission for any of our future novels to be published in the USSR so long as work by Solzhenitsyn is suppressed and Daniel and Sinyavsky remain in their prison camps.

Anatoly Kuznetsov, best known for *Babi Yar* (which was used – amid some controversy – by D. M. Thomas in *The White Hotel*), had fled Russia, and sought asylum in England on 30 July. He had been fearful of his future while Solzhenitsyn was persecuted and Sinyavsky and Daniel put in jail for breach of article 70 of the Russian Republic's Criminal Code, 'anti-Soviet agitation and propaganda'.

Other writers' views were sought: J. B. Priestley told the *Evening News* that opinions were a technicality: 'It is my experience that no permission is ever asked in Russia, as distinct from most other Communist countries. They just publish your books. I think the point was well worth making and I am not objecting to it in any way. If the Russians were to ask my permission I would say no.'

Others wrote to *The Times* along similar lines, one man pointing out that Kuznetsov had left mother, wife and child behind; Donald Gould wrote: 'Mr Graham Greene may persuade his fellow novelists to refuse permission for the publication of their works in Russia, but if he succeeds in his campaign, the last people to give a sample of ersatz caviar for the ban will be the members of the Soviet reading public.

'I visited Russia a couple of years ago at a time when I was editor of *New Scientist*. Time and again I was warmly greeted by ebullient comrades in the science journalism game (the Russians have a voracious appetite for this sort of reading) who informed me of their loyal regard for my magazine, and sought to delight me with the news that they regularly lifted entire articles from its pages for reproduction in their own publications.'

A. L. Rowse said, from All Souls: 'Mr Graham Greene, CH, proposes an embargo on the publication of his and his fellow-novelists' novels in Soviet Russia, on account of the Kuznetsov affair.

'But I remember a previous pronouncement of his on Soviet Russia in your columns, in which he said that if he had to choose between living in Soviet Russia and living in the United States, he would choose Soviet Russia.

'Is he of the same opinion still?'

After Kuznetsov's flight, it was reported that secret police had raided his home and, among other items, 'seized letters . . . from Graham Greene and Alan Sillitoe . . . and Czech publicist Jan Prochazka' (*The Times*, 13 August). 'I have never had any correspondence with Graham Greene, Alan Sillitoe or Jan Prochazka,' Kuznetsov stated, and added that he had burnt anything incriminating.

Greene wrote again, on the 15th:

Published in Russia

— The answer to Dr Rowse's irrelevant question (9 August) is that I would still choose to live in the USSR rather than in the United States if so unlikely a choice were ever necessary. Most of my books are safely published, and perhaps at my age it would be more a question of preferring to die there. He has taken this unimportant remark of mine out of context – the context was a protest against the imprisonment of Daniel and Sinyavsky. I have noticed a curious phenomenon: any protest I make against the Russian authorities in your columns is followed by attacks on myself by such former Socialists as Mr Rowse and Mr [John] Braine. Do they find themselves on an overcrowded lifeboat (or bandwagon) and fear that I am tempted to board? I can assure them that I would prefer to drown than join their political or literary company.

May we return to the point at issue? Many of your correspondents doubt the value of a novelist refusing permission for his work to be published in Russian. From my experience of Moscow I doubt whether they are correct. A novel is not a work of scientific or even, I trust, educational value – there are plenty of foreign novels from which the Russian authorities can choose, and I do not believe they will consider sufficiently reliable the works of writers who condemn the Daniel–Sinyavsky trial. I appeal again to those European writers who are most read in Russia to refuse their permission. Their refusal, even if ignored, will not remain unknown to Russian writers.

P.S.   So Russian police discovered letters of mine in Mr Kuznetsov's apartment. Needless to say I don't know

Mr K and have never written to him. Their lie is satisfactory sequel to my protest in the *Times*, for authorities
can hardly continue to publish in Russia novels of Mr K's
correspondent.

At a PEN Meeting on 28 March 1968 Greene said: 'I am an
admirer of the Soviet Union; I don't appear here as an attacker. I
am an admirer of the Soviet Union, and an admirer of the
Communist system. But in any government there grows up a
hideous Establishment of stupid men. I have slight hopes –
because I notice that a distinguished officer of the KGB, in an
interview with a Western journalist, criticized the Daniel–
Sinyavsky trial. This is my old friend and colleague, Kim Philby.

'One of the traces left on the world by Christianity, I think, is
a phrase like "There but for the grace of God go I", or in
Donne's more literary fashion, "For whom the bell tolls". We
can sympathize with a forger, or a blackmailer, or even that
man, even that genocide, who drops the bombs on innocent
peasants in Vietnam. What seems to me appallingly absent
among these stupid men is a feeling of community. I wrote – if
you'll forgive me being personal – I wrote to the Union of
Writers in Moscow, asking them to hand over my royalties
which are banked there to the wives of Sinyavsky and Daniel.
After about three months I got a cold response that they could
not hand over *my* money to anyone but myself. Legal enough,
fair enough. But I knew the answer to that, and so I wrote to Mr
Alexander Chakovsky, the editor of the *Literary Gazette*, who is
also a member of the Supreme Soviet, and asked him if I took
out a deed of attorney at the Russian Embassy in Paris and sent it
to him, whether he would draw out my money and hand it to
these ladies. I didn't expect a very good response, but I didn't
expect really such a reply, smooth as ice. Can I read it to you?
"My dear Greene, It goes without saying that I remember our
encounters quite well, and those are very pleasant memories
indeed. There's no need to tell you that I am prepared to comply
with any of your requests if it is within my power to do so. I am

extremely sorry that in this case I have to start with a refusal. The fact is we do not see eye to eye with regard to the matter raised in your letter. My attitude towards this matter being what it is, I would not like to be involved in it or get in touch with persons who in one way or another are connected with it. This is the reason why I cannot comply with your request. Please accept my best wishes for the New Year."

'One must say that no bell tolls in Mr Chakovsky's ears: no thought that when we defend others we are defending ourselves. Because, one day, God knows, we shall need to be defended.'

'If I live in a capitalist country, I feel Communist; if I am in a Communist country, I feel a capitalist,' Greene told Gaia Servadio ten years later (*Evening Standard*, 9 January 1978). 'They don't publish me any longer. I think I still have some money in a Soviet bank, but I should go and collect it, which I don't think of doing at the moment. Once I was informed that I could have gone to the Soviet Embassy and collected my royalties, in pounds. I thought that if I had gone, I could have been photographed opposite the gate of the Soviet Embassy with a briefcase full of banknotes.' Once an agent, always an agent? 'I suppose so, but a writer is always an agent: a double agent.'

The letters in *The Times* prompted Kim Philby to break his seven years' silence, since his defection in 1963. He approved of Greene's decision and hoped that conditions in the USSR might change, 'not only because what you did is just and honourable, but also because it might result for us in some unexpected gratification, some meal together, for instance, when we could talk like in old times ...' (interview with Anne-Elizabeth Moutat, *Sunday Telegraph*, 10 May 1987).

*

(145)

Haiti Massacre

— American methods of war are contagious, and it is not surprising to find them imitated in Haiti by President Duvalier to whom Mr Nelson Rockefeller, as Mr Nixon's representative, paid a courtesy call last year. A massacre very similar to the affair of Pinkville [May Lai] took place last year at Cap Haitien, the little town well known to tourists who visit the ruins of the citadel and Christophe's palace of Sans Souci.

To make Haiti seem respectable again for American tourism Papa Doc has turned to killing so-called Communists. During last summer he claimed to have killed eighty-five in the Port-au-Prince area – a success he is believed to owe to the assistance of the CIA. In Cap Haitien last May the massacre was directed by Colonel Jean Beauboeuf, and it was so effective that news of it has only recently reached the outer world. After killing the known left wing sympathizers in Cap Haitien the Ton Ton Macoute proceeded with a plan of slum clearance, indiscriminatingly machine-gunning the inhabitants of the poor quarter of La Fossette, men, women and children.

The number of the dead will never be known for unlike American conscripts members of the Ton Ton are unlikely to suffer from bad consciences, the world's press is busy elsewhere, and the American leaders can hardly disapprove of flattery by imitation.

On 16 January, Delmore Méhu, Chargé d'Affaires, at Haiti's London Embassy wrote: '. . . en toute simplicité je crois devoir signaler que cette déclaration [de Greene] est sans fondemont. Le département du Nord est l'un des Bastions du Duvalierisme. Le Gouvernement Haitien a repoussé cinq invasions dans cette région grâce au soutien total de la population. Le seul crime du

Président Duvalier est d'avoir décidé avec conviction de faire une meilleure distribution des richesses du Pays.'

However, the same day's issue reported from Washington under the headline 'Haiti Massacre Charge is Confirmed': 'Mr Graham Greene's letter to *The Times* published on Monday, on the alleged massacres in Haiti has understandably caused a furore in inter-American circles here and some agitation in the State Department. The comparison with the My Lai massacre was gratuitous, but in fact Mr Greene seems not to have been far wrong.

'According to one observer who was in Port-au-Prince at the time, the Central Intelligence Agency (CIA) was not involved, but many people were ruthlessly killed in an anti-communist campaign in the spring of last year. In one incident a group of houses were surrounded and destroyed with the inhabitants inside. About thirty people were killed.

'The drive lasted about a month and there were several more incidents. None was apparently as large as the one mentioned above, but in each three or four people were killed. The total casualties probably did not amount to eighty-five dead, as claimed by Mr Greene, but they must have been high.

'The most disgraceful aspect of the campaign was said to be indiscriminate ruthlessness. Some of the thirty people killed in the first incident were communists, but many were innocent men and women who happened to live in the area destroyed.

'The Haitian Embassy here has dismissed Mr Greene's letter as vilification of its Government and an attempt to sabotage the flourishing tourist trade. In a statement issued "to counteract such a vicious attack" the Embassy said: "The alleged massacre of last year (said to be) similar to the alleged My Lai 4 massacre by American soldiers in Vietnam, was a phase of the fight of the Haitian Government and people against communist guerrillas, trained in Russia and Cuba, according to the documented complaint backed by all kinds of proofs and brought before the council of the Organization of American States last year . . . The communist young men made prisoners during the clashes who had been trained in Russia, according to their statements, having expressed their disenchantment, were granted mercy by President Duvalier last November and are now living in safety in Port-au-Prince with their parents."

'The statement also said that there was a lawsuit pending in a French court against Mr Greene because of the film *The Comedians.*

'Clearly there was an anti-communist campaign last year, and it is a fair assumption that the Ton Ton Macoute did not wage it with meticulous attention to due process.

'Observers are agreed that there was a communist or radical movement in Port-au-Prince and perhaps a plot against President Duvalier.

'There is also agreement that President Duvalier wanted to show the United States that he is a good anti-communist. The American Embassy in Port-au-Prince was not impressed. Relations between the two countries have long been cool, and they were not improved by the killings.

'Mr Greene's other charges cannot be proved. The CIA is officially said not to be represented in Haiti. Likewise, the Special Forces (Green Berets), which are active in many Latin American countries, are said not to be defending President Duvalier.'

*

The Times / 11 May 1970

Withdrawing from Cambodia

— To those who are ignorant of geography like our Foreign Secretary [Michael Stewart] Mr Nixon's promise to withdraw his troops from Cambodia within seven weeks may seem to be a conciliatory gesture. But in fact he can do nothing else. Before the rains and the annual flooding of the Mekong they must either go or decide to act as pioneers in underwater living.

Air Chief Marshal Sir Donald Hardman wrote (16 May): 'Our Foreign Secretary may be ignorant of geography as Mr Graham Greene states . . . but Mr Greene is plainly ignorant of history. It was thought by many quite impossible to continue operations in Burma in 1945 after the monsoon had broken. There is no need for me to say what happened. Good luck to President Nixon in his agonizing decision.'

*

[19 May 1970]

Solitary Voice

— With regret I ask you to accept my resignation as an honorary foreign member of the American Academy – Institute of Arts and Letters. My reason – that the Academy has failed to take any position at all in relation to the undeclared war in Vietnam.

I have been in contact with all your foreign members in the hope of organizing a mass resignation. A few have given me immediate support; two supported American action in Vietnam; a number considered that the war was not an affair with which a cultural body need concern itself; some were prepared to resign if a majority of honorary members were of the same opinion. I have small respect for those who wished to protect themselves by a majority opinion, and I disagree profoundly with the idea that the Academy is not concerned. I have tried to put myself in the position of a foreign honorary member of a German Academy of Arts and Letters at the time when Hitler was democratically elected Chancellor. Could I have continued to consider as an honour a membership conferred in happier days?

'The authorities seem to have missed my attempt to organize a mass resignation of the foreign members of the Academy of Art and Letters as a protest against the Vietnam war, an attempt which failed,' wrote Graham Greene about his FBI files obtained under the 'Freedom of Information' Act (*Spectator*, 7 April 1984). 'My only supporters proved to be Herbert Read and Bertrand Russell,' both dead by this time.

*

Times Literary Supplement / 30 October 1970

'The Wrong Box'

— In your review of Hemingway's posthumous novel (16 October) you write of Scribner's, 'his canny and close-mouthed publishers'. Your phrase brings back to my mind the strange case of *The Wrong Box*. Scribner's were R. L. Stevenson's publishers, and they despatched the proofs of this book to him in Samoa. I suppose that the mails between Apia and New York were not much better then than they are today, and Scribner's, having received no word from Stevenson, grew impatient and went ahead with publication. Very soon after publication the corrected proofs arrived, and word was sent to Stevenson that the corrections would be made in a future edition. No such corrected edition ever appeared, and *The Wrong Box* has never been published in the way the author intended.

Soon after the war I was shown those proofs in Scribner's Rare Book Department in New York. [He was planning a biography of Stevenson.] Most of the changes might be regarded by those who have no interest in an author's style as unimportant, but in the last chapters whole pages had been almost completely rewritten. In those days I was a director of Eyre and Spottiswoode and I suggested to Scribner's that we should produce together for the first time in England and the United States the real *Wrong Box*. The project was turned down by Scribner's. Why? Did they fear in their canny way that it would reduce the value of the proofs in the Rare Book Department, or were they afraid that publication might draw attention to their possession of the proofs, which normally belong to the author or his heirs. Where are those proofs now and will we ever read *The Wrong Box* in its true version?

John Carter, the book-collector and bibliographical scholar, wrote the following week to say that the Scribner Rare Book Department sold the corrected proofs 'to that dedicated collector of R. L. Stevenson, the late Edwin J. Bieneke, as recorded by my then colleague Professor David A. Randall in his recently published (and enormously readable) book of reminiscences, *Dukedom Large Enough*. They were earlier described in the spacious catalogue of his great collection published by the Yale University Press, and are now in the rare book library at New Haven which bears his name.' Publication was urged on Scribner's by Carter and Randall, but it was probable 'that "the fifth floor" at 597 Fifth Avenue took a sceptical view of yet another half-baked idea put up by those crazy characters downstairs in the rare book department'.

Simon Nowell-Smith pointed out that, in the matter of proofs, there is also a 'conflict of interest between owners of physical objects, owners of copyrights, and scholars. It is not for me to resolve the conflict'.

Ernest Mehew wrote with a sample of the differences between the proofs and published book (at first titled *A Game of Bluff by Lloyd Osbourne and Robert Louis Stevenson*), a fuller version of which he also sent to Greene, and told him about 'a small group of people which meets at the Athenaeum every three years or so to talk about *The Wrong Box* and to eat the meal described in Chapter XV'. Greene replied, 'May I say that I envy you your occasional meeting to eat the meal . . . but I am afraid I would refuse the tomato sauce.'

'Doctor Yogel (in *A Gun for Sale*) has something of a certain police doctor near Blackfriars to whom I once went in my youth, terrified that I might be suffering from what used to be called by an ironic euphemism a social disease; he told me not to eat tomatoes, an instruction which I have obeyed to this day.' (*Ways of Escape*.) 'For a brief period of a month or so I was a member of the Athenaeum but I resigned on the grounds that I couldn't take a friend there because the food was too bad.' (Interview with Duncan Fallowell, *Penthouse*, Vol. 17, No. 9, p. 109.)

'I thought of entering them [the corrections] in my copy,' continued Greene to Mehew, 'but I think I will still wait in the hope that one day we shall see a proper edition.'

The Wrong Box has now been edited by Ernest Mehew and recently published (1989) by Reinhardt Books, under the imprint of The Nonesuch Press.

*

The Times / 17 February 1971

'Butchery' and 'Casualties' in Vietnam

— One has become accustomed to the mistakes of Mr Bernard Levin on the subject of Vietnam – the usual errors of slapdash journalism, but from General Lord Bourne one would expect more precision. He writes on 12 February, 'I have visited South Vietnam and confirm the great efforts of a country which has suffered under Communism once and is determined not to do so again.'

South Vietnam has suffered under the Japanese and the French, it has suffered under President Diem and his successors, it has suffered under the Americans, but when has it 'once' suffered under Communism?

General The Lord Bourne wrote to Greene the same day: '. . . Viet-Nam (which had not then been divided) lived under a Viet Minh, or Communist, regime from the time of the Japanese realization of defeat in the spring of 1945 until General Gracey arrived in Saigon in command of 20th India Division on 13 September 1945. The Indo-China war started only a year

later. Several Ministers of President Thieu's government confirmed this personally to me during my visit in September
1970.'

On 19 February Herb Greer, author of a book on Algiers and
a history of CND, said: 'During the famous Tet offensive Hué
was occupied by the communists. Some 3,000 people were
butchered there at that time – under the communists. Perhaps
that example, which might be enlarged on, will serve Mr
Greene's stated taste for precision.'

Four days later Greene wrote:

> – I objected (17 February) to General Lord
> Bourne's lack of precision when he spoke of South Viet-
> nam having 'once' suffered under communism. This use
> of words gave his letter a sense he may not have intended.
> Mr Herb Greer (19 February) shares his imprecision and
> tries to justify it.
>
> Of course areas of South Vietnam, like Hué, have
> suffered from communist offensives in a civil war which
> unlike the Spanish has been supported on one side only by
> foreign troops. No one will dispute that, and probably
> unlike Mr Herb Greer I have been caught up myself in a
> similar offensive. Incidentally why do supporters of the
> Pentagon always write of men, women and children being
> 'butchered' in a communist offensive, and yet the poor
> victims of an American offensive become only 'casualties'?

Greer wrote on 5 March: 'Graham Greene imputes non-
existent motives to me. I neither share nor justify anyone's
imprecision about events in Vietnam. Nor do I "support" the
Pentagon. My Lai was butchery too. Mr Greene's label "suffered from Communist offensives" applied to cold-blooded
political mass murder is a masterpiece of imprecision, eclipsing
anything you've printed from Lord Bourne or myself ...
Whom do I support? Why, in this argument, I support Bernard
Levin. So, inadvertently, does Mr Greene.'

*

Catholic Debate

— You report (7 September) that in an appeal for harmony in the Roman Catholic Church Bishop Harris said: 'Christ came to reconcile.' Isn't this rather unorthodox? In my copy of the New Testament Christ said: 'I came not to bring peace but a sword,' and spoke of new wine having to be put in fresh wineskins and cursed Capharnaum. If Christ had come to reconcile would he have been crucified?

*

Interrogation Methods in Ulster

— To be at the same time a Catholic and an Englishman is today to be ashamed on both counts. As a Catholic one is ashamed that more than a thousand years of Christianity has not abated the brutality of those Catholic women who shaved a young girl's head and poured tar and red lead over her body because she intended to marry an English soldier. As an Englishman the shame is even greater.

'Deep interrogation' – a bureaucratic phrase which takes the place of the simpler word 'torture' and is worthy of Orwell's *1984* – is on a different level of immorality from hysterical sadism or the indiscriminating bomb of urban guerrillas. It is something organized with imagination and a knowledge of psychology, calculated and cold blooded, and it is only half condemned by the Compton investigation.

Mr Maudling in his blithe jolly style, reminiscent of that used by defenders of corporal punishment when they remember their school days, suggests that no one has suffered permanent injury from this form of torture, by standing long hours pressed against a wall, hooded in darkness, isolated and deprived of hearing as well as sight by permanent noise, prevented in the intervals of the ordeal from sleep. These were the methods we condemned in the Slansky trial in Czechoslovakia and in the case of Cardinal Mindzenty in Hungary.

Slansky is dead, he cannot be asked by Mr Maudling how permanent was the injury he suffered, but one would like to know the opinion of the Cardinal on methods which when applied by communists or fascists we call 'torture' and when applied by the British become downgraded to 'ill treatment'. If I, as a Catholic, were living in Ulster today I confess I would have one savage and irrational ambition – to see Mr Maudling pressed against a wall for hours on end, with a hood over his head, hearing nothing but the noise of a wind-machine, deprived of sleep when the noise temporarily ceases by the bland voice of a politician telling him that his brain will suffer no irreparable damage.

The effect of these methods extends far beyond the borders of Ulster. How can any Englishman now protest against torture in Vietnam, in Greece, in Brazil, in the psychiatric wards of the USSR, without being told 'You have a double standard: one for others and another for your own country.'

And after all the British tortures and the Catholic outrages, what comes next? We all know the end of the story, however long the politicians keep up their parrot cry of 'no talk until violence ends'. When I was young it was the same cliché they repeated. Collins was 'a gunman and a thug'. 'We will not talk to murderers.' No one doubts that it was in our power then to hold Ireland by force. The Black and Tans matched the Republicans in terror. It was the English people who in the end forced the politicians to sit down at a table with 'the gunman and the thug'.

Now too, when the deaths and the tortures have gone on long enough to blacken us in the eyes of the world and to sicken even a Conservative of the right, there will inevitably be a temporary truce and a round-table conference – Mr Maudling or his successor will sit down over the coffee and the sandwiches with representatives of Eire and Stormont, of the IRA and the Provisional IRA to discuss with no preordained conditions changes in the constitution and in the borders of Ulster. Why not now rather than later?

This letter was reprinted in the *New York Times* as an article (2 December), and the following year Home Secretary Reginald Maudling resigned after the revelations of his shady dealings with John Poulson.

'You will remember that it was Sir Walter Nohuly and Scott of the *Guardian* (*not* Lloyd George) who intervened in the horror of the Black and Tans to bring about the resolution of the impasse to which you refer,' wrote one correspondent from Birmingham, who proposed that 'you yourself could take some further action with your own weapons (sling and pebbles from the stream?) and thus fling a shred of credible hope into this circle of hopeless guilt. It might even be the tormenting but positive end to the inexplicable story.'

'I think many many people still have some picture of the old-style IRA which existed during and after the First World War,' Greene told Marie-Françoise Allain. 'I do admire that IRA, but the Provos have turned into out-and-out gangsters, devoid of ideals. One might as well be in Chicago. They bully little shopkeepers, who, unless they give way, are punished by knee-capping. They terrorize the Catholics. They own the taxis. They own the big self-service stores. They win fortunes thanks to terrorism . . . I'm just as averse to Protestant terrorism . . . The only man who can walk through Belfast in perfect safety, I'm convinced, is Paisley. The Provos will never attack him – he's their best ally. So although I'm in sympathy with several of the freedom-fighter movements round the world, I think a distinction has to be made between "armed combat" and "terrorism". Here's an example to illustrate the distinction. A Sandinista I met in Panama came to see me at Antibes. I asked him, jokingly, "Haven't you made a mistake in taking the National Palace at Managua? Wouldn't you have done better to take a Pan Am airliner at the airport? That way, you would have held a whole group of Americans hostage and put pressure on Washington.' His answer was, 'No, that would have been a terrorist act.' The Sandinistas have always behaved very correctly. The real – the official – terrorism was carried out by Somoza.' (*The Other Man*, 1980.)

*

Spectator / 15 July 1972

Gross Outrage

– I am in agreement with your leading article, 'Dictator for London', with one reservation. Poor Mr Harry Hyams, what has he done compared with the enormities practised by Sir Basil Spence OM whose name is not even mentioned in your article? True you condemn his new office block [Home Office] to replace Queen Anne's Mansions as 'this monstrous building', you condemn with justice the 'Knightsbridge barracks complex' as 'even worse than Centre Point', but not once do you name the man responsible for these horrors – Sir Basil Spence.

Centre Point, I grant you, is not exactly beautiful, though if it were surrounded by other skyscrapers it might compare favourably with some of New York's. By its absurd little forecourt it forces pedestrians to walk in the road among the taxis and buses of Charing Cross Road, but when it is attacked for spoiling the environment – what environment? The area where Oxford Street, Tottenham

(157)

Court Road and Charing Cross Road join is not really a beauty spot: a few rubber-goods shops made redundant by the pill have probably been destroyed, but in the wide ugly wastes you don't notice the building until you have to step into the road and risk death from a bus.

The works of Sir Basil Spence are far more hideous. And they really spoil the environment. Mr Peter Walker should take a second look at them before he worries about Centre Point. Sir Basil presumably received the Order of Merit for rebuilding the cathedral in blitzed Coventry – creditably done, though hardly to be compared with the rebuilding of Warsaw and Dresden. Surely what he has inflicted on London with the Knightsbridge Barracks and what he threatens to inflict with his 'latest monstrous building' brings the whole Order to which he has the honour to belong into disrepute.

This letter prompted questions in the House of Lords, and a petition from 100 Tory MPs who deplored the scheme. Lord Molson wrote to *The Times* on 18 July in reply to an interview given by Spence on the 10th: 'He says I shall go down to history as the worst Minister of Works we have ever had because of bad buildings for which I was responsible. His criticism has some justification. I made a mistake when I entrusted to him the designing of the new Rome Embassy. At that time, however, the Cavalry Barracks in Hyde Park were not available as an object lesson. If they had been, he would not have got the job.' Asked to elaborate by the *Evening Standard's* 'Londoner's Diary' (18 July), Molson said: 'Basil Spence and I get on perfectly well, but it is really a question, not so much of the quality of his architecture as the suitability of his style.'

Spence himself issued a warning that day, via the *Architects' Journal*, that legal action would be taken against any who presumed to voice opinions that were not 'objective constructive criticism'.

In the *Spectator*, the subject took another turn, when a man

wrote from Balham (5 August): 'The lambasting of Sir Basil
Spence, OM by Graham Greene CH appeared a petty case of
"the pot calling the kettle black". Having, over the years, read a
lot of this glib old gentleman's writings, I now become more
aware of the kind of things which influenced him in his earlier
life, namely the rubber-goods shops in and around Charing
Cross Road. I hold little brief for much of Sir Basil's works but I
doubt if he ever had the time to browse around the verge of
Soho in search of inspiration, otherwise, like not a few of Mr
Greene's writings, his architecture would show more signs of
permissiveness.'

The controversy took another bound with a letter from G. E.
Fanshaugh, apparently Director of the Eltham Laundry Supplies Ltd: on 2 September he wrote to the *Spectator*: 'I dissent
from Mr Graham Greene's views on architecture which he is
entitled to hold, but I could wish he were not forever silent
about the iniquities of the USSR as recently practised in
Prague. I refer to the monstrous purge and heavy sentences of
imprisonment passed on journalists, writers and many brilliant
men who dared to have a liberal standpoint during the short-
lived Dubcek régime and the courage to make it public. I know
that many French and English writers and even the Italian
Communist Party protested; but Mr Greene who once stated he
"would rather live in USSR than USA" confines his polemics
to sympathy with the IRA internees and castigating Sir Basil
Spence. May one respectfully beg him to use his brilliant pen in
the cause of artistic and political freedom?'

Greene's reply appeared a fortnight later:

Spectator / 16 September 1972

— I have no great faith in political protests against
the misdeeds of the Great Powers made from a safe
distance. Mr Fanshaugh, the Director of Eltham Laundry
Supplies, SE9, holds a different opinion. Neither his firm

nor his name appears in my copy of the London Telephone Directory – as a former sub-editor of *The Times* I check small details like that – so I suspect someone is having a little game with both of us.

However, let me reassure Mr F. whoever he may be. I have already made my futile protest against Russian policy in Czechoslovakia, but on the spot during the Russian occupation – in interviews on radio and television in Prague, and in a public meeting at Bratislava. My protest must be well known to the authorities there (who found it necessary to keep my passport for more than a month) and to my writer-colleagues, so I see no reason to publicize myself further in the security of the West.

*

The Times / 17 October 1972

The Sinking of the *Lusitania*

— Mr Colin Simpson in his new book has resurrected in greater detail the old story that the *Lusitania* was so loaded with armaments that the Germans were justified in sinking her.

As far back as 1924, when I was the undergraduate editor of the *Oxford Outlook*, I published an article on this subject by someone whose later career in journalism foundered in Nazi Berlin. It may be of interest to quote a letter I received then from my uncle, Sir Graham Greene, who had been Permanent Secretary of the Admiralty at the time when the *Lusitania* was sunk. I doubt whether he would have bothered from his retirement to deceive his nineteen-year-old nephew so long after the event. The letter is dated 11 March 1924.

'In the January number [of the *Oxford Outlook*] I notice a reference to the *Lusitania* which seemed to me rather to suggest that the Germans were justified in sinking the ship, because there were some cases of ammunition on board.

'If this was the author's intention, he cannot have considered carefully the facts. To have carried 5,400 cases of rifle cartridges (which only weighed 173 tons) would never have justified the sinking of a ship in any circumstances and they constituted a freight which any steamer might have carried without making the whole vessel contraband and liable to hostile attack.

'The Germans themselves, I believe, did not rely upon this cargo as justifying the destruction of the *Lusitania* but they contended that the cartridges exploding hastened the sinking of the ship.'

Colin Simpson, who also provided material for a BBC television programme on the subject at this time, said (21 October): '. . . I beg to differ. She also carried 1,250 cases of 3in shells, a considerable quantity of fulminate of mercury fuses and a draft of Canadian troops from the 6th Winnipeg Rifles. There are plausible grounds for believing that she also carried a considerable quantity of gun cotton . . . The true manifest of the *Lusitania* was kept secret by the United States authorities until the death of the late Franklin Roosevelt, when it was found amongst his personal collection of naval manuscripts. It bears scant relationship to the manifest on evidence at the Court of Inquiry before Lord Mesey in June 1915 . . . In fact [the Admiralty went] so far as instructing Lord Mesey before the case commenced that "the Board of Admiralty regard it as politically expedient that Captain Turner, the Master of the *Lusitania*, be most prominently blamed for the disaster". As Secretary to the Board of Admiralty, Sir Graham Greene must have been wholly aware as to the true state of affairs.'

John Hetherington (24 October) 'carefully noted what was written to his reply about this by Sir Graham Greene . . . He seems to have avoided making any definite statement; and he wrote when there were living reputations to preserve. I sailed from New York in June 1915, a few weeks after the *Lusitania*, on SS *Cymric*. Strapped on the decks were eighty motor-lorries of military type. As a steerage passenger I was on easy terms with the crew, and I remarked about this cargo. I was told that the hold was full of shells. I said that surely this was contraband. I was told in a very matter of fact way that in the matter of cargo we differed in no way from the *Lusitania* . . . Personnel on the New York landing-stage were mainly of German origin, and would obviously know what we carried. On casting off, we passengers sang *Rule Britannia*, and these men shook their fists at us . . . for three or four days [we] were escorted by two destroyers, who literally made rings round us. In the Irish sea we were tracked by a submarine. It sank the *Carmania*, half an hour behind us.'

After the BBC programme, which implicated Churchill and disputed the accuracy given in his *The World Crisis*, the politician's grandson and namesake announced his intention of studying a transcript. 'If it is nothing more than hypothesis, it is not worth shooting down.' He duly called it, on *Late Night Line-Up*, 'ninety minutes of character assassination' and in *The Times* of 3 November: 'a ragbag of facts, half-truths and innuendo'. He continued: 'It is a matter of regret to me that the BBC sees no reason why this "documentary" co-production by the BBC and Suddeutscher Rundfunk, should not be hawked all over the world without alteration.'

*

Times Literary Supplement / 1 December 1972

Edwardian Occasions

— Your reviewer quotes Samuel Hynes in *Edwardian Occasions* (10 November) as writing that Maurice Hewlett is 'out of print and out of mind'. I am glad your reviewer dissents. 'The Song of the Plow' is indeed a fine poem, and *The Queen's Quair* deserves to be ranked with

Ford's *Fifth Queen* trilogy. Ezra Pound was Hewlett's friend and he quotes with approval in one of his letters Hewlett's views on modern poetry. Isn't it possible that 'Richard Yea-and-Nay' had a strong influence on Pound's Provençal poems, even in its style?

*

The Times / 6 January 1973

Europe's Relationship with the US: Implications of Vietnam

— A few reflections on your sad issue of 3 January.

1. The Prime Minister, at the rather sombre celebration of Britain's entry into the European Community, said: 'Our aim must be that Europe can emerge as a valid partner of the United States in strengthening the prospects for peace and prosperity across the world.' I am sure he was heard in respectful silence, but perhaps there would have been a few half suppressed laughs if he had read the equally absurd statement that: 'Our aim must be that Europe can emerge as a valid partner of the USSR in strengthening the prospects for the liberties of all small nations on our Eastern borders.'

To associate the United States Government, this Christmas in particular, with the idea of peace is surely more than a little misjudged. The B52 bombing of North Vietnam has for the moment ceased, but the indiscriminate bombing of the South continues. To defend an ally now can be defined as killing his population and devastating his country.

2. Sir Edwin Leather (Letters, 3 January) seems to share a rather common ignorance of Vietnamese geography and of the way in which this war began. The North Vietnamese differs from the South Vietnamese perhaps as much as a man of Yorkshire differs from a man of Sussex.

The Geneva Conference of 1954 had no intention of permanently dividing the country. Elections were to be held both in the North and the South and President Eisenhower foresaw a large majority in the South for President Ho Chi Minh – in spite of the million Catholic refugees who had been told by the 'fighting Bishops' of Phat Diem and Bui-Chu that the Virgin had fled south.

It was President Diem, the favoured child first of the French and then of the American colonialists, who refused to hold elections and began the policy, referred to by Sir Edwin Leather, of 'abduction and assassination' directed against Southern nationalists in the countryside who with the communists had fought the French for the liberation of their country. 'Tyrant elimination' was practised first by Kennedy's advisers with great efficiency when President Diem, much to American embarrassment, turned against the Buddhists as well as the nationalists and the communists. It isn't, whatever one may think of Diem (and on the occasion in 1955 when I took tea with him I had the impression of a near-madman), a very honourable episode in American history. (Diem's brother, the Governor of Hué, took refuge in the American Consulate and was handed over to his assassins.)

3. Sir Edwin Leather's statement that no South Vietnamese soldiers were ever on North Vietnamese soil is hardly borne out by what emerged from the Congress inquiries into the Tonkin Bay 'incident', an admitted forgery which was the excuse for the first bombing of the North.

4. Sir Edwin Leather asks whether 'the blood of the South Vietnamese people is not so red as that of the North Vietnamese'. If he knew anything of Vietnam he would know that they are the same people. In any case it seems probable that the Americans have been responsible for the deaths of more South Vietnamese than North Vietnamese.

5. I abhor the Czechoslovak invasion (I was in Prague both during the communist take-over in 1948 and during the Russian occupation in 1969) but I doubt if it can compare in horror and immorality with the indiscriminate bombing by napalm and fragmentation bombs of South and North Vietnam, not to speak of the only publicized massacre of women and children in My Lai.

How heartening it would have been if the new Europe of Nine had celebrated January 1 by a common statement that no visit from President Nixon would be welcomed by any member country before the American intervention in Vietnam had ended.

*

The Times / 15 February 1973

Karel Kyncl

— May I appeal to the Czech authorities through your columns on behalf of Karel Kyncl. In October 1970 Kyncl spoke up at the Union of Journalists in defence of Mr Ludek Pachman, the International Grand Master of Chess, who was then serving a fourteen month prison term. For this crime of defending his friend he was sentenced last summer to twenty months imprisonment. There is sad and alarming news from Prague about his state of health. He has already served more than one half of his term. Are the Czech authorities so insecure that they feel unable to release this distinguished journalist and fellow Communist before the end of his sentence?

From the draft of this letter Greene cut his 'pleasure of getting to know [Kyncl] in Prague in February 1969. In all our conversations at that time he showed himself a true patriot and a defender of the Czech government and of the Communist Party at that moment in its history.' As he explained to Ludek

Pachman, 'that might count against him . . . I have heard much about you from my friend [Josef] Skvorecky and I was delighted to hear that you eventually got your visa for the West.'

'I too have, at one time, shared [Václav] Havel's criminal predicament in Czechoslovakia,' wrote Karel Kyncl in the *Independent* (25 February 1989) when reviewing the again-imprisoned author's *Letters to Olga*, 'and now, while reading his book, am filled with compassion, admiration for his ability to define with such precision some of the most complex topics . . . In Central Europe, writers and thinkers traditionally play more important roles in the public domain than their counterparts in the West. In the absence of everyday politics, it has often been up to them not only to voice the ambitions and longings of nations, but to translate them into reality as well. Seventy years ago, the founder and the first President of Czechoslovakia was a philosopher and university professor, Thomas Garrigue Masaryk.

'No one in that country is naive enough to believe that there will be an early and easy return in Czechoslovakia to common-sense, dignity and democracy. Nevertheless, in systems which lack really binding rules, "even the impossible is possible". Should such an impossibility occur, there would be, I suspect, a substantial drive in the country to have, after more than fifty years, a personality of Masaryk's calibre in the highest office again. Looking around, one can hardly see anybody in today's Czechoslovakia whose moral integrity, perception, clarity of thinking and humane qualities would fulfil the required standards better than Václav Havel.'

*

Time / 14 May 1973

Topplers and the Toppled

— You write that 'Ngo Dinh Diem and his ambitious brother Ngo Dinh Nhu . . . were toppled in a 1963 coup that had active US encouragement' [2 April]. Well, perhaps 'toppled' is not so bad a word to choose for 'murdered', though it would be more accurately applied to the fate of Louis XVI and Charles I, who certainly lost their 'tops'. (You do not mention a third brother, the Governor of Hué, who took refuge in the US Consulate and was handed over by the American authorities to his 'topplers'. The fourth brother, an archbishop, was, luckily for himself, in Rome, though President Kennedy might have had scruples in toppling a member of the ecclesiastical hierarchy. Did it ever occur to him that he who lives by toppling will die by toppling?)

Now there is another word, insurgent, which you use to describe the opponents of Lon Nol in Cambodia, who was himself surely an 'insurgent', with American aid, against the neutral Prince Sihanouk. Perhaps it is time that Lon Nol was 'toppled'.

*

Time / 6 August 1973

Watergate

— As a foreign observer who had some experience of the Viet Nam situation at the time when President Diem was still alive, I am puzzled by one of the accusations in the Watergate case. Why would Hunt find it necessary to 'fake' a State Department cable linking the Kennedy Administration to the 1963 assassination of Diem? Isn't this rather like 'faking' evidence that Senator Edward Kennedy was somehow concerned in a girl's drowning at Chappaquidick?

*

Kidnapped

— I was very interested in the parallels Mr David Holloway found (4 October) between my novel *The Honorary Consul* and Sir Geoffrey Jackson's *People's Prison*, which I look forward to reading.

Just for the sake of the record – my novel was more than three years in writing and I began it some fifteen months before Sir Geoffrey was kidnapped.

Once again, it should not be assumed that journalists take any notice of a letter to the press; Geoffrey Jackson wrote to the *Evening Standard* (4 November 1980): 'May I dot a "small i" regarding the Londoner's Diary [18 November] on the prophetic quality of Graham Greene's novels.

'It stated I was kidnapped in Uruguay shortly after the publication of Greene's *The Honorary Consul.* I was, in fact, kidnapped in 1971, while Greene's admirable novel appeared in 1973, at the same time as my own *People's Prison.*'

*

Unholy Waugh

— There was once a West African tribe which by long tradition employed, when a chief died, the oldest unmarried woman (habitually, because of her low status, used to dispose of the village night soil) to spit upon the grave – thus disposing of any petty jealousies which might otherwise pursue the chief beyond the tomb.

I am fascinated to see that the *Spectator* follows this old pagan ritual (27 October) and that the editor has hired a certain Beverley Nichols to do the spitting. (He performed the same ritual, it may be remembered, at the

grave of Somerset Maugham [*A Case of Human Bondage*].)
It might have been supposed that a sexual regulation
might have precluded BN from playing the role in this
sacred performance. Perhaps the explanation can be found
in an essay of my own called 'Portrait of a Maiden Lady'
which appeared in the *Spectator* [28 August 1936; *Collected
Essays*]. I wrote there of someone also called Beverley
Nichols, the author of *No Place Like Home*: 'Her emotions
are so revealing: she weeps, literally weeps, over Athens.
She disapproves of women who don't grow old gracefully,
she feels tenderly towards young people ("The silvery
treble of youth that is sweeter because it is sexless"). The
old dear, one exclaims with real affection.'

Can it really be the same dear old lady whom one now
sees employed in what is after all a rather ugly ceremony? I
wonder why Evelyn 'should have invited himself' to sit at
Beverley Nichols's table on an Atlantic crossing? Was it
that no other seat was available? Or was it perhaps the
satirist's curiosity to listen to the conversation of the
author of *No Place Like Home?* ('It was almost indecent,
the way he took out pyjamas and shook them.') Is it even
possible that he insulted the waiter because he could not
express his pent-up emotions to so sensitive a fellow
traveller?

Well, the chief is dead and savage rituals must be
preserved just as night soil must be carted away. Only one
must say this of Evelyn as one cannot of the gentle old
thing with whom he shared the table: Evelyn never waited
till a man was dead to release his venom – he would always
have chosen to spit in a man's face rather than on his grave.

*

A Strange Czech Tale

— In the tragic situation which arose in Czechoslovakia with the intervention of the Russians one is always glad to find certain elements of comedy and perhaps the following story just come to me from a reliable female source who has left the country may be of interest to your readers.

'The absolute ruler of Prague Television is a fearful lady by the name of Balášová, about whose exploits legends are told, only they are not legends. This Comrade Balášová ordered that no employees be admitted to work who wear blue jeans, especially women. So in the morning the door guard checks on everyone and those who wear blue jeans are sent home to change, the time they spend thus is of course regarded as absence without excuse, a very unpleasant thing in a socialist country. However, Comrade Balášová is not satisfied with this mild arrangement. She further issued orders that no female employees or performers can come to work bra-less.

'So the door guard started to check on this piece of female apparel by going over the backs of the entering comrades with his palm. Several of the women hit him on the nose, so a female guard was assigned this duty. Then Comrade Balášová had a photo made of the model male haircut, short, no sideburns. There are four photos, full face, left and right profiles, and from the back. Every performer who is to be seen on the TV screen is compared with these model photos and his hair is "adjusted". If he refuses, he is not allowed to appear on the TV screen.

'Recently, a pop singer from Estonia came to Prague, on contract, to tape a few TV songs. His hair was found lacking in shortness, he refused to have it adjusted, and was sent back to Estonia without having taped his songs. Two

Polish saxophonists consented to wear short-haired wigs, a Hungarian tenor saxophonist refused, and since they had to allow him to appear on the screen – he was a member of a big band – the cameramen received orders never to focus their lenses on him.'

A postscript to this story: 'Comrade Balášová has been finally defeated. After she had successfully banned all long-hairs from the Czechoslovak screen, the TV brought the annual Marathon race, sponsored by the party daily *Rudé právo*, to the screen. This is one of the best-known marathon runs in Eastern Europe, and runners from all over the world come to take part in it. The whole race was broadcast by the TV, with cameras placed on special cars, so that they could follow the leading runner. After about one third of the run had been over, an Argentinian athlete got into the lead and remained in the lead to the end, and won.

'His name escapes me, it sounded somewhat English, like Moore. Anyway, this progressive Marathonian had his hair so long that in order not to have his vision impaired he had to bind it with a female ribbon. And he remained on the screen for over an hour, and was even shown in many close-ups, including the one when he was receiving the Cup from the hands of some CP functionary. So the long-hairs had their revenge, eventually.

'It's the same thing as with literature. What is allowed to a foreign writer of renown is forbidden to the poor local subject of the party. The Hungarian tenor-man was avoided by the cameras on orders from Balášová. But you cannot shun the Marathon winner, especially if he comes from the Capitalist camp.'

*

— I am sorry to rebuke Mr Nigel Dennis, who wrote one of the best short novels of the last half-century, *A House in Order*, for slovenly reviewing. He has obviously not re-read the Sherlock Holmes novels sent him for notice. I do not write in my introduction to one of them that in *A Study in Scarlet* Doyle made a 'plain pinch' out of *The Moonstone* – Mr Dennis means *The Sign of Four*. Nor is the sub-plot of *The Sign of Four* set in America – Mr Dennis means *A Study in Scarlet*.

No wonder he makes the extraordinary statement that *The Valley of Fear* is 'far the best written'. It seems to be the only one he has read – or re-read.

There seems to be an idea that Conan Doyle is not worthy of serious criticism. A sad look-out for all of us in that case. Which of our books will remain in print for the better part of a century?

Nigel Dennis replied: 'Mr Greene is quite right. Though I had re-read all the books carefully, I transposed two of the titles by mistake, giving each the sub-plot of the other. With only a century to run, I had better buck up.'

*

The Economist / 14 December 1974

Salt

— I write to you, believe me quite honestly, for the sake of instruction. In the happy carefree 1960s we were told that any atomic war would practically wipe out the human race. There were, it was true, 'dirty' bombs and 'clean' bombs; nonetheless it was probable that a nuclear war of any size would sooner or later, according to prevailing winds and atmospheric conditions, spread radiation around the globe. A few atomic bombs exploded in Europe would render Europe uninhabitable, and a few weeks later the innocent inhabitants of Polynesia would be dying. A popular novel by Nevil Shute, *On The Beach*, made an impressive film and in a way a comforting one. There are more single suicides than double suicides.

Now it is suggested (30 November) that the USSR might be left by a Salt agreement 'in a position to deliver three or four times as much megatonnage on America as the Americans could deliver [on Russia with their less massive Mirv vehicles]', a name almost as comforting as hansoms. It is this possibility that nourishes American fears that the Russians may be tempted to knock out virtually all the American land-based missiles by a sudden first strike, leaving the Americans to make the hideous decision whether to hit back at Russia's cities and thereby bring retribution on their own.

But would there be 'a hideous decision' to make? In the 1960s we believed – and were told by many scientists – that the first strike would not only kill the adversary but kill the greater part of the world's population. Both east and west winds would sooner or later bear the radiation back over Europe and Russia. Have the scientists managed to produce such strictly local nuclear effects that the aggressor is safe from the effects of his own first strike, or are the Salt teams just playing a game in the agreeable city of Geneva?

*

Tablet / 12 April 1975

Tall Storey

—I ought not to complain of being called a Jansenist by the amiable Mr Burgess ['Graham Greene as Monsieur Vert', 15 March, expanded from an article in *Le Monde*] since it has been doubted whether even Jansenius himself was a Jansenist. Mr [Anthony] Burgess, cradle Catholic though he is, or perhaps because he is, seems rather wobbly in his theology or he would realize that my novels which cast doubt on the doctrine of damnation are tinged with the very opposite of Jansenism, with what he might well consider to be the damnable doctrine of hope. Saint-Simon who was no Jansenist wrote well on the loose use of the term: 'I think that the terms Jansenist and Jansenism are like pitch, used as a convenient method of blackening people's characters, and that out of a thousand so dubbed, less than two merit the name.'

'I chose Heinemann', wrote Anthony Burgess in *Little Wilson and Big God* [1987], 'because, at that time, I greatly admired the novels of Graham Greene, and Heinemann was Greene's publisher... At the time of writing the novel I had been undergoing a phase of Catholic guilt which had, in part, been promoted by ... *The Heart of the Matter* ... Trevor Wilson, a Malayan Information Officer with whom I had dined in Kota Bharu, had given me some silk shirts, made in Kuala Lumpur, to take back to his friend Graham Greene ... He took me to lunch at the Café Royal and, as it was Friday, we ate fish ... My own Catholicism, being of the cradle variety, was suspect. I was evidently not to be taken as a professional novelist, rather as a colonial civil servant who had had the luck to find excellent fictional material in the course of his duties. I was an amateur. This was pretty much my own view of myself. I shook hands with Greene, whom I was not to see again till we were both settled on the Côte d'Azur.'

'He amuses me,' commented Greene in 1982. 'And he always accuses me of being Jansenist or Manichean or something and I say it is because you were born a Catholic and therefore you don't know any theology. Whereas I am a convert and had to work it up.' (Interview with Duncan Fallowell, *Penthouse*, Vol. 17, No. 9, p. 46.) 'He came across and interviewed me for the *Observer* [reprinted in *Homage to Qwert Yuiop*] ... he put words into my mouth which I had to look up in the dictionary to see what they meant.' Relations had continued such that, in the long-running dispute about Ford Madox Ford's *Parade's End* series, Greene could at least call Burgess 'the best knock-about comedian in contemporary English criticism' (*Observer*, 14 March 1982).

By August 1988, however, Greene was telling Graham Lord of the *Sunday Express* that 'Burgess is just bad-tempered and unpleasant' and that he had written to him, 'you are either a liar or there's something wrong in your head and I hope it's the second and you should see a doctor'.

Not a dispute over Ford or Jansenism, this was prompted by events described in another letter to Burgess, which Greene read to Nicholas Shakespeare (*Sunday Telegraph Magazine*, 28 August 1988): 'My dear Anthony Burgess, I hear you've been attacking me rather severely on the French television programme *Apostrophes* because of my great age and in the French magazine *Lire* because of my correspondence with my friend Kim Philby. I know how difficult it is to avoid inaccuracies when one becomes involved in journalism but as you thought it relevant to attack me because of my age (I don't see the point) you should have checked the facts. I happen to be eighty-three not eighty-six. I trust you will safely reach that age.

'In *Lire* you seem to have been quoted as writing that I had been in daily correspondence with Philby before he died. In fact I received ten letters from him in the course of twenty years. You must be very *naif* if you believe our letters were clandestine on either side. Were you misinformed or have you caught the common disease of journalists of dramatizing at the cost of truth?

'Never mind. I admired your three earliest novels and I remember with pleasure your essay on my work in your collection *Urgent Copy*, your article last May in the *Daily Telegraph* and the novel (not one of your best [*Devil of a State*]) which you dedicated to me.'

As Greene told both Lord and Shakespeare, Burgess had been

saying in interviews (e.g. with John Walsh in the *Standard*) that he was living with a woman whose husband walks by at night and shouts up at the window '*Crapaud! Salaud!*' 'But I live on the fourth floor. And with this traffic, how can her husband come shouting through the window?'

Burgess was reported as being 'too busy' to comment.

'I fear that letters he wrote to me,' he said later, 'including the two vituperative ones which closed our vague relationship, have been destroyed.' (Letter to the editor, 31 May 1989.)

*

New Statesman / 18 April 1975

French Withdrawal from North Vietnam

— I cannot agree with your leading article of 4 April which states that 'the appalling scenes of misery and despair on the eastern seaboard of Vietnam are reminiscent of nothing so much as the ignominious exit of the French from the area just over twenty years ago'. There was nothing 'ignominious' in the French withdrawal from the North. The French had fought a misguided colonial war culminating in the stupid and heroic defence of Dien Bien Phu, but unlike the Americans they did not withdraw their troops until a million refugees had been shipped South (the figure is probably exaggerated, although the Bishops of Phat Diem and Bui Chu had encouraged their flocks to go by being the first to flee). I was in Haiphong in 1955 when the refugee ships were beginning to sail, and I was in Saigon when the refugees disembarked, and there was nothing comparable to the scenes taking place today. I have photographs I took of the refugees' arrival: food stalls on the water front, smiling faces . . . no reason for panic. The French screen held long enough, and the problem of the refugee camps had still to come.

*

Grigsoniana

— It was curious that you separated Geoffrey Grigson's letter from all the other letters on 'Writers and the Closed Shop' (16 May) by giving it a separate title, 'Grigsoniana' – to suggest, I suppose, that Mr Grigson is an eccentric when he writes of your own closed shop: 'Your *dramatis personae* reveals that your reviewers for the week included at least sixteen academics.' This week, the list of contributors whom you identify – certainly many of them need identification – numbers twenty-two of whom twelve at least are academics, and surely George Steiner is an honorary academic, making thirteen.

Mr Grigson has a distaste for the academic clichés, and I would add the academic assumptions. Mr Steiner, for example, in an unusually lucid piece of writing on J. C. Powys seems to assume that 'a wealth . . . of symbolic incident' is necessarily a desirable quality (desirable of course it is in the academic market for theses and Litt. Ds).

I wonder how Vladimir Nabokov with his sensitive ear will react when he tries to read aloud to himself the friendly article by Alex de Jonge, a Fellow of New College. 'Ms Mason has a sound grasp . . . Ms Mason's insistence . . . Ms Mason declines . . .' Ms obviously mustn't sound like Miss or Mrs or why use it? How then do we read it aloud? (Surely all of us read aloud with an inner ear anything worth reading.) Perhaps it sounds something like Emz. 'Emz Mason declines . . .' In my day at Oxford we had to read a weekly essay to our tutor. How do undergraduates today read aloud to Mr de Jonge a reference to Emz Dalloway? I'm afraid, sir, you will find a lot of us Grigsonians as we struggle through your no longer anonymous columns.

Three weeks later Greene added, under the title 'Ms':

— The solution of pronouncing Ms as Mistress proposed by Kenneth Johnson had occurred to me, but 'Mistress' like 'Master' has rather changed meanings since the Middle Ages. To many married women Mistress might seem to suggest a somewhat loose relationship, while to some husbands it might convey the suggestion that his wife was the dominant partner, however certain he was of her fidelity. Why can't we just call people by their names — de Jonge rather than, say, Master de Jonge and McCarthy rather than, say, Mistress McCarthy?

*

Bookseller / 21 June 1975

Capri

— The latest Bodley Head catalogue which I have just seen in describing *An Impossible Woman, The Memoirs of Dottoressa Moor of Capri*, states that I feel her book 'stands comparison with Axel Munthe's *Story of San Michele*'. The assertion which was made without reference to me, although I am the editor of Doctor Moor's auto-biography, is quite untrue. *The Story of San Michele* was a bogus and sentimental bestseller and it would never have entered my mind to compare it with Doctor Moor's truthful and moving account of her life in Capri.

'As for Munthe's famous book I only like the end, the dream sequence, the fantasy which is no longer reality,' said Dottoressa Moor in her book. 'At first the book held my attention, but it is quite different from Capri as it is, the real Capri. It was a dream Capri, like clouds, not like those dangerous limestone crags which are Capri. But when Norman Douglas called him a "portentous fake" he was not fair. Munthe was a solitary, an original. He could, under some circumstances, be very theatri-

(178)

cal, there perhaps he faked, and then again he would become a simple person, modest, depressed, quiet, almost silent ... Norman liked only knowledge – Munthe's world was a little chimerical, and Norman despised this. He felt only contempt for the "afterlife" to which Munthe paid such great attention.'

*

Tablet / 31 January 1976

Out of Context

— Your broadcasting reviewer writes that in a television interview I 'expressed the view' that: 'Even the Church can't teach me that God doesn't pity the young' – certainly a statement I never made. He is quoting not the television interview but a line of dialogue from *The Heart of the Matter*. The sentence was used by Scobie as an angry and emotional response to a priest's rather stupid reaction to a young man's suicide. I am not Scobie, I have never known such a priest, nor have I ever been the witness of such a suicide. Something said by an imaginary character in an imaginary situation in an imaginary story should not be quoted out of context as an opinion of the author.

*

The Times / [6 February 1976]

Second Opinion

— It is with a good deal of sympathy that I have read the rather long letter from Dr Brian A. Richards in your issue of 5 February. He writes that as a general practitioner 'my particular field of study and interest within that occupation is in sexual problems at GP level. I have practised this for over a decade.' Well, like most of your older readers, I can say I have studied sexual problems – perhaps not at GP level, whatever that may mean –

for more than half a century, and I can recognize that Dr Richards has a sexual problem which a decade of study has not enabled him to solve. As he writes, 'everyone has a sexual problem at least once in a lifetime. For many it is long and painful' (even a decade is quite a long time). 'Aid can none the less be found. It would be unethical for me to offer my own services' (well, in my case not exactly unethical but I'm afraid after fifty years of study I simply haven't got the time) 'but if the writer would care to approach me, I will, in complete confidence, refer him to a colleague for assistance.'

*

Spectator / 20 March 1976

Helmets

— There is another important objection to motor-bicycle helmets which Mr Waugh has omitted. (It is true that there seems a connection between these helmets and obesity, judging from the motor-cycle police in this country, but that may after all come from a lack of exercise.) Here motor-cycle helmets are more and more used in bank robberies, for they are less conspicuous than a stocking mask, especially the latest mode which provide a tinted shield against the sun. Not of course that one wants to make things difficult for bank robbers (we had eight in this region last month), for they may keep away tourists who are a pollution problem; but one would like to help the Sikhs.

In his 'Another Voice' column (28 February), Auberon Waugh discussed the emending of the law so that Sikhs would not be able to claim a conflict between turban and helmet. 'Motor-bicycle helmets are not only unsightly, unmanly and destructive of religion and morality, they are also injurious to the health.

Headaches and giddiness are the first symptoms, usually leading to impotence and baldness, sometimes to blindness and insanity. They upset the fluid distribution of a woman's body, making her masculine and arid, while men become plumper and more effeminate. Mr Anthony Crosland, Secretary of State for the Environment, has been heard openly boasting that he intends to make *all* Sikhs wear these fiendish contraptions, not just on motorbicycles but at all times, even in their most intimate moments. This is in revenge for a humiliation he once suffered at a Punjabi restaurant in Knightsbridge.'

Although victorious on the helmets front, the Sikhs now [1989] face a further safety question, that of hard-hats on building-sites.

*

New Statesman / 23 April 1976

Wrong Date

— The author of your profile of Queen Elizabeth writes that 'when she came to the throne ... the latest shocking novel was Graham Greene's *The Power and the Glory*'. My novel was published in 1940 and the Queen came to the throne in 1952. The wise and patronizing style in which the profile is written recalls to mind the article by Mr Paul Johnson in the Sixties when he advised the Queen on the subject of Prince Charles's education. Perhaps the mistake in dates makes my attribution unlikely, but then I have always regarded Mr Johnson, the historian, as the *New Statesman*'s reply to Lady Antonia Fraser.

*

Greene Guile

— I do not at all approve of Mr Auberon Waugh's suggestion of attacking the man [Sir William] Ryland [Chairman of the Post Office Board] by putting firecrackers in letter-boxes. Not only does this smack of violence, but it will help Ryland in his plan to deliver as few letters as possible at the highest cost. Our object should be to bankrupt the Post Office, so that it may be taken over quite cheaply by some efficient business organization – say, Marks and Spencers.

My plan is very simple and costs practically nothing. Let 10,000 readers of the *Spectator* (as a beginning only) pledge themselves to post one letter a week to a friend in an empty unstamped envelope, first warning the friend to refuse delivery of the surcharged envelope, and to reply by one similar letter a week. Any urgent message can be conveyed on the flap of the envelope: 'Aunt Helen seriously ill.' 'Off to Lyme Regis with the children for a fortnight.' If the postman is inquisitive and catches you reading the flap, there are plenty of reasons for refusing the letter and the surcharge. 'Don't know these people from Adam. Mine's a very common name,' 'Oh yes, I know the writer only too well. Been pestering me for years. I've warned her she must write only through my solicitors.'

20,000 letters a week – 140,000 letters a year, 140,000 surcharge stamps, 140,000 letters returned to be dealt with by the Dead Letter Office – but of course that's only a beginning. Let the idea catch on, and let 100,000 people adopt my method of communication, and you have, at no cost to anyone but the Post Office, nearly a million and a half letters a year trundling to and fro. Of course sooner or later the man Ryland will get a Bill passed through Parliament forbidding any words being written on the flap of an envelope. Well, that Bill will cost a pretty penny, and while it is being read three times in the Commons and passing through the House of Lords, there is plenty of time to circulate an agreed code of signals. The misspelling of a name will mean something, the misspelling of an address something else, besides more work for the Post Office.

My dream begins with 10,000 readers of the *Spectator*, but if the snowball rolls and we have a million letter writers and their friends – then more than a hundred million letters will have to be delivered and serviced and returned in the course of a year with nobody contributing a penny to the cost. I begin to be sorry for the man Ryland.

One man wrote to Greene to say that his plan might not work: 'In the last week I have had five letters delivered to me which have been stamped by someone in the Post Office to indicate that insufficient postage has been paid. No attempt has been made to get me to pay the amount indicated. The good old industrious postman simply shoves them through the letter-box making sure he creases them as much as possible. When Rhodesia declared UDI Her Majesty's Government declared that stamps issued by the rebel regime would not be honoured in this country. I happened to write a letter which was published in *The Times* about this, and it provoked notes from rebels who intended that I should pay the excess, and suffer. I received all the letters, and paid not a penny.'

In *As I Walked Down New Grub Street* (1981), Walter Allen recalled another plan which Greene had for the postal service. Allen had recently taken part in a 'Chamberlain Must Go' march. '"If they really wanted to get rid of Chamberlain," Graham said, "I could do it for them tomorrow." How? I asked. There was any number of ways, he said, and proceeded to tell me two. You had visiting cards printed bearing the name of various members of the Cabinet. You then made a selection of pornographic books up into parcels and dispatched them to Mrs

Chamberlain, Lady Simon, Lady Inskip and the rest as from Sam Hoare, Leslie Hore-Belisha and Kingsley Wood. A cross-traffic of such parcels, Graham asserted, would cause the government to cave in in a matter of days.

'Or there was that actor who was giving such a brilliant impersonation of Chamberlain in the current show at the left-wing Unity Theatre. Surely he could be used. You got hold of half-a-dozen out-of-work actors who could also make up as Neville, found out the date of the next Tory meeting he was addressing in Birmingham Town Hall, lined up your Chamber-lains on the day in question, and an hour before the meeting began you wired the organizers as from Chamberlain: "Delayed stop Shall arrive Birmingham thirty minutes late stop Do not hold back start of meeting." By that time, the first ersatz Chamberlain is already on the train, and you send off the others at half-hourly intervals. Thirty minutes or so after sending the first telegram, you dispatch a second: "Urgent stop. Have reason to believe Chamberlain due to arrive Town Hall now not genuine stop Arrest." Chamberlain arrives with three or four other Chamberlains angrily denouncing one another as im-postors, and in the confusion is promptly arrested and clapped in handcuffs.'

In the *Evening Standard*'s 'Londoner's Diary' (18 January 1984), it was noted: 'Graham Greene, an outstanding creator of bizarre plots, has also on occasion been the originator of some equally bizarre party games, as Maeve Peake, widow of the novelist, Mervyn, recalls, one in particular in an article on bohemian Chelsea, just published in the journal of the Chelsea Society, and written shortly before her death last August. "One evening, Graham Greene came to supper with us and, after we had eaten, suggested that we should play the telephone game which was rather rudimentary and childish. You telephone someone taken at random from the telephone directory and proceed to lead the recipient of the call on a wild goose chase . . . Mine was rather flat but Mervyn said he was a chimney sweep and was coming to clear the chimney. When the telephone said that he had no such thing as a chimney, Mervyn said he would bring his own – and the line went dead. Graham Greene's was very much more sinister, involving the smuggling of diamonds to Amsterdam, stolen passports, etc, and it sounded so much like a Greene story that we felt as though we were taking part in *The Third Man*." '

'He is a great one for practical jokes. I think also he is a secret agent on our side and all his buttering up of the Russians is "cover" ' (Evelyn Waugh to Ann Fleming).

*

The Times / 2 July 1976

Celebrating 4 July

— Those of us who hesitate each year to join with our American friends in celebrating 4 July should think again. 4 July is the date when George Washington surrendered unconditionally to the French at Fort Necessity in 1754 – a thought for President Giscard in this bicentenary year.

Parkman describes the event in his great book *Montcalm and Wolfe*:

'Whatever may have been the feelings of Washington, he has left no record of them . . . he was deeply moved by sights of suffering; and all around him were wounded men borne along in torture, and weary men staggering under the living load. His pride was humbled, and his young ambitions seemed blasted in the bud. It was the 4th July.'

*

Spectator / 12 March 1977

Critical Confusion?

— In criticizing a new novel by Hammond Innes the reviewer Nick Totton disparages surely for quite

(185)

wrong reasons the work of Rider Haggard with whom he compares Innes. He writes (19 February) that the Africa of Innes 'is still dominated by White Hunters of elemental force. And the Africans still play second fiddle in a land that is once again their own … in which blacks are childish, ridiculous and dependent.' There was nothing childish, ridiculous or dependent about Haggard's African characters, about the Zulu Umslopogaas who makes Allan Quatermain, the only White Hunter I remember in his work, play very second fiddle, about the tyrant Chaka, the horrifying Gagool, and Dingaan, a kind of Amin Dada of his day, 'who had the fierce heart of Chaka without its greatness'. In perhaps his best African novel, *Nada the Lily*, white men hardly appear at all. I think Nick Totton is confusing Haggard with Hemingway.

*

Spectator / 20 August 1977

Caodaists

— I can't help wishing that Marina Warner would reread *The Quiet American* (*Notebook*, 6 August). After her moving description of the idyllic, perhaps simple, but altogether peaceful Caodaists in Vietnam in 1972 she writes: 'In *The Quiet American* Graham Greene casts them as supporters of a Third Force, a supposed independent Vietnamese party.' If I could persuade her to take another rapid glance at my book she will find that it was not I who 'cast them', but the CIA in one of its manic moments. The 'peaceful' Caodaists in the days of the French war had their own private army which nominally supported the French, and their own munition factory where I watched the exhaust pipes of old cars being turned into mortars, perhaps good enough for one shot. The Pope's chief of staff Colonel Thé, rebelled and took to the Holy Mountain from which he arranged with CIA support the terrible bomb explosion in the square before the Continental Hotel in Saigon. *Life* magazine was able to publish a full page photograph of the explosion, showing a man with his legs blown off before he had time to fall to the ground – a photographer could hardly have been more on the spot. Thé made his peace with President Diem and was conveniently shot in the back after he brought his troops into Saigon. When I asked Diem how he had come to make his peace with a man who had killed so many innocent Vietnamese – wasn't he responsible for the bomb? – Diem said 'Peut-être' and broke into uncontrollable laughter. The *Life* photograph was reproduced in a CIA propaganda magazine in Manila as an atrocity committed by Ho Chi Minh, although by that time Thé had proudly claimed it as his own.

Marina Warner writes: 'Amnesty now wishes to investigate Vietnam, for it fears religious persecution is taking place. The fate of some Catholic priests and Buddhist monks is known or at least suspected (*sic*). But of the Cao-dai there is no word.' Amnesty would be well advised to look more than twice at her portrait of the friendly gentle comic Caodaists devoted to equality and charity.

*

The Times / 24 May 1978

Is this a rekord?

— May I suggest that the number of misprints per page in an English daily newspaper would be a worthy candidate for the *Guinness Book of Records*? Just to establish a claim I nominate page 4 of *The Times* of 12 May which contains thirty-seven misprints. They include two well worth preserving: 'entertoinment' has a fine Cockney ring and 'rampaign' combining in one word the ideas of campaign and rampage in an article on vandalism, deserves to find a permanent place in the Oxford Dictionary. I was glad to note too the firm attitude taken to juvenile delinquency – two defendants aged 3 and aged 0 were committed for trial at the Central Criminal Court.

*

Sunday Telegraph / 28 January 1979

An Honourable Performance

— Mr Philip Purser writes that Lauren Bacall was 'insanely miscast in her third picture *The Confidential Agent* and having given – as she admits – a lousy performance, she nevertheless bitterly resented the cool notices that came her way'. I also as the author of the book resented those cool notices. This remains the only good film ever made from one of my books by an American director and Miss Bacall gave an admirable performance and so did Charles Boyer. For some reason the English critics thought that a young American actress should not have played an English 'Honourable'. However the Honourable in my book was only removed by one generation from a coal miner and to me there seemed to be an extraordinary chauvinism and snobbism in their criticisms. Her performance was admirable.

*

Spectator / 17 February 1979

Denning and Definitions

— I am delighted by Miss Christine Verity's definition (27 January) of an intellectual which certainly excludes me from that undesirable category. 'Denning is not an intellectual. Scarman is the serious operagoer while

Denning delights in Gilbert and Sullivan.' That excludes me all right because I don't like many operas – but then – a horrible thought? Am I fully excluded? I don't like Gilbert and Sullivan either. 'Journalistic profiles' of Lord Denning (Miss Verity's, I suppose, is an intellectual profile) 'reveal a man of simple tastes' – simple tastes – another definition is given by Miss Verity. Lord Denning lives in the village where he was born. I think I have simple tastes, but I don't live in the village where I was born. 'He is a keen gardener' – I am not. 'He enjoys amateur dramatics' – I don't. Am I condemned? Are these the only simple tastes that qualify? He 'goes regularly to church'. From that Miss Verity assumes 'ethical or intellectual matters have not tormented him'. I go irregularly to church, but if I went regularly I would certainly assume that I were tormented by 'ethical, etc.'. Surely that would be a reason for going regularly. If Miss Verity goes to a psychoanalyst regularly, I would assume she was a little bit troubled about herself.

Miss Verity is glad that few cases involving definitions of obscenity have come before Lord Denning, 'as his position is less than clear'. I must say that I am not quite happy about Miss Verity's definitions either.

*

Spectator / 24 February 1979

Down Mexico Way

— Mr Peter Nichols writes (3 February): 'Readers of Mr Graham Greene will have no difficulty in recalling that the last priest left alive in Mexico was knocking on a door at the end of *The Power and the Glory*.'

I hope they will have great difficulty in recalling what I never wrote. My novel was not a fantasy of the future: it was based on the real situation in one state (Tabasco) of

Mexico in what was then the recent past. There have always been plenty of priests in Mexico, but in 1938 there was no priest or church left in Tabasco. I was optimistic enough to describe the return of a priest to Villahermosa coming probably from Mexico City.

On 3 June 1938 Greene had written to *The Times*:

— I have lately returned from Tabasco, and I should like to correct a misunderstanding which may possibly arise from the report in *The Times* of today of the shooting of Catholic worshippers in Villahermosa. The late dictator, Garrido Canabal, did a great deal more than close the churches, though the fact is little known even in Mexico City: he destroyed every church in the State except one, which is now used as a school, about twenty miles from the capital. Of the Cathedral no trace is left: the site is occupied by a cement playground with hideous iron swings unused in the tropical heat. Your Correspondent in Mexico City speaks of an attempt to reconstruct the Church of the Immaculate Conception. This must be the one church in Villahermosa of which some trace does remain: a backwall with a rectangle of broken stones from which material is — sometimes — taken for mending the streets. Before the Catholics can reopen their churches they must build them again from the foundations.

*

Spectator / 17 March 1979

Perceptive

— I must thank Mr Richard West for his understanding notice of *The Quiet American*. No critic before, that I can remember, has thus pinpointed my abhorrence of the American liberal conscience whose results I have seen at work in Mexico, Vietnam, Haiti and Chile. I would like to correct him on one point — it is absurd to speak of my friend, Omar Torrijos of Panama, as 'right wing' – original too since his enemies like to label him as communist because of his friendship for President Tito and Dr Castro. 'Left wing' certainly, social democrat perhaps, but the nineteenth-century term which suits Torrijos best is the one we apply to men like San Martin and Bolivar, 'patriot'.

*

New Statesman / 5 May 1979

Any Old Iron

  — Mr Larry Adler writes that 'in the *New Yorker* of 26 March Graham Greene is quoted' – no matter about what. This gives me an opportunity to warn away any readers putting trust in a so-called Profile by Mrs Penelope Gilliatt which appeared in that number. It will be safer for them to assume that almost anything there I am made to say is probably – to put it kindly – inaccurate. Her imagination extends from recording the presence of vultures in Antibes to a mysterious Czech official of the Ministry of Foreign Affairs who, she writes, abused me on the BBC (using by an odd coincidence the very words of Doctor Duvalier). An even more mysterious Englishman apparently invited me to visit 'an internment camp' in Argentine, but I'm afraid both the camp and the Englishman are products of Mrs Gilliatt's rather wild imagination.

*

New Statesman / 25 May 1979

Jolly Good Chaps

  — I am glad to read (11 May) that the new jolly good chaps in Mrs Thatcher's cabinet are as well educated

as the old jolly good chaps who have left us: Mr Healey –
Balliol College Oxford; Dr Owen – Sidney Sussex
Cambridge; Mr Michael Foot – Wadham Oxford; Mrs
Shirley Williams – Somerville Oxford; Mr Mulley –
Christ Church Oxford; the two Mr Silkins – Trinity Hall
Cambridge; Lord Elwyn-Jones – Gonville and Caius
Cambridge; Mr Varley – Ruskin Oxford.

Mr Benn does not appear in my edition of *Who's Who*, so
I assume he is young enough to have gone to a comprehen-
sive school and failed to enter a university. But after all,
higher education isn't everything, and he has money
enough to overcome the disadvantage. I am, however, a
little distressed that the new jolly good chaps are overwhelmingly Cambridge, while the old ones inclined to
Oxford.

Perhaps one advantage of the new lot is that they have
made what fortune they have out of business – or inherit-
ance (like Mr Benn) – and not out of politics like so-and-so
and so-and-so.

*

Spectator / 22 September 1979

Open Door Policy

– I am surprised that Russia has not taken advantage of the strange moral position over Vietnam taken by
the Western governments and their odd interpretation of
the Helsinki Agreement. Western governments protest
against the USSR for refusing to let certain of their
people immigrate; they protest against the Vietnamese
Government allowing 'the boat people' to go. They even
demand that Vietnam close its frontiers. (And of course
they protest against the invasion of Cambodia which put
an end to the genocidal regime of the Khmer Rouge.
Apparently it would have been acceptable if Hitler had

confined his massacres to Germany and not crossed the frontier.)

Why hasn't Russia taken this superb opportunity to grant visas to the West to anyone who asks for one? It is highly unlikely that there would be a mass immigration of the proletariat – and that in itself would be a good propaganda point. As for the intellectual dissidents, many like Solzhenitsyn have complained at being forced to leave their country, so perhaps the exodus of the middle class would not be very spectacular. But suppose even the exodus were spectacular ... the Security Services of the West would be overwhelmed by the numbers they had to vet; our unemployment figures would soar, and what a triumph for the USSR when the Western governments very soon had to plead to Russia to close her frontiers as now they plead to Vietnam?

*

The Times / 22 January 1980

Civil Defence

— Let us hope that the official guide to survival is rather more realistic than that printed in the telephone book of the Panama Canal Zone for 1976.

'Your first warning of an attack might be the flash of a nuclear explosion. If outdoors take cover instantly in any building, or behind a wall, or in a ditch or culvert, or even under an automobile.

'If no cover is available, lie down on your side, curl up, cover your head with your arms or hands. Never look at the flash or the fireball.

'If indoors, go to the strongest part of the building and keep low.'

Sydney Edwards had asked Greene whether there were any countries that he would still like to visit. 'Panama. I have a curious attraction. But *not* to write – except to pay my expenses if I can. The squabble between Panama and the United States over the Canal I think is of great interest.' (*Evening Standard*, 28 November 1975: the circumstances in which he did go there the following year have been described in *Getting to Know the General*.)

*

The Times / 12 April 1980

Exodus from Cuba

— Is there not a simple explanation for the policy of Fidel Castro who is allowing those Cubans who wish – for various reasons – to leave their country to do so? I have always believed there is a certain hypocrisy, in view of the Helsinki Agreements, in the attitude of the West towards the boat people of Vietnam. There was great sympathy, of course, at first, but the sympathy quickly diminished as the numbers increased, and when the boat people became too much of a good thing, the governments who had been signatories of the Helsinki Agreements protested against a state which let its people go. One wondered, if Russia should learn that lesson, what would happen if she opened her frontiers to all who wished to leave. The Western security services would certainly be unable to cope. (Who is a genuine refugee for political reasons, who is a criminal, who is a KGB agent?) It wouldn't be very long, in spite of the Helsinki Agreements, before Western governments protested to the Soviets at this appalling freedom of movement.

Cuba perhaps is giving a dress rehearsal of what would happen. We accept a few well-known dissidents, but would we in the West, any more than Peru, be able to receive thousands of 'refugees'? At the next Helsinki follow-up in Madrid who would be accused then of closing their frontiers to free movement, Russia or the West?

*

Times Literary Supplement / 30 May 1980

Location Work

— Constantine FitzGibbon in a charitable spirit has much exaggerated the help I gave to Norman Douglas towards the end of his life (Letters, 9 May). I was certainly not in a financial position to give money to my friend Mario Soldati 'to buy the film rights to *South Wind*'. What happened was this: we both wanted to find some 'pocket money' for Norman and we hatched a plot together. Together we went to Mr Carlo Ponti, the film producer, and we persuaded him that if he bought a film option on *South Wind* I would write the script of the film and Mario Soldati would direct. All that I and Mario contributed were a few weeks of unpaid work in Capri trying to produce a treatment which would be acceptable to Mr Ponti and not a betrayal of the book. Unfortunately no script emerged, but Norman had his pocket money and Mr Ponti very generously never asked us to refund what he had paid for the option. Norman knew all about our little plot and appreciated the joke.

*

The Times / 16 August 1980

A Settlement for Belize

— It is difficult to understand what possible trust the Government can put in any assurance given by the military dictatorship in Guatemala. Even sending Mr Ridley to talk to the Guatemalan Government will cause a suspicion in Belize that a compromise is being discussed and Belize fears with reason that if Guatemala gets an inch Mexico will demand two inches. Until a strong national guard has been organized in Belize she must depend upon the protection of the Commonwealth after independence, but during a short stay in Belize two years ago I had the impression that the Government would welcome a mixed Commonwealth force rather than a purely British one which had underlined her colonial status.

After all the talks in Mexico, Guatemala, London and Belize, I hope the British Government realize the complete ineptitude, I would even say, judging from their Press, the illiteracy of the Opposition in Belize. Mr George Price is a socialist, so the Opposition describe him as a Communist, in spite of the fact that he is a practising Catholic who planned to be a priest and only left his seminary after his father's death in order to support his family. Anyone less likely to ally himself with Dr Castro it is difficult to imagine. But then the Opposition pretends to see Communists everywhere. Even I on my first visit was described as a 'so called writer called Greene, a Communist agent of a foreign state'.

*

The Times / 15 September 1980

Arms on the Sly

— So we are selling arms to Pinochet and normal diplomatic relations have been resumed, and we can laugh off Miss Wilson's case (report, 11 September) with reference to 'the Chicago boys' and Pinochet's economic policies. When I was young Zaharoff was regarded with disfavour for his trade in arms. There was even a royal commission on private arms traffic – not that it came to any useful conclusions. Now the arms traffic is nationalized and Mrs Thatcher has taken on the role of Zaharoff.

The state sells arms to make a profit, as Zaharoff did. No moral principles are involved.

Why does Pinochet need arms? Is he threatened by any of his neighbours – Argentina, Bolivia or Peru? If he were threatened, Zaharoff-Thatcher would have found a yet more profitable market for arms by selling to all four. Pinochet needs the arms to support his internal control which involves the torture of his opponents.

I wonder how Palmerston would have reacted to the torture of Miss Wilson, and I wonder what Mrs Thatcher's representative will say in Madrid when the question of human rights is raised: 'Oh, but we didn't torture Miss Wilson, we only sold arms to her torturer.'

Your contributor, Mr Douglas-Home, in his article on the 'Chicago boys' (11 September) seems to excuse Pinochet's 'intervention' (a cosy word for armed rebellion) because of the very high rate of inflation under President Allende. But who caused the high rate? How much of it was caused by the transport strike now admittedly engineered by the CIA? A little patience – for Allende was determined to play the constitutional game – and the Christian Democrats would have been back in power in a couple of years.

'Yes, *if* there is an election,' the leader of the Christian Democrats commented to me at the time. 'It's not Allende's intention which I doubt, but I repeat *if* there is an election.'

Of course there was no election, and the then leader of the Christian Democrats is in exile. Pinochet's rebellion was not so much against Allende's government as against the continuation of any constitutional government.

'It was rather a personal attack,' Greene said to Marie-Françoise Allain, *The Other Man* (1980). 'I nicknamed her "Thatcher-Zaharoff", after the notorious arms dealer, Sir Basil Zaharoff, who had been active after the First World War. I also allude to him in one of my early books, *A Gun for Sale*: at the time, a Royal Commission was holding an inquiry into arms sales, which came to nothing, as might have been expected. Nowadays the State profits just as shamelessly from the international arms race, and moral sense has gone by the board.'

*

[22 December 1980]

Monsieur le Grand Chancelier de la Légion d'Honneur
— It is with great regret that I am returning to you my insignia as Chevalier of the Légion d'Honneur granted me during the presidency of Monsieur Pompidou.

For the last two years, I have been an unhappy witness, as a resident of the Alpes Maritimes, of the corruption in the police and even the department of justice. Assaults on the person remain unpunished and indeed have not been heard by the court. Plaints have been killed at birth because police officers and at least one official at the office of the Procurer of the Republic have been bribed with gifts from members of the criminal milieu of Nice (their identities are common knowledge).

For this reason I am asking you to have my name crossed from the list of the Légion d'Honneur so that I can feel at full liberty to speak out on behalf of the victims.

The Grand Chancelier – Général de Boissieu – replied sympathetically, but said that, short of criminal proceedings being taken against a recipient, the award is for life. He could not comply with the request. However, an award given for great merit need not prevent his airing something which he had so strongly expressed.

The 'Dark Side of Nice' was first described in a letter to the *Times* a year later.

*

Heroic Failure

— A petty reason perhaps why novelists more and more try to keep a distance from journalists is that novelists are trying to write the truth and journalists are trying to write fiction. Atticus [Stephen Pile] writes that *Night and Day* of which I was joint editor was closed because of a review written by me of a film *Wee Willie Winkie* which 'was so defamatory that Lord Stewart adjudged it a gross outrage. The damages were £2,000 and the magazine closed'. I have never even heard of a Lord Stewart – Atticus is perhaps referring to Lord Hewart – a notorious judge in the 30s, but then why did he not check the facts? The damages were not £2,000 and the paper closed many months *after* the libel action from high costs and lack of advertising support. It was nearing the rocks long before the libel action. I sincerely hope that Atticus is equally inaccurate when he writes of the difficulties of the admirable *London Magazine*.

The *London Magazine* (prop. Alan Ross) was being sued – successfully – by the American writer Donald Windham after it had published an article by Dotson Rader about his collection of letters from Tennessee Williams.

'I kept on my bathroom wall, until a bomb removed the wall, the statement of claim that I had accused Twentieth Century Fox of "procuring" Miss Temple "for immoral purposes",' recalled Greene in 1972. *Night and Day* was a weekly magazine, co-edited by Greene and John Marks, with Selwyn Powell as art editor, published by Chatto & Windus from July to December 1937. An anthology from it was published in 1985, which, as well as reprinting the article for the first time, includes an account of the libel-suit brought on her behalf by the producers of this version of the Kipling story.

'This libel is simply a gross outrage,' commented Lord Chief Justice Hewart, who the previous year had also found against the *Spectator* and Rose Macaulay for commenting adversely upon the fact that Lord de Clifford, while motoring along the Kingston by-pass, had been involved in an accident which left a pedestrian dead: charged with manslaughter, de Clifford had been acquitted by the ancient, otherwise disused right to be tried by his peers.

In the *New Statesman* of 1 May 1964, Greene gave a view of court-proceedings from another angle – the jury's – under the title, 'The Rude Mechanicals':

– As I read Mr Ludovic Kennedy's admirable account of the trial of Stephen Ward, I was irritated at intervals by his references to 'the rude mechanicals', the jury. They were always, in his eyes, so easily deceivable – by prosecuting counsel, by police evidence, by the intonations of the judge. I share his view that the trial of Stephen Ward represented the worst that British justice can do – it belongs to a period of Conservative rule tarnished by the naive figure of Mr Brooke as Home Secretary (how often as an undergraduate at Balliol I used to study that Humpty Dumpty face opposite me at breakfast and wonder how it had ever earned a scholar's gown), a period which has included yet another suicide, that of Mr Soblen, the still unexplained death of Mr Woolf, not to speak of all the half bricks belonging to the W1 police station. All the same I feel Mr Kennedy underrates 'the rude mechanicals', and I was not surprised, when, towards the end of the book, he admitted that he had never served on a jury.

I have the advantage over Mr Kennedy there; I have served once. We had no cases to catch the headlines and perhaps it was for that reason we felt carefree each time we adjourned, without the responsibilities of a murder or of a political case like that of Stephen Ward. Indeed I gained the impression that, if I had committed a murder, it was at this moment of time I would have the best opportunity to escape punishment. For we had, all of us, read detective stories, and we had a built-in conviction that the obvious culprit was innocent, that the police were not so clever as an amateur, and as for the judge – he was an old man, he belonged inevitably to the non-criminal classes, he regarded the police with less cynicism than we.

The first case we heard concerned the theft of lead by two men from a church roof. The police evidence was reasonably complete, although it included a witness, I think, who was an informer. The judge summed up unmistakably against the two prisoners. We adjourned.

I am not a fanatic for punishment – I may even have a prejudice in favour of the criminal classes if they confine their activities to stealing from those who are richer than themselves. I was not the foreman. I had no responsibility. There was a long pause, after the foreman had asked for our opinions, and at last someone spoke up. He said: 'I think they've got the wrong men.' We went ahead from there.

'The police witness – do you really believe what he said?'

'My opinion is the witness was really the guilty man.'

'The judge said . . .'

No one paid any attention to that.

'I certainly didn't like the face of that witness.'

'I'm certain he did it himself.'

Was there one voice raised in favour of the judge's summing up? I can't remember it. Personally I played no part. Surely if my fellow jurymen felt there was a reasonable doubt, there must be a reasonable doubt. I was no more anxious than they were to find anybody guilty. The case was thrown out. I heard later from a policeman that the men had been convicted many times before for stealing lead, but I don't regret our decision.

During the course of that carefree week we found

everyone innocent, whatever the judge said. We even succeeded in stopping one case without hearing the evidence for the defence – a doctor who was accused of being drunk in charge of a car which had collided with a military lorry. The police evidence rested on a sergeant-major who resented his word being questioned, and none of us were very military-minded, and a police doctor – a foreign refugee – who had examined the accused and asked him various questions. He had asked him what year and what month George VI had died. I was probably the only juryman who could even roughly remember, and that was because of a night in Saigon when a strange Vietnamese had run after me in the street, while I was on the way to take a few pipes of opium with a French friend, and said to me, 'Mes condoléances.'

'Pourquoi?'

'Votre roi est mort.'

Even the judge was surprised. He said: 'I'm not sure that I remember the date exactly myself ... Why did you choose ... ?'

'I thought', the doctor said in a heavy moral accent, 'that every Englishman would remember a date like that.'

Yet the rude mechanicals, I can assure Mr Kennedy, threw the case out – and this time without the disapproval of the judge.

I was a little anxious because I had a date in Paris at the weekend. The clerk of the court had assured me that the cases would be finished by Thursday or Friday at latest, but somehow in spite of all my efforts they weren't. There was, for me, an anxious moment in court when the clerk spoke to the judge. The judge said: 'I understand that one juryman claims he has important business next week.' He turned to me and said: 'Where is your business, Mr Greene?'

With a little hesitation I said: 'Paris, my lord.'

There was a titter in court, and the judge made a little

pause. Then he went on: 'If counsel are prepared to do so, we will sit in court on Saturday morning.'

I thought it was a generous gesture since we had found everyone innocent in spite of all his summings-up. Because of our independence I don't like Mr Kennedy calling us so often in the course of his book 'rude mechanicals'. Not for one moment had we regarded *our* judge as 'an oracle, mouthpiece of wisdom, purveyor of uncontaminated truth'. We hadn't really thought about him much at all.

*

Spectator / 14 February 1981

'Ethnocide' in the Soviet Union

— Doesn't your article [24 January] a little resemble what *Pravda* might write about our near destruction of the Welsh language? Surely any Empire has to impose a *lingua franca*? How is it that educated Indians (and Africans from our former colonies) all speak English? Scientific education demands a *lingua franca* – I imagine that it would be difficult to teach advanced physics in Welsh, and perhaps that applies to Ukrainian and Byelo-Russian.

*

Time / 2 March 1981

— You quoted me as saying about Salvador Cayetano: 'His eyes, they are hard. I wouldn't like to be his prisoner.' This gives the impression that I am a supporter of the inhuman junta in San Salvador against which Cayetano is courageously fighting. The opposite is true. I was not criticizing Señor Cayetano but describing what I believe to be the result of the imprisonment and cruel torture he has suffered.

*

— As a former member of the staff I, of course, welcome Mr Philip Howard's statement in your issue of 23 May that '*The Times* is the best newspaper in the world'. Although as a reader I have now a certain loyalty towards *Nice-Matin*. He goes on justly enough with a panegyric on your former editor, Sir William Hayley, who was much concerned with accuracy and elegance. Sir William will surely have been distressed when he finds on page 5 of the same issue a suggestion, in the form of a photo caption, that the late Sir Maurice Oldfield was a leader of the unsuccessful Ripper hunt in West Yorkshire. Perhaps after all the *Nice-Matin* . . .

This letter went unpublished, prompting one to *Private Eye* instead (19 June):

— I would like to join in Auberon Waugh's Clarion Call. Rather more than a week ago *The Times* suggested that the late Sir Morris Oldfield was a Yorkshireman who unsuccessfully hunted the Ripper. They refused to print my letter correcting their mistake, so I changed my subscription to the *Nice-Matin* in which crime reporting is much better done.

And then a letter to its editor, Richard Ingrams (25 June): 'I do wish your correspondence editor would print letters as they are written. My letter becomes meaningless as Maurice Oldfield [whose cover as "C", Head of SIS, was blown by *Newsweek* in 1973] is given the name of Morris Oldfield.' (Peter Mackay's *Inside Private Eye* – 1986 – notes that Greene is the only man to whom he has seen Ingrams 'visibly defer'.)

In his 'Diary' column, Auberon Waugh had written of Henry Fairlie's return to *The Times* and its sloppy grammar, quoting: '"the problems in trying to understand if President Reagan and his present popularity is [*sic*] genuine. His aimiability [*sic*] seems

to conquer, but how deep are his triumphs?" Oh, God. Can
nothing be done to save *The Times*?'
  (In 1973 Greene told Paul Rees [*Time* 8 October]: 'The local
paper, *Nice-Matin*, is very good indeed. I read *The Times* for
news, and the *Daily Express* for nonsense.')

*

The Times / 13 November 1981

The Right to Die

  — The Roman Catholic Bishops' Conference of
England and Wales have issued, according to your Religious Affairs Correspondent (7 November), a statement
which concerns the moral problems involved in the recent
trial of Dr Arthur for the attempted murder of a Down's
syndrome baby. (I hope I am in the majority in welcoming
his acquittal.)
  I think it important to point out to non-Catholics that
the Roman Catholic Bishops of England and Wales are
expressing a personal opinion; they are not the voice of the
Church, which includes a good many other nations than
England and Wales – even Scotland and Ireland seem to
be absent.
  As so often with bishops in committee they seem to
stray a long way from their first intention. I feel sure that
their first intention was directed, rightly or wrongly, to the
protection of new-born children – 'innocent people'
(whether the doctrine of original sin allows even a foetus
to be regarded as innocent is a theological problem I leave
to them). But the bishops seem to have enlarged their
statement to include the duty of all individuals, always
qualified by that adjective 'innocent', to live even against
their will. To quote your correspondent, 'it makes no
difference whether the innocent person is in full vigour or

is handicapped, whether life is just beginning or drawing to its close'.

But who among us is 'innocent'? I certainly don't feel myself innocent, and therefore by my guilt I can surely claim the right to die when I choose, by whatever means I prefer, like all my other non-innocent companions. It is only the poor innocents who haven't that liberty according to the Bishops of England and Wales.

'One is tempted sometimes to stir up a little discussion,' wrote Greene to Father Russ later in the month. 'As for infallibility I do follow Hans Küng. I can't accept that infallibility should be allowed to extend from the very limited infallibility of the Pope to any magisterium of Bishops or indeed laity. Perhaps one might say that the great strength of the Catholic Church lies in the fact that it was founded by St Peter who was certainly not infallible as he lied at the very beginning. I am writing flippantly and I am grateful to you for not taking my letter very seriously.'

As one of his *Observer* 'books of the year' for 1980 Greene had chosen Küng's *The Church Maintained in Truth*: 'a short but profound book. Roman Catholics can be proud of their dissident.' And, in 1982, his *Infallible?* 'A very valuable and very readable criticism, which Vatican II failed to provide, of Catholic teaching on infallibility.'

In *Time's Thievish Progress*, John Rothenstein recalled a Catholic congress in Brussels during the fifties which illustrated 'Graham's attitude towards the conventional pieties. Delegates on the platform included archbishops, bishops and eminent laymen. At a certain point one delegate after another delivered a message of greeting from "the Catholics of Brazil", "the Knights of Saint Columba", and the like. When it was Graham's turn, he said "I bring you greetings from the almost-lapsed Catholics of England."'

*

Corruption in Nice

— After the murder of a general on the streets of
Rome around Christmas, 1980, I received a telephone call
here in Antibes (though my number is not in the directory)
from a rather rough voice which spoke in English unintel-
ligibly. I told the voice that I could not understand a word
it said. It then asked me if I spoke French. I admitted that I
could at least understand French. It then asked me in a
foreign accent if I were ready to receive three members of
the Red Brigades. I said, 'No.' He replied abruptly, *'Pourquoi?'* I answered: 'Because I would have to leave France
next day.'

The Red Brigades were at that moment trying to gain
press publicity, and a reporter of an Italian magazine was
under arrest for publishing an interview with a member of
the Brigades.

I reported the telephone call to a member of the Ministry of Justice, and he agreed with my impression that Nice
was very likely as much a hide-out for members of the Red
Brigades as the Basque area of France for members of
ETA. The criminal milieu of Nice, a city noted for its
corruption, has an Italian connexion which has led to the
closing of the casinos – La Méditerranée and the Ruhl, and
the disappearance (and almost certainly the murder) of
Mlle Roux, the owner of certain key shares in the
Méditerranée. Whether the man who spoke to me on the
telephone (how did he obtain my number?) was really a
member of the Red Brigades, or whether he was a member
of the milieu of Nice I cannot be sure.

The corruption of Nice by the criminal milieu, of police
officers, certain magistrates and some avocats, is a subject
well described in a novel by Monsieur Max Gallo, *La Baie
des Anges*. If old age permits I hope to deal with it too in a

non-fiction book based on personal experience. As for the
title I shall have to borrow from Zola, *J'Accuse*.

*

Clarin (Buenos Aires) / 20 May 1982

Les Iles Malouines

— Thank you for your letter of 15 April. I am afraid
it will be difficult for you to publish anything I may write
about the present situation in Buenos Aires. That is the
difference at the moment between your country and mine
where I would be at liberty to write anything.

However let me try and explain my feelings.

I think the first fault was that of the British Foreign
Office. They should have brought the negotiations over
the Islands to an end satisfactory to both countries many
years ago. The Argentinian government had every reason
to suppose that the UK felt no real support for the
islanders. It was Argentina who built the landing strip and
it was Argentinian planes with our consent that were the
only real means of communication between the islanders
and the mainland. Moreover one quarter of the inhabitants have only been given a limited British citizenship.

However I think that the junta were completely wrong
in the action they took, probably to draw attention away
from the cruelty of their rule. It was an error too to land in
South Georgia which has never been in the hands of either
the Spaniards or the Argentinians. Now the unnecessary
struggle is taking place and the only satisfactory end it
seems to me and to many of us would be the downfall of
the military dictatorship in Argentina and then a quick
settlement by agreement with a civilian government
whose promises could be trusted. This would include
Argentinian sovereignty over the island, with compen-
sation to the inhabitants, and, for those who wish to
remain, the protection of British citizenship and a Consul

to look after their interests. One can only hope and pray that something of this sort will take place without the loss of many lives on either side.

P.S. I am afraid that as I write my hopes that the whole thing would come to an end without much bloodshed have been disappointed. I enclose a piece which appeared in the Catholic weekly *The Tablet* and represents very much my view. It appeared of course before this tragic sinking of the cruiser. This seems to me an almost unforgivable error. The intention was obviously to damage the ship without loss of life but no account had been taken of the state of the weather and the enormous seas.

On 15 April a journalist had written to Greene from Buenos Aires to ask his opinion about les Iles Malouines, as they are also known. 'Je considère que votre opinion est essentielle pour orienter les jeunes intellectuels de l'Amérique Latine qui sont confus et bouleversés dans ce moment chaotique en ce pays où vous avez été invité autrefois par Mme Victoria Ocampo [dedicatee of *The Honorary Consul*], la sœur d'une très bonne amie à moi, Mme Silvina Ocampo.'

Greene addressed his reply 'Señor', a greeting cut from the printed translation. He was presently thanked by the journalist: 'je suis heureuse de l'avoir publié, car maintenant la paix et la voix diplomatique semblent si lointaines. En tout cas, votre opinion a contribué, bien sûr, à la cause du *common sense* contre l'esprit belliciste et fou qui domine les gouvernements de nos deux pays. Je dois vous dire que malgré les difficultés de censure et auto-censure votre lettre a été publiée, grâce à un enjeu politique imposé par un secteur des forces qui appuient le remplacement de la junte militaire par un gouvernement civil . . . Un dernier détail: je n'ai pas mis mon nom sur le journal, à cause de ma sécurité personelle. Vous savez, être journaliste, dans mon pays est devenue très dangereux. Justement, il y a quinze jours trois journalistes anglais ont été kidnappés par un

groupe paramilitaire (ou parapolicier) pendant 8 heures. Ils ont
été libérés après, tous nus, à quarante-cinq km de Buenos Aires.
Pourtant, je suis une femme de cinquante ans et je pense que j'ai
encore beaucoup de choses à faire, plus généreuses pour moi et
pour les autres, qu'avoir des ennuis avec les gens les plus
canailles et les plus réactionnaires de mon pays.'

*

The Times / 10 September 1982

Le Carré Interview

— I am only too accustomed to the errors which
appear in almost every interview to blame Mr John le
Carré for what has been put into his mouth by your
reporter (feature, 6 September). Certainly Mr le Carré
would never have described Sir Maurice Oldfield as the
Head of MI5 and I am sure that Mr Wapshott (perhaps I
should describe him as Mr Badshott) is responsible for his
description of my relationship with Mr le Carré.

I think Mr le Carré and I have only met twice – once
over drinks with our German publishers in Vienna, and
once by chance when we sat together at a musical in Paris
in which our French publishers had an interest. Certainly,
though I admired his novel, *The Spy Who Came in from the
Cold*, and expressed my admiration to his publishers, I
never took him 'under my wing' (I haven't wings wide
enough) and we have never been 'close friends' – 'casual
acquaintances' would be more accurate – nor have we ever
drunk 'for hours', 'swapping stories', any more than I have
ever 'dumped' him.

I feel sorry for Mr le Carré as I often feel sorry for myself
when I have been unwise enough to give an interview to a
journalist.

'He [Anthony Burgess] put words into my mouth which I had to
look up in the dictionary,' Greene told Duncan Fallowell,

(*Penthouse*, Vol. 17, No. 9, p. 46). 'I hope it [Duncan Fallowell's interview] didn't have as many errors as Mr Wapshott was responsible for in *The Times* the other day which beat even Auberon Waugh's errors of fact in the *Sunday Telegraph* [*Magazine*, 12 September]. I don't know Mr Wapshott, but I can forgive Bron for any number of errors because he enlivens my life week by week in the *Spectator*.' (Letter to Alexander Chancellor.)

'Thank you for your kindly reference in your "Notebook" (27 November),' wrote Greene to the *Spectator* (1 January 1983). 'Perhaps William Hickey's "mini-paroxysm" [in the *Express*] was only a disguised defence of a fellow gossip writer whom I dubbed "Mr Nicholas Badshott" a while ago in a letter to *The Times* in which I exposed his inventions concerning Mr John le Carré and myself. I have never heard of one dog defending another dog, but sometimes perhaps it sometimes happens – all honour for such a rare canine friendship.'

Greene has a pile now several feet high of carbon-copies which decline interviews. In 'Congo Journal' (1959; *In Search of a Character*, 1961), he reveals a tactic which can go wrong: 'March 6: Leopoldville: usual trouble with a journalist. Made an appointment for tomorrow evening when I shall be gone . . . March 7: Brazzaville: Forced to give interview I thought I was going to dodge . . .'

'Bitterly disappointed and puzzled you gave interview to my immediate rival *Daily Mail* featured prominently Monday Stop . . . never dreamt you would stick one on me,' cabled the *Daily Express* in May 1975.

'It's got so I hate to say who I am or what I believe,' Greene told Michael Mewshaw (*London Magazine*, June 1977). 'A few years ago I told an interviewer I'm a gnostic. The next day's newspaper announced I had become an agnostic.' 'I . . . manage to fend off most pursuers. In your case, I somehow failed.' (Interview with Jay Parini, *Andy Warhol's Interview*, October 1988.)

*

Degree of Comfort

— I doubt whether Mrs Fabienne-Smith's 'simple rule of thumb' for understanding Centigrade weather reports (double the Centigrade figure and add 30) will work for readers of *The Times* who on 22 October learnt:

Rio de Janeiro C24 F91
Rome C24 F75

and on 21 October:

Corfu C24 F73
Malta C24 F75
Florence C22 F72
Bermuda C22 F77

Other curious factors seem to be at work.

*

Miracles

— There are certainly signs of controversy in Nicaragua between Archbishop Obando and the Sandinista government, but not between the Catholic Church and the government – the Church is not the hierarchy.

Archbishop Obando played a courageous and honourable part during the civil war. A pastoral letter legitimized the Sandinistas' revolt, and he helped in arranging the exchange of hostages and prisoners after the seizure of the National Palace in 1977. After the fall of Somoza the relations between him and the new government soured. Why?

One distinguished old priest to whom I spoke in Nicaragua believed the reason to be wounded vanity. The

Archbishop was in the habit of appearing on television every Sunday celebrating the Mass. The government decided that the Mass should be celebrated on television in a different parish each Sunday – a decentralization of worship which the Archbishop refused to accept with the result that he lost his Sunday television audience.

One has the impression that he now takes any opportunity to embarrass the government of what is a very Catholic country. For example he did not discourage the 'miracle of the Virgin of Cuapa', a very dubious event which became part of a Marian campaign launched with political motives and aided by the opposition paper *La Prensa*. The Virgin was a small statuette in the church of Cuapa which gave off drops of what was first called perspiration and then tears. The drops were gathered by pilgrims who placed cotton wool around the feet of the statuette. The tears were said to be for a sinful and revolutionary Nicaragua. One can imagine with what scepticism the Vatican would have treated a similar 'miracle' in Italy, as they treated the 'breathing' statue of the Virgin in Assisi in the fifties.

Not so the Archbishop who visited the church and expressed his astonishment at handling the wet statuette. Unfortunately for him the miracle was exposed. The statuette had been put in water at night and then into a deep freeze so that it could weep during the day.

One can only hope that the Pope and his advisers will treat the evidence of tension between the government and Catholics more carefully than the Archbishop treated the miracle of Cuapa.

*

Young Writers

— Mr Philip Howard [Literary Editor] is not very well informed about publishing history. He writes of 'the vast sales that Graham Greene attracted forty years ago'. In 1943 I could have just qualified for inclusion in a similar list as today's 'Young Novelists' but where were my 'vast sales'? I had been in debt to my publishers for nearly ten years when at last I broke even in 1938 with *Brighton Rock* (the 'vast sales' amounted to 8,000 copies at the published price of 7/6d [and serialisation in the *Evening Standard*]). As a result my publishers risked an improved first printing of 3,500 copies of *The Power and the Glory* in 1940. Just as most young writers today I had to find other sources of income. It was not until 1949, at the age of forty-five, twenty years after my first published novel, that I was able to rely on my novels alone. Has very much changed since those days, except perhaps that publishers now have not the courage or perhaps the means to help support a promising young author through the lean years.

*

Belize

— Professor [John] Vincent may be good at history but he seems weak on geography when he describes Belize as a country of 'jolly black men' [2 March]. Half of the population are Creoles of mixed descent. The 'jolly black men' represent only 10 per cent, an indigenous people with their own Carib language. Mayan Indians still speaking the Mayan tongue form 17 per cent of the population. 16 per cent are of European origin – there are German Menonites, and there are Asians and Chinese – not to speak of a large number of Spanish speaking refugees from the terror in Guatemala. Professor Vincent's picture of 'jolly black men' seems a long way from the complexities and anxieties and the sometimes violent rivalries of Belize.

*

Observer / [5 September 1983]

The Burning of the Books

    – I understand that two of my books – Spanish editions of *Ways of Escape* and *Travels with my Aunt* – are up for burning by the Customs and Excise. By contract they were sent by the Argentinian publisher to my agents in England marked Not For Sale. It doesn't worry me because I can obtain any copies I want in this relatively free country of France. However I am amused by the irony of the situation. I began to sell my Spanish rights to an Argentine publisher nearly forty years ago to escape Franco's censorship. Now if I am to obtain the Spanish copies of my own books it is just as well that I live in France and escape British censorship.

In his 'Notebook' column of 4 September, Michael Davie had described the banning, and impounding, of imports from Argentina which was imposed as a result of the Falklands war. Anomalies were legion. Rare music, originally printed in England, was about to be burned by the Customs. 'Books are banned, but newspapers and periodicals are not. The tortured government explanation is that newspapers and periodicals reflect current Argentine thinking, whereas books do not. Books, you see, are commodities.' The Minister of Trade, Paul Channon, was asked to comment, but he refused, saying that he was 'unbriefed'.

*

Contraception

— In your issue of 1 October you state that the Pope has said that it is a denial of God even 'to think or say anything' suggesting that artificial contraception can be justified in any circumstances. One can only hope that he has been clumsily or incorrectly reported. Pope Paul VI, even in his encyclical *Humanae Vitae*, left the final decision to the human conscience, and I was taught more than fifty years ago – long before Vatican II – that one should follow one's conscience, even if it was in conflict with official teaching, because the conscience had been implanted in man by God, though of course it might err under the pressures of human life. Surely those who use 'artificial' means of contraception are no more attributing to themselves 'a power that belongs only to God: the power to decide in the final instance the coming into existence of a human being' than if in marriage they abstain from sexual relations because they cannot afford another child, or because the child might be born diseased, or a dozen other reasons which satisfy their conscience. Are they not equally attributing to themselves 'a power that belongs only to God'? For surely if there is a God, we can leave it to Him that nothing we can do in error will effect His power for a final good.

*

Short Memories

— What short memories politicians have. Mr Michael Heseltine says that it is because we retain our deterrent that 'we have lived in peace for the longest period of contemporary history'. Surely it is nearer the truth to say that the longest period of peace (even then only relative peace) was between 1918 and 1939, before there was any question of the deterrent. Since 1945 – to name a few – there have been the Korean war, the French war in Vietnam, the American war in Vietnam, war in Malaya, war in Kenya, war in Angola, war in Nigeria, war in Ethiopia, war in Nicaragua and San Salvador, war in Chad, war in Israel, war in Lebanon. Surely it can be argued that without the nuclear deterrent, which has sometimes deterred the two great powers from intervening with sufficient strength to keep the peace, there would have been far fewer wars.

*

Spectator / 17 December 1983

The *Spectator* Competition

— A rumour has even reached Europe that 'the magnificent 1934 Daimler Saloon' offered in your Competition had to have its venerable carcase towed to the spot when it was photographed with the ever-young Dame Edna Everage. Can this be true? After your previous prize, a second-rate picture by a second-rate artist, one had hoped for a prize of unquestionable value to atone for the heavy brain work required – perhaps some cases of good wine, preferably not chosen by Mr Auberon Waugh who admits to an odd taste for an 'anal' flavour. (How does he recognize it?)

Sources close to the *Spectator* say that the Daimler did have to be towed to the Ritz for an enticing cover photograph which was part of one of the magazine's sales-drives. The following February Alexander Chancellor reported to Greene that the competition winner had now sold the Daimler, for £2,000. 'I was interested by the news of the Daimler's sale,' replied

Greene on 3 March. 'A friend of mine here who is a great expert on cars said that the Daimler's year was notoriously bad and he put the value at £200.'

Auberon Waugh, in his Wine Club article, had written about Chaumes-Chambertin (EB) 1971, £118.26 a case: 'It is a dusky, slightly sewery smell which I, at any rate, find delicious . . . but non-Burgundians sometimes find disconcerting. My wife, who is no Burgundian, characterizes it as the smell of a railway station in a novel by Zola. The taste which follows is rich, powerful, deep, with enormous flair and just that touch of dirt to make one think one is being something rather naughty in drinking it.'

There could be an as-yet untapped source of supply: in an interview with Roy Perrott (*Observer*, 16 November 1969), Greene said: 'I want to go to Samoa next. There's a quaint restaurant there called Aggie Grey's where they serve the wine in bottles labelled Armagnac for some reason. Tastes like syrup of figs.'

*

The Times / 13 January 1984

A Wronged Man

— Mr Louis Allen's memory or his information is at fault (*The Times*, 7 January). It was not the Foreign Office who removed our admirable and very knowledgeable Consul General in Hanoi, Trevor Wilson, during the French war in Vietnam. He was expelled as *non persona grata* by the very man to whom Mr Heren gives rather exaggerated praise, 'General Jean de Lattre de Tassigny, a great soldier who knew and respected the quality of his enemy'. Unfortunately for Mr Trevor Wilson he did not qualify as an enemy. The General had little respect for friends, including many of his own senior officers when they questioned his judgement. Alas, I must admit a certain responsibility for Mr Wilson's expulsion. Mr Wilson was my friend, and in the eyes of General de Lattre I was a spy, though it was never clear to me for whom he imagined I was spying.

Ah well, may the General rest in peace, but for once let us not blame the Foreign Office for Mr Wilson's removal from Hanoi.

Louis Allen replied: 'Graham Greene need not be conscience-stricken about the removal of Trevor Wilson from what was French Indo-China and is now Vietnam. Long before General de Lattre de Tassigny suspected Mr Greene of being a spy, General Salan had taken it for granted that Trevor Wilson was a British secret agent. It was, paradoxically enough, the success of Trevor Wilson's diplomatic endeavours with Ho Chi Minh that enabled the French to land in Tonkin on 16 March 1946; but no doubt his reputation as a secret agent was handed from one French general to another and when Mr Greene arrived on the spot, with his own wartime career as an agent of British Intelligence in West Africa well known to the French, they must certainly have thought they had one British spy too many on their hands. The activities of the OSS in 1945 must already have given them perfectly justifiable mistrust of the clandestine organizations of their Allies.'

On 9 February, Greene wrote:

— I have the impression that Mr Louis Allen (24 January) is only half informed about the situation in Hanoi when Trevor Wilson was made *persona non grata* by General de Lattre. It is quite true (I once had a conversation with Monsieur Soustelle on the subject) that the American OSS were not trusted in Algeria by the French authorities. The OSS were playing the silly game of finding a non-existent Third Force as they also did in Vietnam, a Force which would be anti-Communist and anti-French (Colonialist). This had nothing to do with

Trevor Wilson in Vietnam. For his services in Algeria during the war he had been decorated by General de Gaulle. When the Chinese forces occupying Haiphong were proposing to resist the landing of General Leclerc, Wilson, as British Consul General in Hanoi, gave a lift in his jeep under the British flag to General Salan whose uniform was hidden in the boot. The General put it on after his arrival at the Chinese headquarters and success-fully arranged a peaceful landing for General Leclerc. Whether in the eyes of history this was to prove a good thing, who can say? Certainly at that moment Trevor Wilson rendered a signal service to France which General Salan did not forget.

General de Lattre was another matter. In 1951 Trevor Wilson and I had visited the Bishop of Phat Diem who had a private army of a sort aiding the French. Unfortunately before my return to Indo-China de Lattre had, for per-sonal reasons, attached his son to a Vietnamese company fighting with the French in the Bishop's region, and he had been killed in an ambush. De Lattre, a sick man, connected his death with our visit to the Bishop. Here were three dubious Catholics somehow getting together ... In the three years that followed I had as a correspon-dent of the *Sunday Times* and the *Figaro* excellent relations with General Salan, but the damage had been done as far as Trevor Wilson was concerned.

The Times was on strike again, and publication of this letter, written on 24 January, was delayed.

*

Tablet / 14 January 1984

Bed and Board

— The Holy Father in his Christmas message seems to have a curious interpretation of the Scriptures.

He spoke of 'the absolute poverty' to which Christ was born. Surely this is going against the Gospels. Joseph was a carpenter and a carpenter at this period was an honourable profession and in medieval times he would obviously have been a member of a Guild. He was a descendant of David and he would have had to have had at least two mules to transport him from Nazareth to Bethlehem. The birth in a stable was purely accidental because there was no room in the inn. Joseph was obviously in a position to pay for the room in the inn if it had been available. Surely this can hardly be considered extreme poverty.

*

Spectator / 21 April 1984

Dr Norman's Illusions

— As I know little or nothing about Namibia I am not ready to dispute what Dr Norman writes ('Two essays in illusion', 31 March) of the situation there, but I cannot accept his remarkable understatement of the issues in Central America. 'Many of the existing governments subject to subversion are not themselves very creditable.' The death squads in El Salvador and the murder of Archbishop Romero – are they in his eyes 'not very creditable'? Yet he regards the removal of the Misquito Indians in Nicaragua from the Atlantic war zone, penetrated by the Contras of Somoza's National Guard and Pastora's *Arde*, where non-combatants are a serious encumbrance, as an 'outrage'. Tomas Borge, the Minister of the Interior, has frankly admitted that the removal was clumsily done without proper explanation, but I have talked to an American nun who had lived under the Somoza regime and had visited the Indians in their temporary quarters and she told me that they have never before been so well housed, well fed and well cared for.

Dr Norman writes on Nicaragua that 'a unitary Marxist state' is 'in course of construction'. 'Unitary'? With the Foreign Minister a Catholic priest, the Minister of Culture a Catholic priest, and a Jesuit priest in charge of education and health?

*

Spectator / 28 July 1984

Papal Bank

— I for one would be interested in learning from Jock Bruce-Gardyne (7 July) how far he thinks the run on Continental Illinois has been influenced, not only by the Argentine debt, but by the disclosure of the bank's relations with that dubious institution known as the Vatican Bank and its governor, Archbishop Marcinkus, and with the fraudulent Michele Sindona, now serving a twenty-five-year sentence in the USA. However lacking in literary merit, Mr Yallop's *In God's Name* has been unfairly neglected, particularly in its financial researches, by reviewers who have seemed unfairly biased in favour of the living Pope.

On 14 October 1985 Greene told John Wilkins, editor of the *Tablet*:

— I have only had two encounters with Archbishop Marcinkus, one in person and one on the telephone. He came with me to see Pope Paul VI, who had invited me, as a possible translator, but this was not necessary as I and the Pope managed to get on without him in French. My second meeting on the telephone was due to a misunderstanding my agent had over a number of dinars which were blocked for me in Yugoslavia. Somebody suggested that I should ask Archbishop Marcinkus whether they could be transferred through the Vatican Bank. My informant knew Marcinkus and offered to act as intermediary. I suggested that he should offer 25 per cent commission to the Bank, but this was rejected firmly by Archbishop Marcinkus with the phrase 'that's chicken food'. I had to raise the offer to 40 per cent. The phrase 'chicken food' seemed to give me a little insight into the Archbishop's character. We spoke later on the telephone because he wished me to meet the Archbishop of Zagreb on my way to Yugoslavia and the whole affair came to very little because my agent had been wrong in his estimates. I am afraid this is all. But the chicken food has always rung in my head when I see the name M.

'The scandalous reign of the American Archbishop Paul Marcinkus at the head of the Vatican Bank was declared at an end yesterday as the Holy See paid a humiliating price for a financial bail-out from the US church,' reported Michael Sheridan from Rome (*Independent*, 10 March 1989). 'American bishops meeting in Rome informed the Vatican that vital funds from US Catholics would be forthcoming only in return for strict accountability and scandal-free management ... Archbishop Marcinkus was involved in financial transactions with two notorious Italian frauds, Michele Sindona and Roberto Calvi ... Archbishop Marcinkus escaped trial in an Italian court on charges of fraudulent bankruptcy thanks to the terms of a Concordat between Italy and the Vatican. Milan magistrates fought all the way to the Constitutional Court for his extradition. Mr Calvi and Mr Sindona both died in mysterious circumstances.'

*

Tablet / 25 August 1984

Pope Scoop

— I applaud Mr Peter Hebblethwaite's article 'Pastor on the Revolution'. There seems at the moment in the

Catholic Church one law for the Pope and a different law for priests. In his unfortunate visit to Nicaragua the Pope proved himself a politician rather than a priest and yet he condemns other priests for playing a similar role in politics.

In his article (4 August) Peter Hebblethwaite had written: 'The Nicaraguan revolution ended in the overthrow of the Somoza family in July 1979. For the first time in history Christians were fully involved in a revolution. It was made with them, not against them. This was a great gain for the Church, said Jesuit Father, Fernando Cardenal, brother of Ernesto, the poet and minister of culture who was admonished by Pope John Paul at Managua airport when he visited Central America.

'"But," Fr Cardenal went on, "it would be a terrible blow for the Church if one or other of us abandoned the revolution, for then the Church would no longer be present to bear witness to God. If the Church ordered Christians out of the revolution, the revolution would become atheistic."

. . .

'But still the priests remained at their posts. They felt they were understood by Cardinal Agostino Casaroli, secretary of state. He maintained that whatever Canon Law said about priests in politics, there were "emergency situations" in which exceptions were possible.

'It was difficult to deny that Nicaragua was in an "emergency situation". Especially since it was at precisely this same time – the summer of 1981 – that the 8,000 *contras* began their systematic attacks from across the border. This was accompanied by a propaganda campaign designed to portray the Sandinistas as the stooges of Cuba and the Soviet Union. This background explains why the government ministers and Fernando stayed at their posts. They were "disobedient" because they thought that their removal had become a political matter. The religious, pastoral, and canonical charges that were made against them seemed like mere pretexts.

'They were certainly not in heresy – the fantasy that they had wished to found a rival and anti-hierarchical "popular church" was soon exploded; nor did they wish to be in schism from their point of view.

'That was why the papal visit proved so disappointing from their point of view: to deplore the excesses or errors of the Sandinistas was one thing and would have been acceptable; to find nothing good to say about the revolution at all was a bitter blow. And in Nicaragua there is concern at the way Cardinal Joseph Ratzinger's condemnation of liberation theology can be linked with President Reagan's Santa Fe speech against liberation theology – the religious and the political going hand-in-hand. Not unnaturally, the Sandinistas feel that the whole world is conspiring against them.'

*

The Times / 11 September 1984

Liberation Theology

— One supposes that if Catholic bishops, like Anglican bishops, were made members of the House of Lords, the present Pope, if he proved logical, would tell them either to refuse their seats or cease to fulfil their priestly functions, especially if they supported the governing party with their votes. But in fact would he? Unlike John XXIII he himself seems to take a political and partisan line. To him, as to President Reagan, Marxism is the great enemy, black against white, and the word Marxist becomes more and more a vague term of abuse. Is anyone completely Marxist any more than any one is completely Christian? Doubt like the conscience is inherent in human nature (perhaps they are the same thing) but one might expect the Pope to remember that Marx as a historian condemned Henry VIII for closing the monasteries.

*

Johnson's Ignorance

—Mr Paul Johnson, in his review of *Getting to Know the General*, which I have no desire to defend except on points of fact, seems so bent on burying his perfectly honourable left-wing past that he has failed to read carefully the book he was given to criticize.

General Torrijos is described throughout his review as President of Panama. He was never President, and when I wrote that the only privilege of the President was a reserved parking space for his car I was of course not referring to Torrijos, as Mr Johnson assumes, but to the President of Panama, a rather nominal post in the years before the Treaty. When Mr Johnson writes 'he (Torrijos) sounds like any other Latin American general to me', he is exposing his ignorance of Latin America. The words 'to me' seem a little over-confident and egotistic. Perhaps after Mr Johnson left the world of the *New Statesman* he should have travelled a little further than the safe haven of Mrs Thatcher before he ventured to write about the situation in Central America and the character of Latin American generals.

Beneath Greene's letter was one from J. Plested in Leigh-on-Sea: 'Paul Johnson would have us believe that President Allende, during the short term of his Presidency, was a total incompetent in economic affairs in comparison with the latter-day saint General Pinochet. Is that so? The massive debts currently owed by the Pinochet regime to the international banking system, together with those of Mexico and other nations, with their massive "knock-on" effect in the prolongation of the Western economic crisis, would suggest otherwise. The Teddy Roosevelt axiom that "the bastard is up to his eyeballs in debt, but he's our kind of bastard and it's our money anyway", may be the mode of progressive right-wing *salon* opinion. However, the fact that right-wing military revolutionaries backed by the CIA murdered a legitimately elected President appears to those of us who are more careful in our choice of polemic the treacherous act it undoubtedly was . . . In seeking answers to the fundamental question of "why these Hispanic societies find it so extraordinarily difficult to devise forms of government", surely Paul Johnson should address that question to the White House.'

*

Tablet / 2 March 1985

A Misguided Pope

— Those Catholics who like myself feel no great attachment to the ideas of Erasmus will be disappointed to find that Pope John Paul II is apparently a real disciple. How could the Pope's political stand in Central America have been more closely described than in these timid words of Erasmus? 'It is neither safe nor pious to harbour and spread suspicions of the public authority. It is better to endure tyranny, so long as it does not drive us to impiety, than sedulously to resist.' Small comfort there for the victims of the death squads in El Salvador or the victims of the *Contras* recruited from Somoza's National Guard in Nicaragua, both supported by President Reagan, though I doubt if he is a reader of Erasmus.

*

Spectator / [3 May 1985]

Presumed Ignorant

— I am sure I shall not be the only reader to protest against the disastrous change in the typography of the *Spectator* so far confined to the first half but threatened for the whole paper. Is it too late to think again? The new typography shows a complete contempt for the intelligence of your readers. Do you really believe they cannot read a short article without reading at the head banal explanations of its meaning – 'Christopher Andrew explains how . . .' and without glaring subtitles worse than in the popular press which interrupts the poor author's narrative?

'the cost of keeping one destroyer in home
BALDWIN'S BUNGLE
waters.'

You have for some time been quoting my opinion in your advertisements that the *Spectator* is the best written weekly in England. That was certainly true in the past. Will it remain true if you become the most vulgarly produced weekly in England?

'The appearance at great length of Barbara Cartland as a reviewer in the *Spectator* is the last straw [on *Legacy* by Susan Kay: Betty Trask Prize – Bodley Head]. Will you please see that my name does not appear any further in advertisements for the *Spectator*,' wrote Greene to Charles Moore (21 October 1985); later, in declining to write a preface for the *Spectator*'s anthology of its World War Two years (1989), he said that he remains 'a loyal reader'.

*

Tablet / 31 August 1985

Shouting the Odds

— We are all human and I wonder whether Peter Hebblethwaite's attack on David Yallop and his book *In God's Name* may not have been influenced by the references to Mr Hebblethwaite in the book.

Concerning the new election, 'Followers of Hebblethwaite's writings must have had a particularly hard time backing the winner. In the *Sunday Times* of 13 August Cardinals Felici, Villot, Willebrands, Pellegrino and Venelli were added to his list of tips. The following Sunday he told his readers, "The new Pope: it could be Bertoli." The Sunday after that even Luciani got a mention. It was reminiscent of a racing correspondent reviewing the form for the Grand National or the Derby. If he mentioned every horse then after the race his paper could quote his comment about the winner.'

Mr Hebblethwaite replying to Mr Smyth's criticism in your issue of 3 August writes 'I did not speak of financial matters because I was concentrating on the "sources" that could throw light on the events of 28–29 September 1978, when the alleged murder plot was carried out.' He has neglected therefore the most convincing part of Mr Yallop's book which went into the financial motives which could have underlain a murder at considerable length and these have never been answered.

*

Spectator / 26 October 1985

The Neat Answer

    — I am shocked by Mr Waugh's reference to vodka – 'the dullest and most brutish way of imbibing alcohol which mankind has yet invented'. As he refers to it as 'the national drink of Russia' perhaps his judgement is tainted with right-wing prejudice or perhaps he has only drunk the degraded Western versions often called Smirnoff to mislead. He will find admirable the Polish and Finnish vodkas and also the exported Russian each differentiated by a distinct and subtle flavour – a pure drink unlike whisky without colouring matter and of the same strength.

*

Papal Error

— The Pope when he speaks of religious persecution in Nicaragua seems to be lamentably ill-informed. I have just returned from that country, and I can only speak of what I saw – big placards displayed on the roads marked 'Revolution Yes, But Christian', the open churches and the traditional celebrations on the eve of the feast of the Immaculate Conception held in the cities and villages. I walked between six and eight in the evening along the streets of Leon in the barrios of the poor. Every little house stood open to the crowds and displayed altars decked with flowers and the image of the Virgin. The crowd would shout 'Who has brought us happiness?' and the answering cry was 'Mary the Immaculate' while the host of each house distributed sweets, if he could afford or find them, or cheap jewellery or in one case small home-made brooms. This may be described as Mariolatry but hardly religious persecution, nor were these celebrations a protest against the government. My companion that night in the streets of Leon was my friend Tomás Borge, the Minister of the Interior, whom no security guard could possibly have protected in those crowds.

*

Catholics and Voodoos

— In your issue of 18 January you write that the Catholic population of Cuba 'has dwindled from 95 per cent to a nominal 40 per cent'. I think that the word 'nominal' should have qualified both figures. The 'popular religion' of Cuba before the revolution was Voodoo, though as in Haiti the Voodoo worshippers would have claimed to be Catholics. Indeed in Haiti the ceremonies ended in time for the worshippers to attend early Mass at 5.0 a.m. I have been present at Voodoo ceremonies in both countries: they much resembled each other, though perhaps the Cuban ceremony was a bit Low Church, for I don't remember the priest in Cuba biting off the head of a live cock. I wonder whether the drop from 95 per cent of Catholics means a drop in the Voodoo congregation.

I believe that your reference to the Catholic church 'being actively repressed since 1959' should be qualified. Certainly the Papal Nuncio in 1963 and 1966 (the only years I can personally vouch for) was on excellent terms with Fidel Castro to whom he always brought a present of his favourite cheese when returning from visits to Rome.

It must be remembered that practising Catholics (mainly middle class) in Cuba were equally ill at ease under the dictatorship of Batista who sent his henchmen to beat up the Archbishop of Havana in his own palace.

*

Sunday Telegraph / 23 February 1986

Mr Greene Sees Red

— I am – I hope you will agree – a friend of Mr Alexander Chancellor. Does this mean that I am seeing Blue? Surely I can be a friend of both Mr Chancellor and Señor Tomás Borge without sharing either of their political views. I like reporting facts, neither Blue nor Red, such as the lack of religious persecution in Nicaragua.

Later that year to become the *Independent*'s Washington correspondent and subsequently its *Magazine* editor, Alexander Chancellor wrote in his *Sunday Telegraph* column (16 February): 'The Order of Merit is in the Queen's personal gift and has nothing to do with politics, as Graham Greene emphasized last week after being named a member. Whether or not he would have accepted an honour on the recommendation of Mrs Thatcher is a moot point, for Mr Greene appears to be becoming increasingly left-wing in his old age.'

He wrote of Greene's recent visit to Nicaragua, where he was shown around Leon by Tomás Borge, whom Patrick Marnham had described in *So Far From God* as being hardest of the hard left and, questioned about the Christian basis of Communism, saying 'State coercion is an act of love.'

'I am glad that the Queen can overlook Mr Greene's predilection for this sort of fellow,' continued Chancellor. 'He deserves all the honours she has to bestow.'

*

The Times / 20 March 1986

Queries for Reagan

— Isn't it about time that a very big question mark was aimed at President Reagan?

'Why do you persist in calling the Nicaraguan Government a communist government? Wouldn't it be equally true, or equally false, to call it a Roman Catholic government? I can understand and even sympathize with the objections you might have to a Catholic government, but, of course, the support you give the terrorists would be less excusable in the eyes of your countrymen.'

How can the Nicaraguan Government be classified simply as communist? The key positions of foreign affairs, health and education and culture are all held by Catholic priests. The official in charge of economic research is a priest. An English priest is organizing rural libraries in the countryside.

It is true that the Archbishop is opposed to the present Government, but the Church does not belong to the Archbishop, it belongs to the Catholic people, and I watched last December how the population celebrated with a faith and a fervour which I wish I could have fully shared the Feast of the Immaculate Conception.

There are Marxists in the Government, yes, but Marxism is an economic theory not a heresy. President Ortega has visited Moscow, yes, and Mrs Thatcher, we are told, also hopes to visit Moscow.

*

Sunday Telegraph / 30 March 1986

Figure of Fun

— I have no wish to be unpleasant in dealing with Mr William Buckley, perhaps the most extreme right-wing spokesman in the United States outside the White House, for he has always to me been an endearing figure of fun. English humour is often puzzling to Americans, and Mr Buckley hasn't realized that my suggestion that President Reagan might well call the Nicaraguan government Roman Catholic was not seriously meant. Alas, these English jokes! I must try to avoid them. My main point that there is no religious persecution in Nicaragua remains unanswered. Mr Buckley should visit Nicaragua and see for himself as the North American bishops have done and fairly reported.

Your editorial with its attack on the political role of the Catholic church requires a more serious reply (by the way there are three not two Catholic priests in the government).

You write 'so far as politics are concerned Catholic priests are very poor judges as to rights and wrongs, since they tend for good reasons to want to be on the winning side'.

Was Archbishop Romero who was murdered in El Salvador at the altar by those in power trying to be on the winning side? Is Archbishop Damas who has followed on the same lines in bravely condemning the death squads trying to be on the winning side? and the Archbishop of Santiago in his courageous opposition to Pinochet? True enough many church authorities in the Thirties were fellow travellers with Fascism, but we must remember that even then the voice which spoke out loudest in Spain against Franco after his victory was the voice of Archbishop Segura of Seville.

The *Sunday Telegraph* (23 March) contained an editorial and articles by Buckley and Norman Podhoretz after President Reagan's Latin American policy had suffered a rebuff when the House of Representatives rejected his proposal for military aid to the Nicaraguan Contras. The editorial opened: 'Now that the Queen has rightly seen fit to elevate Mr Graham Greene to the illustrious ranks of the Order of Merit, his political views cannot any longer be received with the indulgent tolerance traditionally granted in this country to mere great men of letters,' and closed: 'Western liberals generally are beginning to judge communism more kindly because of its supposed innocence by association with Catholicism. This is a dangerous trend. The Catholic Church has always been a weather-vane turning in response to where the winds of authority blow strongest. Thus it will ever be, and woe betide the secular affairs of mankind if and when great liberals begin to believe otherwise.'

*

Tablet / 19 April 1986

Wrong Then and Wrong Now

— I congratulate Mr Harriott on the best article which I have read exposing the dishonesty of President Reagan in his policy towards Nicaragua (22 March). I wish

(234)

it would be read and published in the United States. One of the lies which the President persists in repeating is that there is religious persecution in Nicaragua. If any religious persecution exists it is exercised by Archbishop Obando – so unfortunately created a cardinal – on the priests who support the government. Nicaragua is surely the first socialist government to include in the draft of a new constitution religious freedom, political pluralism and a mixed economy.

For what then are President Reagan's hired killers fighting? Presumably for an authoritarian government to guard United States interests as effectively as Somoza, Papa and Baby Doc, Pinochet and Trujillo.

In his 'Periscope' column John F. X. Harriott wrote: 'Human nobility is less in the spotlight these days than human depravity, so let us begin with a shining example. In February, Church Action For Central America published the following letter: "Dear Mr President: According to despatches of today, 3 January, from Managua, my son, John F. Hempfel, was killed in action by General Sandino's troops. For the death of my son I hold no malice against General Sandino or any of his men for I think, and I believe that 90 per cent of our people agree with me, that these people in Nicaragua today are fighting for their liberty, as our forefathers fought for their liberty in 1776, and that we as a nation have no legal or moral right to be murdering these liberty-loving people in a war of aggression. What we are doing is nothing less than murder, for the sole purpose of keeping in power a puppet president, and acting as a collector for Wall Street which is certainly against the spirit and letter of our Constitution. My son was twenty-nine years old, served three years of his third enlistment, survived honourable service in the World War against Germany, only to be officially murdered in a disgraceful war against this little nation. My father served through the Civil War. Both my grandfathers died in action in the same war, and I am proud of their records. So this is not from the pen of a red Radical but from one who loves justice and fair play. I have four sons and if necessity arose I would be willing to sacrifice, not only all four sons, but my own life as well in a war of defence. But I am not willing to shed one drop of blood in a war of aggression, such as this one is."

'That memorable letter was written by John S. Hempfel of Fergusson, Missouri, to President Calvin Coolidge in 1928. *Plus ça change.* The mounting number of protests, demonstrations and vigils by ordinary Americans, especially in the Christian Churches, against Mr Reagan's present policy towards Nicaragua, reveals the same decency of sentiment, the same concern for justice and fair play. They too see that whatever the motives for that policy it is certainly not the wishes and interests of the people of Nicaragua. It is surely high time that the governments friendly to America loudly, publicly and collectively joined their voices to that protest against a rhetoric and a policy that disgraces Mr Reagan himself, his country, and the cause of democracy.

'During recent weeks Mr Reagan's rhetoric has descended to new depths. The Contra guerrillas, a murderous rabble who in two years have taken 8,000 innocent lives and are bent on restoring a system that looted and brutalized Nicaragua for generations, are hailed as freedom fighters to be bracketed with the early American revolutionaries. Churchill, the spirit of Dunkirk, and other grotesque analogies are invoked in their cause. One does not have to believe in Utopias or regard the Sandinistas as angelic to recognize that they have been unmercifully caricatured and calumniated, and subjected to virulent propaganda on the flimsiest of evidence.

'Their remarkable achievements in popular education, literacy, health and hygiene, land distribution and production of essential foods, have all been consistently belittled, and standards of rectitude applied to them which have never been remotely demanded of the tyrannical military dictatorships infesting Latin America. In Guatemala 100,000 people have been killed by government forces and 40,000 people have

(236)

"disappeared" in under thirty years, yet that regime has been tolerated and supported by the United States. Nicaragua's rulers have employed none of the bleak apparatus of tyranny – death squads, torture and the like – so commonplace elsewhere, and very few Latin American governments have half as strong a claim to represent the genuine democratic wishes of their people. Yet they have been forced to suffer military harassment and economic strangulation which other uninhibitedly cruel and ruthless regimes have been strikingly spared. That is applying double standards with a vengeance.

'As Mr Hempfel's letter illustrates, the problem long antedates the rise of Soviet Russia as a superpower or any imagined threat which Nicaragua might present to the security of the United States. According to Mr Noam Chomsky and other American critics of Mr Reagan's policy, Nicaragua's real sin is to insist on using for its self-development resources which the United States wishes to control and exploit as in the past, so provoking the fear that if they get away with it other small countries will follow suit. In short, that democracy and social justice are expendable if and where they threaten North American standards of material prosperity. That policy is as abhorrent to many Americans today as it was in 1928. Too many innocent lives have already been lost because of it. And in the interests of democracy, justice and fair play Mr Reagan should call off his dogs. Now.'

*

Time / [21 May 1986]

Return to Sender

— Before the Tokyo Conference I wrote the following letter to *The Times* which the Editor found 'interesting and distressing' but not possible to print [nor did the *Telegraph*]. I hope you will find it possible even though the Tokyo Conference is over and President Reagan has returned home to seek money again for his 'freedom fighters', the Contras.

'Most people, I imagine, will approve of the strongest measures possible against terrorists, but surely not only against selective terrorists. Here is one of the latest reports of terrorism which one hopes may be considered at Tokyo. It has been made by an American nun, Sandra Price, who is working in a country parish in Nicaragua.

'On 25 March a group of Contras took one of our Catholic catechists, Donato Mendoza, from his home. Two kilometres further on they castrated him, gouged out his eyes, pulled out his finger nails, cut the flesh from his legs, broke every bone in his body, and shot him.

'Three days later, on Good Friday, his naked, mutilated body was found. Donato had always worn a chain and cross as a distinctive mark of his position in the Church. He said he had lost the cross a few days before, while working. It was this chain without a cross which identified his dead body.'

*

The Times / 19 July 1986

Warning Shot

— I am puzzled by a sentence in your leading article (8 July) on Mrs Aquino's problem in the Philippines. 'She has not, despite protestations to the contrary by both sides, been able to attract the unqualified confidence of the United States once enjoyed by Marcos.'

Marcos certainly enjoyed United States support. So did Batista in Cuba, the Duvaliers in Haiti, Trujillo in the Dominican Republic, Somoza in Nicaragua, General Videla in the Argentine, and even today General Pinochet in Chile and the Contras in Nicaragua. This is a queer form of enjoyment which I would be surprised if Mrs Aquino wished to share.

*

Tablet / 6 September 1986

Rich Man, Poor Man

— Piers Paul Read [23 August] in criticizing John Dalrymple's pamphlet seems to be living rather out of the real world. He claims that Dalrymple's sentence 'it is difficult to become rich without making others poor' betrays 'an elementary ignorance of economics'. Perhaps Mr Read's economics may be true in Europe, but he shows his own ignorance of economics in Latin America. There the rich in Salvador, Nicaragua, Guatamala and Chile are deliberately eliminating the poor in order to maintain and increase their riches. This is a world where small children are disembowelled, women raped and burnt alive in order to create a terror which will drive the poor from the little land they occupy.

I think if Mr Read had read the reports from Nicaragua of an English priest, Father Medcalf, he would not have written with such dogmatic assurance worthy of a Marxist that increased prosperity can be created for the rich 'which in time leads to a real and lasting rise in the standard of living among those who are currently poor'.

On 20 September Read replied: '. . . Nor did I wish to suggest that the rich never oppress or exploit the poor as Graham Greene describes, although I should point out that the economic decline of the only South American country of which I do have some knowledge, Uruguay, was due partly to the creation of a lavish welfare state.

'It would be a mistake, however, to base our social morality on the experience of this or any other South American republic.

Indeed it is time we Catholics escaped from our obsession with South America and learned from those communities who have succeeded in raising the standard of living of their people – West Germany, for example, or South Korea.

'What I fear is that Christians in this country, by drawing false conclusions from untypical instances of prima facie injustice, go on to preach a social morality which destroys the spirit of enterprise upon which our ability to be charitable ultimately depends; and at the same time distract the faithful from the essentially spiritual nature of the Church's mission.'

On 11 October Fr Geoffrey Pye of Leigh-on-Sea wrote: 'Please permit me to protest against Piers Paul Read's extraordinary remark that "it is time we Catholics escaped from our obsession with South America". Does he realize that the largest number of Catholics in any one continent live in Latin and Central America and that the Hispanic influx, largely from South America, is radically changing the make-up of the Catholic Church in the United States? Would to God more lay people understood the problems between rich and poor as well as does Graham Greene and that more priests would make as courageous an option for the poor as has Fr John Devine, who I know sees the salvation of his poverty-stricken Indian parishioners not in material terms but in spiritual terms of human dignity and Christian liberation.'

*

The Times / 15 December 1986

The Nuclear Umbrella

– Surely the disaster at Chernobyl has demonstrated, as far as Europe West and East is concerned, that a nuclear umbrella would remain, even if all nuclear weapons were destroyed. Is a conventional war in Europe possible when it would involve the probable destruction – or at least the cracking of – a dozen Chernobyls in

England, France, the USSR? Will either side carefully restrain from any 'accidental' bombing of a peaceful nuclear plant? In fact the peaceful nuclear plants provide Europe with a cheaper umbrella than that provided by nuclear weapons.

*

Spectator / 28 February 1987

Lectured in Moscow

— Your Portrait of the Week (21 February) is in one respect badly drawn. In Moscow the other day we were none of us lectured by Soviet 'cultural workers'. I had the boring experience of being lectured by several English and Americans, an Egyptian, an Italian, an Ethiopian – I don't remember a single 'Soviet cultural worker'. Poor people, they had to listen to us.

*

Sunday Telegraph / 24 May 1987

Nothing to Hide

— There was nothing secret about my meetings in Moscow with my friend of the war years, Kim Philby, to justify your startling headline. ['Graham Greene and Philby in secret Moscow meetings', 10 May.] As your correspondent Madame Moutet correctly reports, two of the meetings were at parties of writers or artists. Apparently a journalist regards any meeting one may have with a friend abroad as secret if he is not invited to the party or informed about it.

*

Sweet Waste of Effort

— I continue to be puzzled by the label Marxist–
Leninist which you and many other papers attach to
the government of Nicaragua. It is not that to me
Marxist–Leninist is a pejorative term but is it the
correct one? I would have thought that Nicaragua was
the first Latin American country under authoritarian
rule (Somoza supported by the United States) to
have reverted by revolution in the direction of democracy. You write that 'education is now indistinguishable from indoctrination'. Can you give us details
with what the schools are now 'indoctrinated'? What
books are the children reading? What subjects are they
taught?

You might indeed have reason to fear that under a
Minister of Education who is a Jesuit priest the 'indoctrination' may be too Catholic, though that seems hardly
necessary in a country quite as Catholic as Poland, but of
course there may well be understandably a bias towards
liberation theology. But Marxist–Leninist?

On 17 October Charles Mosley wrote: 'Owing to absence
on holiday I have only just seen Graham Greene's letter in
your 29 August issue in which he questions the statement
that in Nicaragua "education is now indistinguishable from
indoctrination".

'I have seen a first-grade reader published under the imprint
of the Ministry of Education, Managua, Nicaragua. On page 48
it says "*¡Viva el FSLN!*" On page 54 the letter F is illustrated by
the word *fusil* (rifle) and a picture of what I take to be (I am
admittedly no small-arms expert) an automatic rifle. On page 59
the text reads "DEFENCE – The valiant militia march in the
square. They all hold their rifles in their hands. The militia are

of the people. The people are ready for defence. The militia defend peace. Long live the militia!"

'On page 92, under C, the text reads "Carlos – Carlos Fonseca taught us the way. He is the founder of Sandinista Front of National Liberation [Frente Sandinista de Liberación Nacional (FSLN)]. He fell at Zincia. Carlos lives on in the hearts of the people."

'On page 100, illustrating the two letters "gu" (used frequently in Spanish hence translated here as one letter), is the single word "guerrilleros".

'On page 73, under a picture of lemur-eyed children of the sort one sees in the kitscher sort of Italian restaurant, the lesson goes "Toño, Delia and Rodolfo belong to the Association of Sandinista Children [Asociación de Niños Sandinistas. (ANS)]. Sandinista children use a neckerchief. They take part in the tasks of the Revolution and are very studious."

'On page 127 the text reads "The children of the Revolution – We children are the fledglings [*mimados*] of the Revolution. We study to prepare ourselves and be useful to our country and our people. We children help in the defence of the Fatherland, looking after our schools and teaching materials, participating in the preservation of water and lighting [i.e. not wasting electricity] and carrying out the tasks that are given us. As we are the fledglings, the Revolution concerns itself with giving us education, health and recreation. And above all it guarantees us peace."

'In another book published under the same imprint – a first-grade mathematics primer – three circles enclosing each a brace of hand grenades are shown, followed by "$2 + 2 + 2 = 6$". At the top of the page are three groups of a brace of automatic rifles.

'There's plenty more along these lines, but I hope I have quoted enough to convince even Mr Greene.'

In the issue of 31 October (at a time when the *Spectator* was going through another astonishing spate of misprints) 'Grahame' Greene wrote:

— I obviously misunderstood Mr Mosley's statement that in Nicaragua 'education is now indistinguishable from indoctrination'. I thought that he meant indoctrination in that economic bogy Marxism. The free education books from which he quotes contain no hint of Marxism judging from his own choice of quotations, and I certainly won't dispute that there is a form of indoctrination – the indoctrination in patriotism during a war waged against terrorist members of Somoza's National Guard, mercenaries paid under the table by the United States and conscripts kidnapped from villages near the Honduran border.

I remember as a boy of eleven being indoctrinated by posters of Lord Kitchener pointing his finger at me from the hoardings and apparently saying 'England has need of You.'

I hope at least that Mr Mosley will agree with me that in time of war an appeal to children to help, as he quotes, to look after their teaching materials and economize on water and electricity (no word of Marx!) is an acceptable form of indoctrination.

*

Tablet / 26 September 1987

Price of Protest

— A Catholic priest, Fr Roy Bourgeois, is serving a nine-month sentence for protesting against the training of Contras at a military base in Florida. He was given four months on the charge of trespass (he had simply 'crossed the line' marking the US Government property, knelt down and prayed, holding a small white cross with the names of Nicaraguan civilians killed by the Contras). He also got five months for violating his probation for a similar protest at the same military base four months earlier.

*

Commonweal / 23 October 1987

Stigmata

— In your issue of 14 August which has only just reached me, Mr Christopher Buckley tells 'a true story' told to him by someone 'very close' to me (I am unaware of anyone close to me who knows Mr Buckley) about a Mass I attended said by Padre Pio. I did once attend such a Mass, but there is not a word of truth in the rest of his story. The church was not 'packed' (it was five o'clock in the morning), there was no bleeding of the stigmata, I left at the end of the Mass quite normally, there was nothing to 'horrify me', no priest came running with a message to me, I would have been at breakfast and not sitting with a bottle at 'the edge of town' – in fact there was no town only a village.

I trust that the lies in this story will be corrected before it appears in book form. I am sending a copy of this letter to the forthcoming publishers of *Once A Catholic*, Houghton Mifflin.

'I suppose this is part of the price of eminence,' wrote *Commonweal*'s Editor, Peter Steinfels, to Greene, 'but it is important to stop legends like this in their tracks. We will publish your letter, and prominently, at the next opportunity.'

In the meanwhile Buckley wrote to Greene, and said that in fact the article was not written by him but 'an interview given to someone assembling a book on the Catholic experience in America. I was not pleased with the misleading way *Commonweal* presented it, and wrote to say so. But down to the heart of the matter. The story about Padre Pio was told me, more or less exactly as it appeared in *Commonweal*, by our mutual friend, Peter Glenville.'

Greene replied (17 October):

   — I'm sorry if I was unfair to you, but Peter Glenville was fantasizing from what must be a very bad memory . . . the facts are these: in the days before a hotel had been built and the situation of Padre Pio was still in a small village I went there from curiosity with a personal friend of Padre Pio. He invited me to visit him on the evening I arrived and I refused because I said I didn't wish my life to be changed by a saint. However, I and my mistress attended the Mass at 5.30 in the morning. Padre Pio was forbidden to serve Mass at the high altar and said it at the small side altar. The few people who arrived for the Mass, all of them women, instead of going to the altar went to queue up at the confessional because he went there immediately after Mass and stayed until lunchtime. I was within a few feet of him. When his sleeves slipped I could see the dried stigmata on his hands. A priest is forbidden to wear gloves and he was trying to conceal them. The one curious thing about the Mass was that I had been warned it was very long. He said the Mass very slowly and distinctly in Latin but there was no sermon and I judged that perhaps the Mass had lasted as much as forty minutes. I was astonished and it seemed to me inexplicable that when we left I found it had lasted for somewhere around an hour and a half and I couldn't imagine where the time had been lost. There was no bleeding and I was not pursued by another priest. We went away that day. These are the facts. Free from what we will call the imagination of Peter Glenville.

Buckley wrote to say that some time had elapsed between his hearing the story and his relating it to the interviewer. 'I am very glad it was your fault and not Peter's,' replied Greene. 'Your apology is a generous one and let's forget the whole matter.'

*

Unwelcome Guest

— I am shocked to hear that Sir James Eberle has invited Adolfo Calero, one of the top terrorist leaders of the Contras, to address a meeting called 'Nicaragua at the Crossroads', organized by the Royal Institute of International Affairs.

No better date than 30 October could have been chosen as a platform by Calero to help him attempt the sabotage of the Guatemala Peace Accord, due to be in place on 7 November. The Nicaraguan government has taken important steps already to implement the accord, which is supported even by Archbishop Obando.

One can only hope that the Home Secretary will refuse entry to Calero as a known terrorist.

*

Bachelors' Advice

— Fr Wermter writes (*The Tablet*, 9 January) that 'it is the women who have to bear the burden of contraception and they have to bear this burden alone'. He is referring to 'the very unpleasant side-effects of the pill and more especially of the contraceptive injection'. He ignores completely the condom (I would prefer to call it by its old frivolous term 'French letter' or *capote anglaise*, for there is humour too in sex relations) which has no 'unpleasant side-effects' for women or men.

Pope Paul VI, to his credit, although he went against the advice of the large majority of the cardinals and bishops forming his commission on contraception, made it clear that his encyclical *Humanae Vitae* was not to be regarded as an infallible pronouncement.

We are now faced with an attempt by certain characters in the Vatican to enlarge the definition of infallibility made by Vatican I (opposed even then by theologians of Newman's standing), and I cannot help feeling that Fr Wermter is trying to find humanitarian reasons for excusing the papal condemnation of contraception.

What we require, if we are to treat Vatican I seriously, is a condemnation of contraception by the Apostles, for infallibility, even by Vatican I, was granted only to questions of faith and morals 'in accordance with the teaching of the Apostles'. Contraception was practised even in Roman times and when was it condemned by the Apostles?

*

Independent / 27 June 1988

Forbidden Visit

— I am disappointed to hear that in a very sad case certain Bulgarian authorities are not following the excellent example given by Mikhail Gorbachev.

Dimitar Botschev is what is known as a dissident living in West Germany. In August 1987 his mother underwent a severe cancer operation from which she has not yet recovered. Some two months ago he sent his parents the invitation for a visit required by the Bulgarian authorities. On 31 May they were summoned to the local police office in Silistrato to be informed that they might visit their son but only separately, which makes the visit virtually impossible. His mother is not in a position to go unaccompanied even to the shop next door. His father is seventy-six years old and ill too.

In 1983 and 1986 they were allowed to visit their son together when they were in better health, and they returned to Bulgaria. It seems unlikely that the authorities in

Silistrato are afraid of their remaining in Germany. To me it seems far more likely to be the fault and callousness of local bureaucrats afraid of Mr Gorbachev's reforms and perhaps revengeful. How many Silistratos are there in Bulgaria?

*

The Times / 19 July 1988

Official Trivia

— I think that Mr Bernard Levin (11 July) takes a rather too friendly view of the American treatment of 'official secrets' compared with our own. He writes that 'the Freedom of Information Act throws open to inspection every file other than genuinely secret ones'.

In 1984 I obtained my dossier, forty-five pages of material of which nearly sixteen had been blacked out in heavy ink. I very much doubt whether I was ever in a position to know 'genuinely secret' information about the USA.

However, it amused me to put up my dossier at Sotheby's [see *Spectator* 7 April 1984]. I received a very good price in return, so that I wonder now whether it might be worth my while to obtain a second instalment and later a third one, a good means of earning a livelihood in old age.

*

Independent / 18 November 1988

Two Europes

— I confess that I am not a supporter of the Conservative party, and yet unwillingly I find myself a supporter of Mrs Thatcher in her hesitation about a so-called united Europe in 1992. The discussions in Brussels seem

(249)

always to centre on three powers, France and Germany and the United Kingdom. But this so-called united Europe includes little more than half Germany, Greece (at the moment probably the most corrupt state in Europe), Italy which is in the hands of the Christian Democrats who are in the hands of the Mafia, and Spain (a little problem there about Gibraltar and a bigger problem about the dumping of drugs) and an unenthusiastic Denmark.

Why not have a second Europe, a northern Europe (all national sovereignties intact) consisting of Norway, Sweden, and Denmark, Finland (very prosperous at the moment), and the United Kingdom having relations with Comecon and the other splintered Europe if they choose to co-operate.

The United States of Europe (a whole Europe) can never exist. We are too diverse in our judicial systems for one thing. Nor does the example of the United States of America encourage the idea as matters stand at the moment.

*

Tablet / 10 December 1988

God as It

— In reference to your Television article of 19 November I feel like many others a certain uneasiness at changing references to God in the Liturgy from He to She. Would it be a possible compromise which would satisfy both the Reverend Suzanne Fageol and Bishop Masters if in the Liturgy we call God It (of course with a capital I)? After all there is a hint of the indefinable and inexplicable in the word 'it'.

*

Spectator / 25 February 1989

A Frenchman's Castle

– I have suffered myself from the French law against Intrusion into the Private Life (a fine and a pamphlet called *J'Accuse* confiscated), but I couldn't agree with you more strongly that a similar law is needed in England.

*

Independent / 27 March 1989

Confiscated Books

– The government of Grenada, which, in spite of the US intervention, remains part of the British Commonwealth, has begun to confiscate books published in England. On 9 March four boxes of literature published by the Pathfinder Press were seized by the police and also a personal copy of my novel *Our Man in Havana*. Surely some protest should be made by the British Government?

*

Spectator / 6 May 1989

Out of Date

– I would like to reassure Sir Raymond Carr (Books, 22 April) that whatever the pimps told him I had no sexual relations with anyone in Haiti, not even with Papa Doc. I certainly drank heavily at Oxford, but I haven't met Dr Rowse for sixty years or more, so perhaps his impressions are a little out of date.

In reviewing A. L. Rowse's *Friends and Contemporaries*, Carr commented on the essay 'Graham Greene: Perverse Genius' which revolved around a post-war dinner in Oxford and a chance meeting in the streets of St James's. Carr reported that 'in Haiti I was repeatedly accosted by pimps who claimed Greene had slept with their adolescent sisters'. Rowse himself says, 'It is not for me to say whether there is any harm in brothels ... I fear that this is very unlike the domestic life at All Souls which I enjoyed.'

*

Independent / 27 May 1989

An Expulsion Born of Ignorance

— I am writing as one who belongs to no political party, but who believes it is high time we had a Prime Minister who is less ignorant of foreign affairs.

Margaret Thatcher's reception recently of President Daniel Ortega showed her complete ignorance of conditions in Nicaragua and Latin America. We find ignorance again in the Government's behaviour, well described in the *Spectator* of 13 May, to our fellow citizens of Chinese birth in Hong Kong; ignorance again and clumsiness too, in the expulsion of the so-called spies of the USSR.

In this days of mutual *glasnost* it's hard to understand into what they are spying. If they were really identified as defence spies, why were they expelled? They must have been a valuable source of information for our MI5 watchdog. The Russians, more wisely, are probably expelling in return the useless and the innocent.

The whole affair is an exhibition of bad diplomacy and another example of the Prime Minister's ignorance of all countries except her own.

*

Net Book Agreement

— A Net Book Agreement was abolished in France during the rule of President Pompidou with disastrous results. Innumerable small booksellers throughout the country had to close and books became available only in big stores. As a result the agreement was wisely reinstated by Monsieur Barre when he was prime minister. I think we should have learnt a lesson from France.

EPILOGUE

'I saw Stokes the other evening. We both lamented that you never come to our club.'

Evelyn Waugh to Graham Greene

INDEX

Ackroyd, Peter, xiii
Acton, Harold, xii
address, forms of, 177–8
Adler, Henry, 63–4
Adler, Larry, 191
Adzhubei, Mr, 127–8
age, old, 72–4
airports, drinks at, 46–7
Aldington, Richard, 20
Aldrich, Winthrop, 31
Algeria, 219, 220
Allain, M.- F., xi–xii, 156, 197–8
Alleg, Henri, 98–100
Allen, Louis, 218–20
Allen, Walter, 9, 183–4
Allende, Salvador, 197, 226–7
Amnesty, 187
Anderson, George, 133
Anglo-Texan Society, xiii, 27–32
ants, pet, 108–9
Apostrophes, 175
Aquino, Corazon, 238–9
Architects' Journal, 158
architecture, 157–9
Argentina, 191, 208–10, 215, 238
arms trade, 95, 109–10, 196–8
art, Catholic, 3–4, 44–5
Arthur, Dr Leonard, trial of, 205–6
Asquith, Margot, 46
atebrin and atropin, 4–6
'Atticus' (Stephen Pile), 199
Austin, Jack, 43
Avis, Derek, 94
Ayer, Professor A. J., 80
Azzopardi, John, 108–9

Bacall, Lauren, 188
Bagnall, Nicholas, 92, 94
Bailey, L. W., 11
Balášová, Comrade, 170–71
Bank of England, 14–16
Barber, Stephen, 126–7
Barkeley, William, 84–7
Bates, Colin (pseud. of GG), 13
Baxter, Mr (pseud. of GG), 10
Beale, Ronald, 51–2
Beauboeuf, Colonel Jean, 146
Beaverbrook press, 97; see also,
    Daily Express; Gordon, John
Beeston, Mr, 127
Belize, 195–6, 214–15
Benn, Anthony Wedgwood, 192
Bentley's Fish Restaurant, 128–9
Berkhamsted School, x, 11
Birch, Lionel, 80, 140
Birmingham, 115, 184
Bodley Head, 108, 125, 126
Boissieu, Général de, 198
books, confiscation of, 215, 251
Books and Bookmen, ix
Bookseller, 178–9
Borge, Tomàs, 221, 230, 231, 232
Bosch, Dr (Dominican
    politician), 118
Bossom, Alfred, Baron, 28, 30, 31
Botschev, Dimitar, 248–9
Boum Oum, Prince, 106
Bourgeois, Fr Roy, 244–5
Bourne, General The Lord,
    152–3
Boyer, Charles, 188

Bradshaw, S., of Liverpool, 5–6
Braine, John, 143
Brazil, James, 137
Brazil, 155
Brighton; Bedford Hotel, xiv–xv
British Broadcasting
  Corporation, 104, 162
Brogan, Colm, 91, 92–4
Brogan Professor D. W., 137–8,
  139
Brook, Peter, 80
Brooke, Henry, 200
Bruce, Donald, 111
Bruce-Gardyne, Jock, 222
Buckley, Christopher, 245–6
Buckley, William, 233
Buddhism, 43, 187
Bui-Chu, Bishop of, 125, 164, 176
Bulgaria, 248–9
bureaucracy, 88–9
Burgess, Anthony, 126, 173–6, 210
Burgess, Guy, 186
Burma, 118, 149
Butler, R. A., xiii, 81, 87–8,
  90–91, 94
Butler, Samuel; Erewhon, 62–3

Cabinet ministers' education,
  191–2
Cabral, Dr Reid, 117
Calero, Adolfo, 247
Calvi, Roberto, 223
Cambodia, 148–9, 167, 192
Campaign, 128
Canabal, Garrido, 190
Caodaists, 43, 186–7
Cape Asbestos Company Ltd, 116
Capri, 178
Cardenal, Fr Fernando, SJ, 224
Carmania, SS, 162
Carr, Sir Raymond, 251–2
Cartland, Barbara, 228

Casaroli, Cardinal Agostino, 224
Castro, Dr Fidel, see under Cuba
Catholic Herald, 3–4, 52
Catholicism; Anthony Burgess's,
  173–4; art, 3–4, 44–5; clerical
  authority, 205–6; Communism
  and, 234; Index, 39; Paul
  Johnson's, 95; liberation
  theology, 223–5, 242;
  Mexico, 189–90; Northern
  Ireland, 154; and politics,
  233–4; religious advertising,
  134–5; right to die, 205–6;
  US, and McCarthyism, 25; see
  also, Papacy and under Cuba;
  Greene, Graham; Nicaragua;
  Vietnam
Cavendish Square Convent, 44–5
Cayetano, Salvador, 203
censorship; Argentina, 208, 209;
  Britain, 7, 36–9, 66–8, 87–8,
  102–4; international, 39, 87–8;
  John Gordon Society and, 79,
  81–2; Spain, 39, 215
Central Intelligence Agency, 105,
  146, 147, 148, 186–7, 197, 227
Centre Point building, 157–8
Chakovsky, Alexander, 144–5
Chamberlain, Neville, 183–4
Chancellor, Alexander, xiii, 13,
  217, 231–2
Channon, Paul, 215
Chaplin, Charles, 24–6, 108
Chataway, Christopher, 80
Chatto & Windus Ltd, 199
Chernobyl nuclear accident,
  240–41
Cherwell, xii
Chesterton, Mrs Cecil, 63
Chile, 226–7, 234, 239; arms,
  196–7; US policy, 190, 238
China, People's Republic of, 120

Chomsky, Noam, 237
Christ, poverty of, 220–21
Churchill, Randolph, 69–72,
    85–7
Churchill, Sir Winston Spencer,
    162
civil defence, 193
Clarin (Buenos Aires), 208–9
Clarke, Kenneth, xvi, xvii
clichés, 92–4
Clifford, Lord de, 200
Cocteau, Jean, 72, 73
Colette, 40–42
Collins, Malcolm (*pseud.* of GG),
    11
Commonweal, 130–31, 134–5,
    245–6
Communism; and Catholicism,
    234; Greene's membership of
    Party, 88
competitions, newspaper, 9–14
Conan Doyle, Sir Arthur, 172
contraception, 216, 247–8
Cook, D. R. (*pseud.* of GG), 9
copyright laws, 126
Cornwell, Rupert, 136
Coward, Noël, 17, 47–8
Crace, Jim, xix
Cripps, Sir Stafford, 15
Crosland, Anthony, 181
Crozier, Brian, 118–20, 121–2,
    122–4
Cuapa, Virgin of, 213
Cuba: arms for, 95, 109–10;
    Batista regime, 74–6, 95, 109,
    110, 231, 238; British policy,
    95, 109–10; Castro regime,
    74–6, 95, 109–11, 194, 231;
    Church, 75, 111, 230–31;
    Dominican Republic and,
    117–18; exodus from, 194–5;
    Greene's affinity for, 136;

torture, 109; US policy, 95,
    106–7, 109, 117–18, 141, 238
Cymric, SS, 162
Cyprus, 49, 50
Czechoslovakia, 8, 155, 165–6,
    191; Soviet invasion, 8, 140,
    159–60, 165; television, 170–71

Daily Express, xv, xvi, 84–7, 205,
    211; *see also*, Gordon, John
Daily Herald, 8
Daily Mail, 211
Daily Mirror, 6–7
Daily Telegraph, letters to, xiii;
    bureaucracy, 88–9; Francis
    Iles, exchange with, xii; Great
    Train Robbery, 112–13; *The
    Honorary Consul*, 168;
    Krushchev–Susskind interview,
    101–2; Mau Mau rebellion,
    33–4; obscenity law, 66–8;
    prostitution, 90–94; publishers,
    129–30; Vietnam, 114–15,
    120–5
Daily Telegraph Magazine, ix,
    27–32
Dalrymple, John, 239
Damas, Archbishop, 234
Daniel, Alexander, 137
Daniel, Yuri, 135–7, 141–2, 143,
    144
D'Arcy, Fr, 65
Davie, Michael, 215
Dawson, Geoffrey, ix
Day Lewis, Cecil, 133
death; right to die, 205–6
Delargy, Hugh, 74
Denning, Alfred T., Baron,
    188–9
Dennis, Nigel, 172
Dennys, Elisabeth, 12–13
Devine, Fr John, 240

Dickens, Charles, 58–9
Diem, Ngo Dinh, 164, 166–7, 187
Dien Bien Phu, 34, 69–72, 105
Dix, F. H. R., 44
Dominican Republic, 117–18, 140, 141, 238
Dostoevsky, Fyodor, 137
Douglas, Norman, 19–20, 178, 179, 195
Duff, Lady Juliet, 80
Dupont-Gonin, Pierre-François, 106
Duvalier, François ('Papa Doc'), xv, 131, 140, 146, 148, 191, 238

Eberle, Sir James, 247
Economist, 172–3
Eden, Sir Anthony, 36
Edwards, Sydney, 193
El Salvador, 221, 227, 233–4, 239
Eleigh, Sebastian (*pseud.* of Hugh Greene), 11, 12
Eliot, T. S., 45, 55
Elizabeth II, Queen, 181, 231–2
Eltham Laundry Supplies Ltd, xxi, 159
Elwyn-Jones, Frederick, Baron, 192
Epstein, Sir Jacob, 44–5
Erasmus, Desiderius, 227
European Economic Community, 163–5, 249–50
Evans, C. S., 130
Evans, Dwye, 129, 130
Evening News, 142
Evening Standard; *Brighton Rock* serialized, 214; interviews with Greene, 56–7, 63, 100, 145, 193; letters, 113–14, 168; 'Londoner's Diary', 59–60, 130, 158, 184–5

Everage, Dame Edna, 217
executors, literary, 126
Exprès, L', 42
Eyre and Spottiswoode Ltd, 28, 150

Fabienne-Smith, Mrs, 212
Fairlie, Henry, 204
Falk, Quentin, 10
Falkland Islands, 208–10, 215
Fallowell, Duncan, 174, 210–11
Fanshaugh, G. E., xxi, 159–60
Federal Bureau of Investigation, 26–7, 138, 150, 249
Feltin, Cardinal Maurice, 40–42
Figaro Littéraire, Le, 40–2
films: author's loss of control, 56–8; *Wee Willie Winkie*: Greene's review, 85, 86, 199–200; *see also under* Greene, Graham
Firbank, Ronald, xv–xvi
FitzGibbon, Constantine, 195
Flaubert, Gustave, 94
Fonseca, Carlos, 243
Foot, Michael, 192
Ford, Ford Madox, 125–6, 163, 175
Foreign Office, 148; and Cuba, 74, 75, 76, 109–10; and Vietnam, 122
Formosa crisis, 42–3
Forster, E. M., 55
Fowles, John, xix
France, 98–100, 185, 251; *see also*, Nice
Fraser, Lady Antonia, *see* Johnson, Paul
freedom of publication, 129–30
Frere, A. S., 66, 67, 80, 114, 129

Gale, George, 77

Gallo, Max, 207
Gaulle, Charles de, 72, 73
George VI, King, 202
Ghana, 61–2
Gilbert and Sullivan operas, 189
Gill, Eric, 3–4
Gilliat, Sidney, 16, 17
Gilliatt, Penelope, 191
Gilmour, Sir Ian, 78, 80, 81
gin, 46–7
Glendinning, Victoria, 20
Glenville, Peter, 245–6
Gliddon, G. M. 125–6
God, sex of, 250
Goddard, Lord Rayner, 68–9
Gonzi, Archbishop, 108–9
Gorbachev, Mikhail, 248, 249
Gordon, John, xiii, 76–88, 140
Gould, Donald, 142
Graves, Robert, 126
Greece, 155, 250
Green, Graham J. Graham, 52
Greene, Sir Graham, 160–1
Greene, Graham; childhood, x,
    xii, 11, 85, 88, 115; at Oxford,
    x, xii, 88, 160, 200, 251–2;
    journalist, x–xi, 116, 117, 132,
    133–4; early novels, xi, 126,
    133, 214; SIS work, xiv, 219;
    Order of Merit, 231–2, 234;
    Catholicism, 137–9, 206, 211;
    politics, 231–2
        films, 10, 16, 148, 156–8;
    Brighton Rock, 6–7, 16; *The
    Comedians*, 148; *The
    Confidential Agent*, 188; *The
    Heart of the Matter*, 16; *Our
    Man in Havana*, 16, 17; *The
    Mau Mau Story*, 16; *The Quiet
    American*, 56–8, 61; *The
    Stranger's Hand*, 10
        writings: *Babbling April*, xii;

The Best of Saki, 23; *Brighton
    Rock*, xiv, 6–7, 16, 214; *The
    Captain and the Enemy*, xi, 13;
    Collected Essays, 5, 23, 169; *The
    Comedians*, xv, 60; *The
    Complaisant Lover*, 102–3, 104;
    The Confidential Agent, xiii, 188;
    The End of the Affair, 46; *Getting
    to Know the General*, 46, 194, 226;
    A Gun for Sale, 198; *The Heart
    of the Matter*, xix, 13, 14–16, 174,
    179; *The Honorary Consul*, 168;
    The Human Factor, xvi; *An
    Impossible Woman*, 178; *It's a
    Battlefield*, xi; *J'Accuse*, xiv,
    207–8, 251; *Life and Letters*, x;
    Lord Rochester's Monkey, 67;
    May We Borrow Your Husband?,
    60, 128; *Memoirs of the Forties*,
    132; *Our Man in Havana*,
    16–17, 251; *The Other Man*,
    157; *The Outsider*, xv; *The
    Pleasure-Dome*, xi; *The Power and
    the Glory*, 181, 189–90, 214;
    The Quiet American, xii, xv, 61,
    126–7, 190–91; *Rumour at
    Nightfall*, xi; *In Search of a
    Character*, 211; *A Sort of Life*,
    ix, 10, 134; *Ways of Escape*, xi,
    xv, 8
Greene, Graham (namesake),
    48–50, 52
Greene, Sir Hugh Carleton,
    11–12
Greer, Herb, 153
Grenada, 251
Grigson, Geoffrey, 177
Grimshaw, Eric, 69
Guardian, 156
Guatemala, 195–6, 236–7, 239,
    247
Guinness, Samuel, 28, 31–2

Hackett, J. P., 65
Hadfield, John, 68
Haggard, Rider, 5, 101, 186
Hailsham, Baron (Quintin Hogg), 58
Haiti, 138, 146–8, 230–31, 251–2; US policy, 130–31, 140, 141, 146, 147, 148, 190, 238
Hall, Radclyffe, 37, 39
Hammerstein, Oscar, 14–16
Hand, Judge Augustus N., 38
Hardman, ACM Sir Donald, 149
Harriott, John F. X., 234, 235–7
Harris, Rt Rev. Augustine, 154
Harris, Wilson, xi
Havel, Václav, 166
Hayley, Sir William, 204
Hayward, John, 67
Healey, Dennis, 192
Heath, Edward, 163
Hebblethwaite, Peter, 223–5, 228–9
Heinemann, William, 107, 108, 129–30, 174
helmets, motor-cycle, 180–81
Helsinki Agreements, 192, 194
Hemingway, Ernest, 150
Hempfel, John S., 235–6
Herbert, A. P., 67
Heseltine, Michael, 216
Hetherington, John, 161–2
Hewart, Gordon, 1st Viscount, 69, 85, 199, 200
Hewlett, Maurice, 162–3
Hickey, William, 211
Hicks, Joynson, 80
Highgate School, 28
Hingley, Ronald, 138–9
hire-purchase controls, 131–2
Hitler, Adolf, 124, 192
Ho Chi Minh, 120, 164, 187
Hoa Hao sect, 43

Hobbes, John Oliver, 89–90
Hobbs, John, 64–5
Hollis Christopher, 64–5
Holmes, Valentine, 86
Home, Charles Douglas-, 134
Home, William Douglas-, 98
Home Office building, 157
Hong Kong, 252
Horizon, xxiii
Howard, Major G. E., 114
Howard, Philip, 204, 214
Howard, Trevor, 10, 16
Hudson, Derek, 23
Hungary, 155
Hyams, Harry, 157
Hynes, Samuel, 162

Iles, Francis, xii
Independent, letters to, 247, 248–9, 249–50, 251, 252
Independent Television Authority, 102–4
Index, Roman, 39
India; Naga Hills, 48–52
Inglis, Brian, 90
Ingrams, Richard, 204
Innes, Hammond, 185–6
intellectual, definition of, 188–9
interviews, giving of press, 210–11
Ionesco, Eugène, 100
Ireland, 39, 154–7
Irish Republican Army, 156, 159
Isherwood, Christopher, 80

Jackson, Sir Geoffrey, 168
James, Clive, his juvenilia, xx
James, Henry, 46
James, William, xiii
Janes, Mr H. S. (of Spectator), 80, 81
Jansenism, 173–4

Jay, Douglas, 133–4
Jeffreys, George, 1st Baron, 69
John Gordon Society, xiii, 10,
  78–88
John XXIII, Pope, 127–8, 225
John Paul II, Pope, 216, 220–21,
  223–5, 227, 230
Johnson, Kenneth, 178
Johnson, Paul, x, 181, 226–7
jokes, practical, xiii; Anglo-Texan
  Society, xiii, 27–32; John
  Gordon Society, xiii, 10,
  78–88; Post Office, xiii–xiv,
  182–4; telephone game at
  party, 184–5
Jones, David, 4
Jones, Glyn, 69
Jonge, Alex de, 177, 178
Joseph, St, 221
Joyce, James, 37, 38, 39
July 4th celebrations, 185
Junor, John, 77
jury service, 200–3
justice, 68–9, 199–203; Dr
  Arthur's trial, 205–6; France,
  98–100, 198, 207–8, 251;
  Ghana, 61–2; Great Train
  Robbery, xiii, 112–14; jury
  service, 200–3; law on
  obscene publications, 66–8;
  libel proceedings against
  Greene, 85, 86, 199–200;
  misprintedly juvenile
  offenders, 188; murder
  penalties, C19th, 58–9;
  obscenity laws, 36–9, 66–8,
  189; peers, trial by, 200

Kavanagh, Dan, xix–xx
Kennedy, Senator Edward, 167
Kennedy, John F., 107, 167
Kennedy, Ludovic, 200, 203

Kennedy, Margaret, 55
Kenya; Mau Mau rebellion, xvi,
  32–4
Kilham-Roberts, D., 54
King, Francis, 128
Kitchener, Herbert H., 1st Earl,
  244
Knightsbridge Barracks, 157, 158
Krushchev, Nikita, 88, 101–2
Küng, Hans, 206
Kuznetsov, Anatoly, 141, 142–3,
  143–4
Kyncl, Karel, 165–6

Lane, Allen, 54
languages, minority, 203
Lansdale, General, 126–7
Lao Dong party, 122, 123, 124
Laos, 104–6, 120
Larkin, Philip, 9
Lattre, General Jean de, 218–19,
  220
Lawson, Nigel, 128
Le Carré, John, 210, 211
Leather, Sir Edwin, 163, 164
Lees-Milne, James, 20
Légion d'Honneur, 198
Levin, Bernard, 68–9, 96–8, 152,
  153, 249
Life, 187
Limburn, George, 116–17
Lire, 175
Listener, xii, 4–6, 5, 52, 226–7
Lloyd, Selwyn, 74
Lon Nol, 167
London Magazine, 20, 199, 211
Lord, Graham, 175
Lord Chamberlain, 102, 103
Lord Chief Justices, 68–9; see also,
  Hewart
Luang Prabang, Vietnam, 104
Lurgan, Lord, 61–2

Lusitania, SS, 160–62

MacArthur, General Douglas, 115
Macaulay, Rose, 200
Mackay, Peter, 204
Maclaren-Ross, Julian, 132
Maclean, Donald, 86
Maland, Charles, 26–7
malarial prophylactics, 4–6
Malraux, André, 98–100
Malta, 108–9
Mankiewicz, Joseph, 57–8
Marcinkus, Archbishop Paul, 222–3
Marcus, Nieman, 31
Marks, John, 199
Marnham, Patrick, 232
Martin, Kingsley, 35–6, 72–4
Marx, Karl, 225, 233, 242
Masaryk, Thomas Garrigue, 166
Matisse, Henri, 45
Mau Mau rebellion, xvi, 32–4
Maudling, Reginald, 154–5, 156
Maugham, W. Somerset, 129, 130, 168–9
Mauriac, François, 42
Mayer, Louis B., 26
McCarthyism, 24–7
Medcalf, Fr, 239
Méhu, Delmore, 146–7
Mendoza, Donato, 238
Menjou, Adolf, 26
Mewshaw, Michael, 211
Mexico, 189–90
Meynell, Alice, 44
Mindzenty, Cardinal Jozsef, 155
misprints, 187–8, 243
Misquito Indians, Nicaragua, 221
Mitford, Nancy, 46
Molotov, Vyacheslav M., 36
Molson, Lord, 158

Monde, Le, 98–100
Monson, Lord, 124–5
Montgomery, Mrs (*pseud.* of GG), 28
Month, The, 62, 65
Moor, Dottoressa, 178
Moore, Charles, 128
Moore, George, 89
Morgan, Charles, x
Morning Post, 23
Moscow, 96–7, 138
Mosley, Charles, 242
Moulik, Dr M., 50–51
Moutat, Anne-Elizabeth, 145, 241
Mulley, Frederick W., 192
Munro, E. M., 22–4
Munro, H. H. (Saki), 22–4
Munthe, Axel, 178–9
Murarka, Dev, 127
Murray, Venetia, 80
Musgrave, Dr Clifford, xv
My Fair Lady (musical), 52–5, 67
My Lai massacre, 153, 165

Nabokov, Vladimir, 78, 87, 177
Naga Hills, Assam, 48–52
Naipaul, V. S.; interview with, ix
Navarre, General, 70
Net Book Agreement, 253
New Scientist, 142
New Statesman: competitions, 9–12; Greene on standards, 73–4;
    letters to: authors of, xix–xx; Cabinet ministers' education, 191–2; Charlie Chaplin, 24–6; old age, 72–4; Cuba, 106–7; Czechoslovakia, 170–71; Dickens and Dostoevsky, 58–9; Epstein's sculptures, 44–5; Ghana, 61–2; Penelope

Gilliatt 'profile' of Greene,
191; John Gordon, 76;
hire-purchase controls, 131–2;
Rider Haggard, 101; Paul
Johnson, 95, 181; jury service,
200–3; Shaw's *St Joan*, 62–5;
Vietnam, 34–6, 118–20, 176
New York Times, 29, 156
News Chronicle, 8, 70, 71
newspapers, Greene's choice of,
205
Nhu, Ngo Dinh, 166–7
Nicaragua: Contras, 227, 234,
236, 238; economic
conditions, 239; and
Guatemala Peace Accord, 247;
Misquito Indians, 221;
patriotism, 244; Pope's visit,
223–5; religion, 222, 230, 231,
232–3, 233–4, (and
government), 212–13, 222,
242–4; Sandinistas, 157,
224–5; Somoza regime, 157,
221, 238, 244; terrorism,
237–8, 244; Thatcher's
ignorance of affairs in, 252;
torture in, 237–8; US policies,
227, 232–3, 234–7, 237–8,
244–5
Nice; corruption, xiv, 198, 207–8
Nice-Matin, 204, 205
Nichols, Beverley, 129, 130, 168–9
Nicolson, Harold, 19–20
Nicolson, Nigel, 20
Night and Day, xi, 199
Nohuly, Sir Walter, 156
Nonesuch Press, The, 67, 152
Norman, Dr Edward, 221–2
Nottingham Journal, x
Nowell-Smith, Simon, 38–9
nuclear accident, Chernobyl,
240–41

nuclear weapons, 66, 172–3, 193,
216–17

Obando, Archbishop, 212–13,
235, 247
obscenity, law on, 36–9, 66–8,
189
Observer: books of the year (1980),
206; interviews, xiv, xv–xvi,
174–5, 218; letters, 46, 107–8,
215; 'Pendennis', 107, 108
Ocampo, Victoria, 209
O'Keefe, T., 80
Oldfield, Sir Maurice, 204, 210
Olivier, Laurence, Baron, 100
Onslow, Katharine (*pseud.* of
Elisabeth Dennys), 12–13
opera, 16–17, 188–9
Order of Merit, 231–2, 234
Ortega, Daniel, 233, 252
Owen, Dr David, 192
Oxford University, 192; *see also
under* Greene, Graham
Oxford Outlook, 160

Pachman, Ludek, 165–6
Paisley, Rev. Ian, 156
Panama, 193–4
Papacy, xiv, 228–9; infallibility,
205–6, 247–8; *see also* John
XXIII; John Paul II; Paul
VI
Parini, Jay, 211
Parkman, Francis, 185
Parliament; MPs' pay, 114, 116;
Select Committee on Obscene
Publications, 66–8; Street
Offences Act (1959), 90–94;
trial by peers, 200
Parsons, Lady Bridget, 80
Pathfinder Press, 251
patriotism, 191, 244

Paul VI, Pope, 216, 222, 247
pay claims, 112, 114, 115–17
Peake, Maeve and Mervyn, 184–5
PEN, 144
'Pendennis', 107, 108
Penguin Books, 125, 126
Penthouse, 174, 210–11
Perrott, Roy, 218
Peter, St; fallibility, 206
Peters, A. D., 55
Phat Diem, Vietnam, xi, 35;
    Bishop of, 124–5, 164, 176,
    220
Philby, Kim, 144, 145, 175, 241
Philippines, 238–9
Pile, Stephen ('Atticus'), 199
Pinker, Eric, 125
Pinochet Ugarte, General
    Augusto, 196–7, 226–7, 234,
    238
Pio, Padre, 139–40, 245–6
Pitlochry Festival Company,
    53–4, 55
Plested, J., 226–7
Podhoretz, Norman, 234
Ponti, Carlo, 195
pornography, 79–80, 183–4; *see
    also*, obscenity
Porter, Charles, 37–8
Posner, Mr Michael, 131–2
Post Office, xiii-xiv, 112, 182–4
Pound, Ezra, 163
Powell, Anthony, 113–14
Powell, Selwyn, 199
Preminger, Otto, 62
Prensa, La (Nicaragua), 213
Price, George, 196
Price, Sandra, 238
Priestley, J. B., 142
Pritchett, Mr V. S., 101
Private Eye, 204
Prochazka, Jan, 142–3

prostitution, xiii, 90–94
publication, freedom of, 129–30
publishers; and authors, 17–19,
    107–8; principles and profits,
    129–30; Net Book
    Agreement, 253
Puerto Rico; Greene deported, 88
Purser, Philip, 188
Pye, Fr Geoffrey, 240

quoting out of context, 179

Rader, Dotson, 199
Radio Free Europe, 135
Rainbird, George, Ltd, 68
Ratzinger, Cardinal Joseph, 225
Read, Herbert, 45, 150
Read, Piers Paul, 239–40
reading aloud, with inner ear, 177
Reagan, Ronald, 204–5, 225, 227,
    232, 234
Red Brigades, 207
Red Cross, 115
Redgrave, Michael, 57
Reed, Carol, 16
Rees, Paul, 205
Reeves, Ruth, 48
religion; censorship, 7; and
    politics, 21–2, 223–5; USSR,
    137–9; *see also*, Buddhism;
    Catholicism
Rhodesia, 183
Richards, Dr Brian A., 179–80
Richardson, Sir Ralph, 17, 103
Ridley, Nicholas, 195
Ripper, Yorkshire; hunt for, 204
Robbery, Great Train, xiii, 112–14
Rochester, John Wilmot, 2nd
    Earl, 67
Rockefeller, Nelson, 140, 146
Rogers, Richard, 14–16
Romero, Archbishop, 221, 233–4

Roosevelt, Theodore, 226
Rosary, Scriptural, 134–5
Rothenstein, Sir John, 45, 206
Rowse, A. L., 142, 143, 251–2
Royal Institute of International
    Affairs, 247
royalties, authors', 17–19;
    Greene's in USSR, 96, 135,
    144–5
Russell, Bertrand, 150
Russia; murder in 19th century,
    58–9; see also, Union of Soviet
    Socialist Republics
Ryland, Sir William, 182–3

Saint-Simon, Louis de Rouvroy,
    duc de, 174
Saki (H. H. Munro), 22–4
Salan, Gen R. A. L., 69–72, 219,
    220
SALT talks, 172–3
Samoa, 218
San Salvador, 203
Santiago, Archbishop of, 234
Sassoon, Siegfried, 65
Savonarola, Girolamo, 93–4
Scarman, Leslie George, Baron,
    188
School House Gazette, x
Schuster, Friedmann, 106
Scrabble, 81
Scribner's, 150–1
Segura, Archbishop of Seville,
    234
Servadio, Gaia, 100, 145
Shakespeare, Nicholas, 175
Shaw, George Bernard, 52–5,
    62–6, 67
Shawcross, Sir Hartley, 28
Sheehan, Bishop (sic), 138, 139
Sheen, Bishop, 111
Sheen, Mgr Fulton, 139

Sheridan, Michael, 223
Shilling, Eric, 17
Shute, Nevil, 173
Sickert, Walter, ix
Sierra Leone, 4–6
Sihanouk, Prince Norodom, 167
Sikhs, 180–81
Silkin, John and Samuel, 192
Sillitoe, Alan, 141
Simpson, Colin, 160–61
Sindona, Michele, 222, 223
Sinyavsky, Andrei, 135–7, 141–2,
    143, 144
Skvorecky, Josef, 166
Slansky, Rudolf Salzmann, 8, 155
Slick, 37
Smith, Janet Adam, 72
Smith, R. (trade unionist), 112
Smyth, Mr, 229
Snow, C. P., Baron, 58–60
Society of Authors, 52, 53, 54–5,
    67
Soldati, Mario, 10, 195
Solzhenitsyn, Alexander, 141, 193
Soustelle, M., 219
Souvanna Phouma, Prince, 105
Spain, 39, 215, 234, 250
Spectator; competitions, xiii,
    12–13, 217–18; Greene on B.
    Nichols, 169; Greene at xi; and
    John Gordon Society, 77–80;
    Lord de Clifford's libel action
    against, 200; misprints, 243;
    style, xiii, 227–8
    letters on: architecture,
    157–9; Caodaists, 186–7;
    Central America, 189–90,
    221–2, 242–4; Noël Coward,
    47–8; definition of intellectual,
    188–9; Norman Douglas,
    19–20; France, personal rights
    in, 251; Greene's disreputable

Spectator – *cont.*
   habits, 158–9, 251–2; Greene's
   FBI files, 149–50; Greene's
   comparison of USSR and USA,
   137–9; Lord Hailsham's
   verses, 58; helmets,
   motor-cycle, 180–81; J. O.
   Hobbes, 89–90; inaccuracies in
   interviews, 211; Bernard
   Levin, 96–8; Lord Chief
   Justices, 68–9; Post Office,
   182–3; *The Quiet American*,
   190–91; Saki, 22–4; Nick
   Totton, 185–6; USA, quality of
   life in, 137–9; USSR, 127–8,
   137–9, 159–60, 192–3, 203,
   241; Vatican Bank, 222;
   Vietnam, 69–72; Auberon
   Waugh, 229; Evelyn Waugh,
   168–9
Spellman, Cardinal F. J., 25, 138,
   139
Spence, Sir Basil, 157–9
Spender, Stephen, 55, 80, 113,
   133–4
Star, x
stars, relative chastity of, 44
Steiner, George, 177
Steinfels, Peter, 245
Stevenson, Noel, 103–4
Stevenson, Robert Louis, 150–52
Stewart, Michael, 148
Styles, John, 83
Suddeutscher Rundfunk, 162
Sukarno, President, 118
Sunday Express, 77, 87, 175
Sunday Telegraph; letters on:
   Greene's politics and OM,
   231–2; Conan Doyle, 172; *The
   Confidential Agent*, film of, 188;
   Haiti, 131; *May We Borrow
   Your Husband*, 128; Nicaragua,

233–4; Philby, 145, 241; Padre
   Pio, 139–40; *The Quiet
   American*, 126–7
Sunday Telegraph Magazine, 175,
   211
Sunday Times, 16–17, 78, 199;
   letters, xiv–xv, 43, 49, 199
Susskind, David, 101–2
Sutro, John; and Anglo-Texan
   Society, 27, 28, 29, 30, 31–2;
   and John Gordon Society,
   77–8, 80–84, 86–7

Tablet: letters on: Fr Roy
   Bourgeois, 244–5; Christ's
   poverty, 220–21; contraception,
   216, 247–8; Cuba, 230–31;
   Greene's beliefs, 173–4; God,
   sex of, 250; Peter
   Hebblethwaite, 228–9; Pope
   John Paul II, 223–5, 227, 230;
   Nicaragua, 212–13, 223–5,
   230, 234–7; quoting out of
   context, 179; religion and
   politics, 21–2, 223–5, 227, 230;
   Vatican Bank, 222–3
taste, 'good', 45
Tayninh, 61
television, 102–4, 162, 170–71
Temple, Shirley, 85, 86, 199
terrorism, 156–7, 237–8, 239, 244
Thal, Herbert Van, 38
Thatcher, Margaret, 191, 232,
   233, 249, 252; and Chile, 196,
   197
Thé, Colonel, 186–7
Thomas, D. M., 141
Thurston, Fr Herbert, SJ, 62, 65
Time, 61, 166–7, 203, 205, 237–8
Times, The, xiii; Greene's career
   on, 116–117, 132, 133–4;
   misprints, 187–8

letters on: airports, drinks at, 46–7; Henri Alleg's trial, 100; Anglo-Texan Society, 27; arms trade, 95, 196–7; authors' royalties, 17–19; banning of *Pygmalion*, 52–5, 55; Belize, 195–6, 214–15; Cambodia, 148–9; censorship, 36–9, 102–4; Chile, 196–7; Christ's purpose, 154; civil defence, 193; Cuba, 74–6, 95, 109–11, 194–5; currency regulations for authors, 14–16; Daniel–Sinyavsky trial, 135–6, 137; Dominican Republic, 117–18; Europe's relations with US, 163–5; Formosa crisis, 42–3; Haiti, 146, 147–8; Douglas Jay, 133–4; Pope John Paul II, 225; 4 July, 185; Karel Kyncl, 165–6; Laos, 104–6; John Le Carré, 210, 211; *Lusitania*, sinking of, 160–62; Malta, 108–9; Mau Mau, 32–3; Alice Meynell, 44; Naga Hills, Assam, 48–52; Net Book Agreement, 253; Nicaragua, 232–3; Nice, corruption in, 207–8; Northern Ireland, 154–6; nuclear accident at Chernobyl, 240–41; nuclear weapons, 66, 216–17; opera of *Our Man in Havana*, 17; Philippines, 238–9; Post Office, 112, 183; quality of *The Times*, 204–5; right to die, 205–6; sexual problems, 179–80; stars, relative chastity of, 44; teachers' pay, 115–17; *The Quiet American*, 56; tyrannies, 140–41; US Freedom of Information act, 249; USSR, 96, 135–6, 137, 141, 142–4, 240–41; Vietnam, 34, 104–6, 152–3, 163–5, 218–20; weather reports, xiv, 212; Trevor Wilson, 218–20; young writers, 214

Times Literary Supplement, 111, 125–6, 150–52, 162–3, 177–8, 195

Tokyo Conference, 1986, 237–8

Ton Ton Macoute, 130–31, 146, 148

Torquemada, Tomás de, 93

Torrijos, General Omar, 191, 226

torture; Brazil, 155; Cuba, 109; France, 98–100; Greece, 155; Nicaragua, 238; Northern Ireland, 154–6; San Salvador, 203; treatment of Great Train Robbers as approaching, 113; USSR, 155; Vietnam, 114–15, 125, 155

Totton, Nick, 185–6

Toynbee, Philip, xv-xvi

Tracey, Michael, 11–12

Ulster, 154–7

Union of Soviet Socialist Republics; and Czechoslovakia, 140, 159–60, 165; Daniel–Sinyavsky trial, 135–7; emigration policy, 192–3, 194; expulsion of diplomats, 252; Greene attends conference, 241; Greene compares with USA, 21, 135–6, 137–9, 143, 144, 159; and Laos, 104–6; minority languages, 203; Moscow, 96–7, 138; *New Scientist* in, 142; religion, 137–9; supports

Union of Soviet Socialist
Republics – *cont.*
tyrannies, 141; torture, 155;
Union of Writers, 135, 144;
and Vietnam, 105; Western
novelists and, 96, 135, 141–5
United States of America;
American Academy, Greene
resigns from, 149–50; Catholic
University of America, 135,
139; CIA, 105, 146, 147, 148,
186–7, 197, 227; and Europe,
163–5; FBI, 26–7, 138, 150,
249; Freedom of Information
Act, 249; Green's attitude to,
xiv, 29, 56, 135–6, 137–9,
190–91, 250; Kennedy
administration, 106–7, 167;
Krushchev's visit, 88; lack of
sense of history, 102; liberal
conscience, 190–91; McCarran
Act, 88; McCarthyism, 24–7;
OSS, 219–20; Reagan
administration, 227, 232, 234;
religion, 21–2, 25, 138, 139;
support of tyrannies, 140–41,
238–9; USSR compared, 21,
135–6, 137–9, 143, 144, 159;
Waugh on success in, 13–14;
see also, Anglo-Texan Society
and under Cuba; Haiti;
Nicaragua; Vietnam
Unity Theatre, 184
Universe, 42
Unwin, Sir Stanley, 17–19, 38
Uruguay, 239

Valli, Alida, 10
Varley, Eric, 192
Vatican, xiv; Bank, 222–3;
Council, First, 248; *see also*,
Papacy

Vaughan, Fr Bernard, 45
Verity, Christine, 188–9
Vietnam, 120–5; boat people,
192, 194; Buddhism, 187;
'butchery' and 'casualties' in,
153; Caodaists, 186–7; China
and, 120; Communist regimes,
past, 152–3; Dien Bien Phu, 34,
69–72; French withdrawal
from North, 176; Greene
compares North and South,
136; Luang Prabang, 104;
partition, 34–6; *The Quiet
American* as portrayal, 56–8;
religion, 35, 36, 118–19,
124–5, 164, 187; 'toppling' in,
166–7; torture, 114–15, 125,
155; US policy, 105, 114–15,
119, 120–22, 131, 141, 153,
167, 190, (bombing), 163, 164,
165; Vietcong, 120–22, 123–4,
125; Vietminh, 34, 35, 36, 146
Villahermosa, Mexico, 190
Vincent, Professor John, 214–15
vodka, 229
Voodoo, 230–31
vulgarity, 45

Walker, Peter, 158
Wallis, Alfred, xxiii
Wapshott, Nicholas, xiii, 210, 211
Warburg, Frederic, 129, 130
Ward, Stephen; trial, 200
Warner, Marina, 186, 187
Washington, George, 185
Watergate case, 167
Waugh, Auberon; Greene's
enjoyment of, 211; on
motor-cycle helmets, 180–81;
on Post Office, 182; on quality
of *The Times*, 204–5; tastes in
alcohol, 217, 218, 229

Waugh, Evelyn, 253; and Alfred
  Wallis Prize, xxiii; on Greene,
  42, 106, 185; Greene defends
  Waugh's shade against B.
  Nichols, 168–9; on *The Heart
  of the Matter*, 16; on Olivier
  in *Rhinocéros*, 100; politics,
  100; on success in USA,
  13–14
Wee Willie Winkie, 85, 86,
  199–200
Wermter, Fr, 247
West, Richard, 190–91
Westminster Cahedral, 3–4
Whitebait, William, 63
Whitehouse, Mary, 12
Whitley, Reginald, 6, 7
Wilde, Oscar, 66
Wilkinson, M. (*pseud.* of GG), 99
Williams, Shirley, 192

Williams, Tennessee, 199
Williamson, Malcolm, 16–17
Wilson, Angus, 80, 113
Wilson, Claire, 197
Wilson, Harold, 47
Wilson, Trevor, 174, 218–20
Windham, Donald, 199
wine, 217, 218
Winick, Helen, 80
Wiseman, Thomas, 5–7, 63
Wolfenden Report, 77
Woolsey, Judge John (US), 38

Yallop, David, 222, 228–9
Young, B. A., of Fulham, 79

Zaharoff, Sir Basil, 196–7,
  197–8
Zest, 37
Zirma, H. D., 33–4